NEW HORIZONS IN CRIMINOLOGY

SPORTS CRIMINOLOGY

A critical criminology of sport and games

Nic Groombridge

First published in Great Britain in 2016 by

Policy Press
University of Bristol
1-9 Old Park Hill
Bristol
BS2 8BB
UK
t: +44 (0)117 954 5940
pp-info@bristol.ac.uk
www.policypress.co.uk

North America office:
Policy Press
c/o The University of Chicago Press
1427 East 60th Street
Chicago, IL 60637, USA
t: +1 773 702 7700
f: +1 773-702-9756
sales@press.uchicago.edu
www.press.uchicago.edu

British Library Cataloguing in Publication Data
A catalogue record for this book is available from the British Library

Library of Congress Cataloging-in-Publication Data
A catalog record for this book has been requested

ISBN 978-1-4473-2315-0 hardcover
ISBN 978-1-4473-2319-8 ePub
ISBN 978-1-4473-2320-4 Kindle

Cover design by Policy Press
Front cover image: istock
Printed and bound in Great Britain by CPI Group (UK) Ltd,
Croydon, CR0 4YY
Policy Press uses environmentally responsible print partners

MIX
Paper from
responsible sources
FSC® C013604

Contents

Acknowledgements

Thanks to Andrew Millie the series editor for inviting me to write this book, thereby making me deliver on something I'd been talking about for ages with anyone who'd listen. So thanks also to the many criminologists subject to my ramblings at conferences and seminars.

Several anonymous reviewers were most helpful in shaping and refining the project. I may have reviewed and judged many books but this is the first I have written.

Thanks also to my family, Hilary and Rhys, for putting up with all this talk of sport. My father, Brian, knew of the book before his death. He could not understand sport , but all his other sons – Ed, Tim and Joe – have been keen participants and spectators, although I don't expect them to agree with any of this. Thanks also to my sisters: Ellie, a stronger woman than she knows, and Jennie, a more committed rugby player than I ever was.

NEW HORIZONS IN CRIMINOLOGY

Series editor: Professor Andrew Millie, Department of Law and Criminology, Edge Hill University, UK

Preface

The Policy Press *New Horizons in Criminology* book series provides concise authoritative texts that are international in scope and reflect cutting-edge thought and theoretical developments. These short, accessible texts explain principles and developments clearly before going deeper into the subject, and are written so that the non-specialist academic, student or practitioner can understand them. Written by leading authors in their fields, the series aims to become essential reading for all academics and students (and practitioners) interested in where criminology is heading.

Criminology is a subject that has always been willing to explore new horizons, to consider other disciplinary influences and to embrace new methodologies. By exploring new possibilities, fresh and innovative ways to consider the traditional core of criminology can be found; and the traditional core itself might also be questioned. The criminological imagination (see Young, 2011) continues to expand, and this new book series aims to reveal to a wider audience these cutting-edge developments.

With numerous high-profile cases of bribery, drug-taking, illegal gambling, violence and simple cheating in sport, there is clearly scope for a sports criminology. Sportspeople play by various laws, rules and norms that would be familiar to the criminologist – all of which can be bent or broken for personal advantage. Furthermore, systems of policing, surveillance, social control and punishment permeate the sporting world. There are also issues of race, disability, gender and sexuality within sport that would interest the criminologist. Perhaps there is much that sport can learn from criminological scholarship, and similarly, much that criminology can learn from sport.

Having an international reputation for his writing on sport and criminology, Nic Groombridge was the obvious choice of author for this book, and I was delighted when he accepted my invitation. His enthusiasm for the subject is evident in his popular blog at http://sportscriminology.blogspot.co.uk, where he states that he is 'a fan of criminology and of sport'. This is certainly evident in this book, which is the first to be published on sports criminology. Nic draws on his experience as a sports fan and (amateur) sportsperson. He also draws influence from the sociology of sport and sports law, but concludes that a sports criminology can say something new, especially if it comes from a critical perspective. His intention is not to carve out a niche for criminologists who are also sports fans, but for a criminological study of sport to also say something to and about criminology more generally.

This is a very readable book, full to the brim with absorbing examples from a range of countries and sports – and also some games. It is clearly of interest to criminologists and other academics, students and practitioners with an interest in sport. But it also comes highly recommended for those who are not necessarily sports fans, but want a new perspective on notions of deviance, crime and social harm.

References

Young, J. (2011) *The Criminological Imagination*, Cambridge: Polity Press.

Author's preface

Although the book addresses some of the more negative aspects of sport, it seems fitting that its gestation should coincide with two of the world's major sporting events – the 2014 World Cup in Brazil had just finished when I started writing, and the 2016 Olympics, also in Brazil, are due to take place around the time of publication. Like many fans, I have gained great pleasure from watching the World Cup on TV over the years. I enjoyed even more being in London during the 2012 Olympics, where I watched live athletics, hockey, cycling, water polo, basketball, the wheelchair marathon and Paralympic swimming.

My own participation in sport is less spectacular, but it ranges from schoolboy rugby union (continued in later life with less success) and judo to low-level athletics (hammer–pole vault–steeplechase combination – my contribution to the Corinthian pursuit of points for my club in Southern League Division 7) and occasional back-of-the-pack triathlons. Nowadays I still manage regular five-kilometre parkruns and the odd 10-kilometre race, but I ran my best marathon (in London, in three hours, one minute and 43 seconds) 30 years ago. I am not taking a standpoint epistemological view and insisting that readers should heed me because I have done, and therefore 'know', sport, but I occasionally mention my sport activities where relevant. I also draw on relevant experiences from my doctoral fieldwork and work for the Home Office.

I like watching, but prefer doing, sport. The pleasure is not unalloyed. Playing rugby as an adult I enjoyed the game but not the sexism, racism, homophobia and public school masculinity associated with it. I have found athletics more egalitarian and, as I age, find myself running increasingly with women - who often beat me – although, given my demographic, it is still a largely middle-class, straight, white activity. There are Marxist critiques of sport (Brohm, 1987 and Perelman, 2012), Foucauldian takes on sport as bio-power (Miller, 2009) and feminist critiques of sport and male violence (Nelson, 1995), but I don't mention them to sportspeople or running partners, at least, not in those terms.

Like any other participant, I am aware that the rules/laws of sport are often observed sporadically and that the rules of substantive behaviour on field/pitch often stand at odds with the formal ones; so far, so sociological. As a criminologist, I see that many actions on the sports field are crime-like – in breaching the law of the country that is sport – as well as actually or potentially criminal. I did not consent to the chips on my teeth (pre-mouthguard days) at the hands of doctors, lawyers, bankers and police officers, and, as we shall see, consent is a key element in some of the arguments around sport and discussed in this book.

Sports law and the sociology of sport are bourgeoning fields, but this book argues that a specifically criminological, and preferably critical, approach has something to contribute to the debate. These law and sociology texts and histories of sport are referenced throughout, sometimes roughly, but within the bounds of what is seen to be sporting (or, fair). In addition, I often refer to media coverage of events, particularly 'breaking' new stories, or those about which no academic has yet published.

I have laid claim to the term 'sports criminology' for both my blog and this book, but other, more long-standing, commentators in the field (acknowledged throughout) may disagree with the appellation. Others will extend it to areas of sport and crime that merely overlap. Indeed, when I mention sports criminology to people they often assume I mean the study of football hooliganism or the involvement of sports stars in crime. Young (2015), for example, bemoans the tendency for the sociology of sport's engagement with violence to be too narrow – for example focusing on European crowd violence, ignoring that elsewhere or aggressive behaviour displayed by ice-hockey players in game. The book touches on such obvious examples of crime and sport, including crowd violence in the US.

Among those already established in the sports criminology field are Brooks and colleagues, who, in an attempt to disentangle 'fraud' from 'corruption', say that 'the problem with developing any typology of fraud and corruption in sport is that different sports react in a completely different way' (2013: 25). Indeed, they note that the same sport – athletics/track and field – in different countries may react differently. Thus athlete LaShawn Merritt, with the assistance of USA Track & Field, was cleared by the Court of Arbitration in Sport (CAS) to run for the US after he had served a drugs ban, whereas the British Olympic Association sought to ban Dwain Chambers for life. Such a 'problem' represents an opportunity for criminology to compare punitiveness and the effectiveness of such bans.

Criminology occasionally beats itself up about its failure to acknowledge gender before returning to study 'criminals' who just happen to be men. Sport is even less apologetic in this regard. Crime and sport are two of the most gendered and gendering activities in modern life, and legislation to counteract this has had little effect on either. As this book discusses both crime and sport, it will often be about men whose crimes are considered from a gendered perspective throughout. Roth and Basow rightly suggest that sports as a social sphere 'offer a unique venue for feminist theorizing, as gender issues are both replicated and magnified within it' (2004: 247).

The embodied nature of sport means that gender is often very obvious. Or apparently so. In the aftermath of the Caster Semenya case, the athletics authorities introduced hyperandrogenism regulations on the range of testosterone that might be considered normal for women against that for men. Semenya was tested in 2009 after accusations that she was biologically male. Gender testing is not normal now, but is still an option where it is thought that excessive levels of testosterone may be creating an advantage. Semenya was eventually cleared to run but in 2015 Indian sprinter Dutee Chand's successful appeal to CAS against the hyperandrogenism regulations (Chand produces a greater than normal level of natural testosterone) has reopened the issue.[1]

Some of the arguments in this book may upset sports fans and participants. Some of those readers may be criminologists. Those criminologists need to look beyond their 'field' to the playing fields outside their window to engage with these arguments.[2]

[1] *Athletics Weekly* (28 July 2015) 'IAAF's hyperandrogenism regulations suspended', www.athleticsweekly.com/featured/iaafs-hyperandrogenism-regulations-suspended-29321 (accessed 11 October 2015).

[2] Standen (2009) argues amusingly for taking sport seriously.

ONE

Introduction: just men fighting?

To get a grip on what sports criminology might be, this chapter explores sports law and the sociology of sport. It argues that sports law and the sociology of sport overlap but also leave gaps which a sports criminology can play with, but the overlaps deserve examination too. An often overlooked but overlapping concern is masculinity. The study of masculinities has started to have a limited practical and theoretical impact on studies of sport and upon criminology. This book will frequently reflect on the fact that it is most often men who commit crime, and it is more common for men than women to play professional sport. A critic might look at sport and dismiss it as 'just men fighting'; and not just with regard to boxing and participants, but to other sports and spectators too. That criticism is taken. Any discussion about men (fighting or not) in this book is conducted from a gendered and, frequently, feminist perspective. The book tackles women's participation in both sport and in crime, although it could be argued that women's sport has a lower public profile that has so far protected it from the levels of corruption that might interest criminologists in any field. But we find that Piepa Cleary, a young cricketer in Australia, has received a six-month ban for bets totalling Aus $15.50 (£7.60) on a Test match between Australia and New Zealand.[1]

This chapter suggests some of the possibilities of sports criminology and, without being too legislative, also suggests areas involving sport and crime that might be regarded as less central to sports criminology, such as crowd violence or crimes by or against sports stars, although all of these will necessarily feature. The issue of what might be considered sports criminology will be revisited throughout and specifically in the concluding chapter. There are other definitional issues too. In proposing a sports criminology, what does this say about or assume for criminology? Before turning to criminology, sports law, the sociology of sport and finally sports criminology, we must first ask what sport is.

[1]   BBC Sport (4 February 2016) 'Piepa Cleary: Player punished for £7.60 bets on Test match', http://www.bbc.co.uk/sport/cricket/35490454 (accessed 17 February 2016).

Sport

Like 'art' or 'obscenity', we are meant to recognise sport when we see it. The sports pages, and increasingly other sections, of print and online media in the UK largely feature football, interspersed with some rugby, cricket and horse racing, and almost invariably prioritise men's participation. Academic writing is similarly skewed. Thus Dart's analysis of the contents of three sports sociology journals over 25 years found:

> A total of 74 sports and activities are identified across the three journals. The most popular sports are those involving teams, but there are examples of individual sports and activities (e.g. running and bodybuilding). What is evident is how 'sport' (as identified in the journals' titles) encompasses a broad range of activities – ranging from fun, amateur, school, competitive to elite levels, as well as related leisure activities. (2014: 654)

Dart's 'wordles' for each journal show the major sports as 'soccer' (*International Review for the Sociology of Sport*); baseball, soccer and basketball (*Journal of Sport and Social Issues*); and basketball, baseball and national football league (*Sociology of Sport Journal*). A far more eclectic approach is taken here. The English Bridge Union has recently been disappointed by the High Court. The Union had argued that bridge is more physically demanding than rifle shooting.[2] Bellringing has recently made similar claims.[3] Bridge had made its bid in the hope of receiving lottery funding. Perhaps the court should have considered

[2] Khaleda Rahman (27 April 2015) 'Judge says card game Bridge is more physical than rifle shooting and rules bid to get recognised as a sport for lottery funding can go ahead', *Mail Online*, www.dailymail.co.uk/news/article-3057633/Judge-says-card-game-bridge-physical-rifle-shooting-rules-bid-recognised-sport-lottery-funding-ahead.html#ixzz3gbeTgzX4 (accessed 11 October 2015).
[3] *Daily Mail* (18 February 2016) 'Bell-ringers want it called a sport... pull the other one!', www.dailymail.co.uk/news/article-3452194/Bell-ringers-want-called-sport-pull-one-Enthusiasts-say-reclassification-raise-profile-attract-youngsters.html#ixzz40VOOKfeM (accessed 18 February 2016)

the game's competitiveness and two recent 'cheating' scandals in the game, as this book shows that one of the marks of sport is cheating.[4]

Indeed, was Weber right about the accumulation of wealth in the United States having 'the character of sport' (2012: 182)? Kane (2005) reminds us of non-Western traditions of sport that are ludic. More troubling is the 'sporting' air of 'nigger-hunting' and lynching described by Jamieson and Orr (2009). Throughout this book sport is generally taken to mean organised, institutional activities, but sometimes games and leisure activities that share similarities will be examined. Space precludes much discussion of video games, eSports and the like (see Groombridge, 2008a).

Criminology

Bosworth and Hoyle (2011) ask their contributors 'What is criminology?' The 35 chapters of their book cannot easily be summarised here, but they reflect the diversity/perversity of the subject. Criminology, for the purposes of argument, might be said to be all of the theories examined in Chapters Four and Five of this book, and more. Chapter Six is more concerned with criminal justice than criminology and Chapter Seven's focus on 'what works' (and what doesn't) draws from prison and probation studies. These theories are set out in ways that cannot truly reflect their histories or the conflicts that have marked their birth. It is, perhaps, a measure of the flexibility of criminology that the 'Foreword' to Bosworth and Hoyle (2011) is by Braithwaite, who describes himself as 'decidedly not a "true believer" in criminology' (2011: vii) and who rarely attends criminology conferences.

Braithwaite notes the reduced 'intellectual factionalism and epistemological dogmatism' (2011; viii) of recent criminology as well as its commitment to justice and normative debate, which stands as a rebuke to some law schools. Some of that 'factionalism' has played out in methodology wars. Both methodology and factionalism are played down in this book, but contending arguments should be clear and the methods used in many studies will be mentioned.

Tellingly none of Bosworth and Hoyle's (2011) contributors mention sport, but, as we shall see, law and sociology have plenty to say. We

---

[4] Patrick Jourdain (27 April 2015) 'International bridge champions accuse teammates of cheating', *Telegraph*, www.telegraph.co.uk/news/worldnews/middleeast/israel/11824257/International-bridge-champions-accuse-teammates-of-cheating.html (accessed 11 October 2015).

shall also see how some of that might be claimed for criminology, even sports criminology.

Sports law

In his book on the subject, James says that 'sport and the law' is the simple application of national and EU law to a sports dispute (2010: 19). He goes on to argue for the specificity of sport and entitles his book *Sports Law*. McFee (2004) spends some time trying to work out whether he is making a contribution to philosophy that takes sport as its subject or to the philosophy of sport. What must be noted here though is sport's claim to, and partial recognition of, its specificity – one might say its sovereignty. Historically, and to date, sport has sought to sustain the reality, and sometimes the illusion of, its own separate jurisdictional competence. Much of Chapter Six focuses on this issue.

Colucci and Jones (2013) introduce their colossal survey of the justice systems of different sports federations and countries with these words:

> In the name of their autonomy and the specificity of sport many associations around the world developed their own justice bodies. Some of them seem to be more effective than others but all share the same goal: to settle disputes, to mediate and to guarantee the correct interpretation of sporting rules and regulations. This is not a simple task since the scope of sports justice is not always easy to describe. In fact ordinary justice maintains its role in granting and supervising certain rights and obligations that are not so different from those protected by sports justice. The lines of distinction become even more blurred when issues of individual or fundamental rights come into play. This has become an interesting paradox, because sports justice and ordinary justice are not always discernible. One possible explanation may be found in the reality of certain countries where the two systems tend to converge. (2013: 21)

Thus in England the decision-making processes and appeals tribunals of national governing bodies are not subject to judicial review (James, 2010: 29). Famously sport has also resisted interaction with (for which read interference by) politics; such as criticising Olympic boycotts and sporting sanctions against apartheid South Africa.

Legal and criminal justice systems have long since superseded sovereignty in all aspects of Western society with the possible of exception of sport and religion, which still has its kings/popes – witness chief executive Bernie Ecclestone's grip on Formula One motor racing and former Fédération Internationale de Football Association (FIFA) president Sepp Blatter's stranglehold on football. Football kept its players in 'bondage' until the *Bosman* ruling 'freed' them to ply their trade throughout Europe without national restrictions.[5] Most sports seek to wash their dirty linen in-house; the law used to condone this. Thus Lord Denning said, in *Enderby Town FC v The Football Association* (1971):

> In many cases it may be a good thing for the proceedings of a domestic tribunal to be conducted informally without legal representation. Justice can be done in them better by a good layman than by a bad lawyer. This is especially so in activities like football and other sports, where no points of law are likely to arise, and it is all part of the proper regulation of the game.

In other words, what happens on the pitch, course or track, or in the ring or court – in as much as it does not breach any national law – is entirely within the ambit of the National Governing Body and International Sports Federation. This makes for a skewed legality; for example, you might succeed in challenging your sport's anti-doping, disciplinary and appellate procedures – like the athlete Diane Modhal, whose drugs ban was overturned after a lengthy battle – but the focus on faulty process does not challenge the necessity for drug testing in the first place. We return to her case when looking at the 'justice' systems of sport in Chapter Six. You will not be able to press the case for a three-legged race or doggy paddle let alone overturn an offside; decision though official observers in the stands and technology do allow some retrospective review by those authorities. What is more, those punishments that are meted out cannot affect the result of the played game, as Sheffield United found when it complained that West Ham had not been punished sufficiently for fielding an ineligible player, Carlos Tevez, in 2007. The £20 million Sheffield received was scant compensation as the result stood and they were demoted.

The Olympic movement makes considerable 'sovereign' demands. As James (2010: 10) notes, 'some sections of the London Olympic

---

[5]   *Union Royale Belge des Société de Football Association v Jean-Marc Bosman* (C415/93), www.ena.lu/judgment_court_justice_bosman_case_c_415_93_15_december_1995-020003031.html (accessed 11 October 2015).

and Paralympic Games Act 2006 appear to have been inserted at the behest of the International Olympic Committee (IOC), rather than on the basis of rational legal debate'. Draconian powers are deployed to protect commercial sponsors from 'ambush' marketing by competitors (Healey, 2009). For the 2010 FIFA World Cup, South Africa passed the Special Measures Act deploying civil and criminal powers against ambush marketers and petty crime alike.[6] While a lawyer might view this in terms of proportionality, the critical criminologist might see it as the criminalisation of fans – a punishment for bearing the logos of non-sponsoring companies, the flags of non-Olympic nations or political slogans.

Judging from the numbers of books, specialist journals and standalone modules on undergraduate and postgraduate degrees, sports law is a growing area. Books on sports law typically set out the law in respect of particular jurisdictions, and journal articles typically analyse or set out notable cases. Largely they follow the black letter law tradition, and often, as textbooks, contain little critical material. Some take sporting celebrity and the extreme circumstances that occur in live sport as vignettes to illuminate the law humorously (Day, 2005). Obviously, the growth of international organisations and law, and the influence of international sports federations with their imbrication in late modern mediatised societies, mean there is a growing confluence of sports, entertainment and media law.

In Brazil, under President Lula, football acquired legal protection – the 'Law of Moralisation in Sport' – and a 'fans statute'. The statute requires the Brazilian FA to hold at least one national competition in which the 'teams know before it begins how many games they will play and who their opponents will be'. Brazil has had a national league only since 1971 and changed its format every year as the *cartolas* (top hats) and former ruling dictators used the sport to serve their own interests. Relegation rules had been changed to support big clubs, or in return for political favours (Bellos, 2003). During the 2010 UK general election, all parties made mention of greater regulation of football.[7]

---

[6] Marina Hyde (20 June 2010) 'World Cup 2010: fans, robbers and a marketing stunt face justice, Fifa style', *The Guardian*, www.guardian.co.uk/football/2010/jun/20/world-cup-2010-fans-marketing-justice-fifa (accessed 11 October 2015).

[7] Nick Harris (22 April 2010) 'Questions of sport for the men who would be minister', *The Independent*, www.independent.co.uk/sport/general/others/questions-of-sport-for-the-men-who-would-be-minister-1950517.html (accessed 11 October 2015).

The most common aspect of recent legal publications on sport in England and Wales is the addition of material on drugs testing and the Olympics. Drugs are seen to be a problem in all sports and all jurisdictions, so this is to be expected. The arrival of the Olympics in London for 2012 ensured that Lewis and Taylor's book on sport law and practice (2008) now includes a special section on this subject, as does James' work on sports law (2010).

In the sports law literature, the term 'drugs' generally means performance-enhancing drugs rather than 'recreational' or illegal drugs. Indeed, Hartley's index refers simply to 'drugs, see doping' (2009: 325), but, encouragingly for the critical criminologist, treats the subject as a human rights issue. Healey (2009) too, in her analysis of Australian sports law, takes much the same line. Gardiner and colleagues (2006), however, discuss the issue in contractual terms, often implied and now more often explicit, between the sports authorities and the competitor, and raise the moral issue of 'cheating'. Modahl's case turned on whether she had a contract with the athletics authorities.

Much of the standard, shared content of these texts is the application of the doctrine of *volenti non fit injuria*, that is, that when stepping into the ring or on to the pitch, you consent, within the rules of the sport, to be injured. Hartley (2009) expands on this by applying arguments from *R v Brown* [1994] (involving homosexual sado-masochism) to boxing, mixed martial arts and cage fighting (Ultimate Fighting Championship). James (2010) glosses over the specific details of this case – you would not know from his account that it involved sex at all. This case is revisited in the conclusion to this book.

Hartley's work promises a bridge to the sociological literature. Concentrating on English law, her work is commended in Helena Kennedy's foreword, which describes it as the 'development of the law through a sociological lens' (2009: xvii). By this, Kennedy seems to be referring to the fact that issues of 'race', religion, homosexuality, age and disability are finally having an increasing impact on sports law. In other words, it is sports law with a strong sociological flavour.

Sociology of sport

In this section, the sport sociology literature is considered before turning to the works of Atkinson and Young (2008) and Blackshaw and Crabbe (2004), which come close to sports criminology.

This literature tends to universalise about sport, but closer attention shows this often to be about US sport and gender and race/ethnicity issues. Alternatively, it focuses on a particular sport and therefore tends towards one country or continent. As sociology it contains more critical commentary, particularly about structural issues such as gender, ethnicity, sexuality and ability, than sports law and often of a campaigning, equal opportunities nature. Empirical research is deployed to promote inclusion and diversity within sport; that is, it is critical of sport's failings in the modern world, suggesting that sport is slow, erratic and ineffective in its response to a modernity entrenched in power and culture.[8]

Coakley and Pike (2009) update Coakley's US-based text for the UK and make extensive engagements with the many issues and controversies raised by sports that might be ignored by sports science students who are very active, and often overconforming, sports people. Coakley and Pike (2009) accord deviance and violence a chapter each. Delaney and Madigan (2009) follow the same scheme, which suggests that deviance and violence are seen to be minor concerns or distractions from the main issue. For sports criminology, they become central along with other harms and crimes. Deviance and violence in Coakley and Pike (2009) are briefly examined below with contributions from some of the other texts in the area.

In their chapter on the subject, Coakley and Pike (2009) identify deviance on and off field and also among spectators, managers, coaches and media representatives. Their discussion even extends to a consideration of whether 'field' sports are deviant. But the majority of the chapter is taken up with the problem of 'overconformity', which is often boiled down to the use of performance-enhancing substances. The various issues raised include the legality of some substances when not taken by elite athletes under the World Anti-Doping Agency's surveillance.

The authors raise the issue of whether sports participation is 'a cure for deviant behaviour' (2009: 204) and summarise Nichols (2007). Unlike many others they also mention Trulson (1986) who found that training in tae-kwon-do allied to associated philosopho-ethical ideals could lower delinquency rates whereas less traditional sports-orientated tae-kwon-do could not.[9] This issue is the subject of Chapter Seven. Interestingly, Coakley and Pike (2009) make no specific connection to the violent deviant potential of such martial arts with their own discussion in their chapter on violence.

---

[8] Jarvie (2007) is particularly scathing of his discipline.

[9] As my judo was learned with extensive use of Japanese nomenclature and traditions of respect, this accords with my sense of what might work.

Violence is also seen to be a form of overconforming deviance, which can occur on or off field, or between athletes or spectators. Here sports law, sports sociology and criminology have all contributed to issues of stadium safety and hooliganism (see Scraton, 1999, particularly for a critical take on this). The nearest to a recognition of the full criminality of some sports deviance/violence comes in a discussion of Smith's (1983) typology of sports violence: brutal body contact; borderline violence; quasi-criminal violence; and criminal violence.

It is telling that such books, and the teaching modules they support or derive from, typically discuss deviance or violence in terms that derive from 'the sociology of deviance'. Such interactionism is posited as a radical move away from its previous functionalism, with Marxist, feminist and minority perspectives name-checked along the way. There is a time warp feel about this, which may reflect not only sportspeople's overconformity, or conservatism, but also that of those who teach them.

Much of the past 40 years of conflict, consensus and paradigm shifts within and between the sociology of deviance and criminology goes missing, although, as we shall see, Blackshaw and Crabbe (2004) and Atkinson and Young (2008) are honourable exceptions. Other developments in sociology have also been ignored; for instance, Bourdieu has specifically addressed himself to sport on several occasions, yet merits only two glancing mentions (Coakley and Pike, 2009: 359, 476). Journals offer a richer intellectual diet, but often bemoan the marginality of sports sociology and its lack of influence on sport (see, for instance, Bairner, 2009 and Jarvie, 2007). Criminologists know that feeling.

Atkinson and Young (2008) specifically address deviance, cite authors familiar to criminology and offer specific chapters on criminal violence in sport, and terrorism and sport. Helpfully they offer sections in which some criminological theories are applied. Four of these are largely recognisable as criminological: violence and aggression; subcultural; victimology; and identity politics. These are then organised into eight 'houses': functionalism and strain; conflict; interactionism; social control; classicism; critical; gender; and integrated theories (2008: 47). Such matters are taken up in Chapters Four and Five here.

In their discussion of violence, Atkinson and Young (2008) take examples from ice hockey, describing a litany of ultra-violence that fails to end in court, or, if taken to court, usually fails to end in prison. Neither this nor various attempts to crack down on violence has any effect on behaviour in the rink. The National Hockey League, the fans and the media discursively circle the wagons and talk away the problem. They cite the work of others or suggest ways to understand the violence as potentially functional, profitable for the owners, a form of tertiary (self-chosen) deviance, a sport-specific failure to inculcate social control, or a failure of the authorities to be rational and proportionate. Race, ethnicity and gender, or combinations of these, are also often seen as issues.

When discussing terrorism, Atkinson and Young (2008) rightly look at the Olympic Games given its history (namely, the attack during the 1972 games in Munich), but other sports mega-events like the World Cup might be perceived to be potential targets. Historically, they point to guerrilla action between Turkey and Greece at the 1896 Olympic Games and the spectre of Irish nationalism that hovered over London in 1908. Thus terrorism may be seen to function for the state to promote appropriate ideas of good and evil; as a means of political and media labelling; as an 'opportunity' for organisers to provide guardianship and talk up security; as justification for rhizomic surveillance; or as an excuse to 'protect' women and bar countries with unacceptable policies towards women.

Interestingly, Coakley and Pike make only one mention of Blackshaw and Crabbe (2004), and then only to observe that 'off-the-field deviance among athletes attracts widespread media attention' (2009: 200). This rather underplays, indeed undervalues, their work. Blackshaw and Crabbe (2004) are specifically mentioned by Atkinson and Young (2008) as notable exceptions in taking criminology/deviance seriously. Where Atkinson and Young explore the possibilities of established and traditional deviance/criminology theories, Blackshaw and Crabbe (2004) engage with Sumner (1994) and cultural criminology.

Building on Downes and Rock (1998), Blackshaw and Crabbe (2009) note the lurking, and sometimes unacknowledged, functionalism in sport sociology's adherence to ideas of the abnormal and pathological. They suggest that overconformist 'positive deviance' is an example of Mertonian innovation and 'negative deviance' as retreatism. They also point out the Weberian interpretivism of work like Snyder's (1994) on a group of college athletes who practised burglary together (a blow for 'sports builds character' functionalism). They swiftly move on to Lyng's 'edgework' (1990) and Rojek's (2000) 'wild leisure' and drag in Sutherland (1949), Box (1971), Croall (1992) and Ruggiero (1996) to discuss white-collar and respectable crime before lighting on Brohm's (1978) Althusserian account of sport as part of an ideological state apparatus. On-field deviance is obvious whereas off-field fraud is as invisible as all other corporate crime. Left realist and feminist critiques are quickly added, followed by actions taken against paedophilia in sport, which are seen to be akin to the risk management approach identified by Feeley and Simon as 'new penology'.

Intriguingly, Blackshaw and Crabbe (2004) claim that 'had he cared to discuss it, Foucault would without doubt have recognised the disciplinary techniques of the emerging institutional regime of sport as a crucial part of the 'carceral archipelago' (2004: 44). They persuasively go on to cite studies in this vein that indicate the disciplinary nature of sport, although followers of sport would also note much indiscipline on the pitch and off, in matters of training and alcohol intake.

As might be expected, some of the most cutting critiques of violence in sport – and sometimes of sport *tout court* – come from a feminist perspective, but, in the sports sociology literature, this is often deployed by men (see, for instance, Messner, 1990). For some, sport itself is deviant and for some too many of its male participants are criminal and hubristically see themselves above the law (Jamieson and Orr, 2009).

New media provides opportunities for fleeting, often gimmicky, commentaries that do not sit easily with academic discourse, but the work of two sports journalists not captured by the 'fans with typewriters' sports media, Andrew Jennings (Transparency in Sport) and Dave Zirin (Edge of Sports), offers plenty of investigative and muck-raking potential with which critical criminologists could find common cause (see also King, 2008). The work of Atkinson and Young (2008) and Blackshaw and Crabbe (2004) seem to me to point the way to sports criminology, as does some of what Redhead (2015) calls 'physical cultural studies' in his ultra-realist criminological take on football hooligan memoirs. Indeed Atkinson predicts the sociology of sport's 'impending demise' (2011: 136) and Silk and Andrews blame its 'debilitating blend of introspective and ineffectual parochialism' (2011: 5).

Sports criminology

The discussion of sports law and sports sociology so far has largely been descriptive. The critical work of Atkinson and Young (2008) and Blackshaw and Crabbe (2004) suggests that a sports criminology may exist already. What does this book offer that is new? It takes on board their criticisms of criminology. However, their criticism assumes a monolithic and rather conservative criminology. In Chapters Four and Five a variety of criminologies are shown either directly or indirectly to have relevance to sport and vice versa; that is, those criminologies might have explanatory power in respect of criminal acts or harms within sport, or those criminologies might already have engaged with sport, if only metaphorically.

It should be clear that both law and sociology have engaged with sport. This book shows that criminology has done so tentatively and seeks to encourage more engagement. That engagement goes beyond football hooliganism and athlete deviance. It can move from the criminalisation of kids playing street games, to events on pitch, into board rooms and on to the exclusive hotels favoured by international sports associations when deciding the venue for the next sporting mega-event and back to the dreams and merchandise sold to those street kids.

Here in this book, in Chapters Four and Five, and in this section, some more of the 'precursors' to sports criminology beyond Atkinson and Young (2008) and Blackshaw and Crabbe (2004) are set out. Yar (2014) admits that his interest in sport as a site of criminological interest only came during a period of enforced inactivity that found him in front of the television watching the Tour de France, and cycling will feature strongly in this book as a sport, as site of drug taking and as a spectacle. More directly, Kudlac (2010) concentrates on the crimes of athletes at school, college and in the professional game; on crowd violence; on the possibilities of crime as desistance; and on the issue of sports gambling. He makes much use of criminology, and as such, this book refers to his work throughout.

From a cognitive psychology perspective, while Morris and Lewis (2009) make no reference to the sociology of sport, sport law or criminology in their discussion of 'diving' in football, they do make proposals for the use of video evidence that has resonance with Chapter Six. As they conclude that 'deceptive intentions in this context are to a degree manifest in behaviour and are observable' (2009: 1), their work understandably received some attention from psychology and sports science, but could have been expected to have gained wider recognition. Two philosophers of sport (Pfleegor and Roesenberg, 2014) merely cite these findings to remind us that deception is at the heart of sport. They open with Diego Maradona's so-called 'Hand of God' goal against England in the quarter final of the 1986 World Cup.[10] As they say:

> Disguising movements, shots, throws, passes and other
> movements to throw off one's opponents and/or create
> competitive opportunities are part of learning and executing

[10] Video replays show it clearly to be his hand not his head that steers the ball into the net.

specific sport skills. Deception can also occur outside the contest during closed practice sessions or by limiting one's disclosure of information to opposition. Although the latter instances may be interesting, this review will delimit its focus to in-contest forms of deception that directly involve the motives and interactions of athletes during competition. (2014: 1)

All of these types of deception can be within the rules of the sport but all can be against the law. A feint is permissible and may receive praise from crowd and commentators, but the 'simulation' of 'diving' may only please the winning side's fans.

The following quotes from Atkinson and Young (2008: vii, emphasis in original) indicate some of the problems that a critical sociology of sport has with criminology and therefore potentially with sports criminology:

> ... in the subfield of criminology, deviance and social control, sport is rarely considered seriously despite the many and varied controversies, corruptions and illegalities *out there*.
>
> When, for example, sport is mentioned in criminology/ deviance texts, or when deviance is addressed in sociology of sports texts, little clear conceptual distinction is made between hard-line actions that fall under the purview of law as crime and softer manifestations such as violations of norms or mores.
>
> Occasional summaries of or references to (criminal or norm-breaking) rule violation in sport may be found in the respective literatures, but they usually serve as small case examples, empirical oddities, or points of discussion rather than legitimate academic concerns ...

In spite of, or perhaps because of, the grey areas surrounding criminology, this book lays claim to the formulation of 'sports criminology' and suggests that some things that apparently fall within its domain might be precluded. In its initial formulation, sports criminology was seen as occupying an area between sports law and the sociology of sport, as discussed earlier. Further reflection has resulted in the consideration of sport criminology, criminology of sport and their plurals. Foreshadowing the conclusion, this book should really adopt the plural and be called *Sports criminologies*, and would include zemiology, victimology and penology in official/administrative and radical/critical versions. That would be a cumbersome title; the issues deserve unpicking.

We might start with another formulation: that of sports-related crime (SRC), a term coined by Haberfeld and Abbott (2014), and used in their book arising from an Interpol global experts meeting in 2012. It is unsurprisingly focused on criminal justice; crime is seen as unproblematic and the sport in question turns out largely to be Association Football. SRC is largely seen to comprise match fixing associated with betting and politics. Clearly these topics will come up throughout this book, but are too limited for a critical sports criminology.

Some of the materials discussed here move smoothly, or unconcernedly, from considering sport and crime or sport and deviance to considering sports*men* and crime/deviance. There is some allure in covering the burglaries of footballers' homes, but these might well be addressed within criminology 'proper' or under the aegis of 'celebrity' (Penfold-Mounce, 2010) – that is, the only connection with crime here is that a sportsperson has been the victim. Similarly, accusations of sportsmen's violence against women (Benedict, 1997, 2004; Benedict and Yaeger, 1999) are important, but could be considered to fall outside a 'sports criminology'. The work of Jefferson (1998) on the boxer Mike Tyson might be considered appropriate, as it explores the continuities between Tyson's sport and life, but it is also a depiction of the psycho-social method and a contribution to the masculinities literature (see also Wacquant's [1995] personal engagement with boxing). The overlaps between the masculinities, sports and crime literatures need further examination.

A rising concern in sports law and sports administration (not to mention more widely) is child protection. Clearly this is also of interest for criminology, but not necessarily sports criminology, as sport is the context rather than a defining characteristic here. Should the study of paedophile priests lead to a religious criminology?

One of the difficulties in defining a sports criminology might be the absence of the term in standard criminology texts. The only mention of sport in *The Sage Dictionary of Criminology* is by Jupp (2001: 203) as a throwaway example of 'hidden crime' – bribery to effect a sport result. There are two references to sport in *The Oxford Handbook of Criminology*.[11] The first, by Heidensohn and Gelsthorpe (2007: 390) – again a throwaway example – mentions sport in a discussion

---

[11] The fifth edition is no better.

of masculinity. The second, by Morgan and Newburn (2007: 1048), notes that sports projects are well represented in youth justice provision. Even in Newburn's (2007) own magnum opus, there are only four occurrences of the word sport: one is metaphorical (2007: 275); another refers to some work of Eynsenck on personality (2007: 163); a third relates to the tendency of the press, in the past, to report assaults on the police as being akin to a 'spectator sport' (2007: 45); and the fourth notes the motor sport elements of joyriding (2007: 468).

A very modern example of Jupp's 'hidden crime' might be seen in reports and speculations about rule manipulation in cricket – a wide ball here, a full toss there – that might allow the spread better[12] to benefit without attracting any attention (Qureshi and Verma, 2013). Similarly, snooker has seen concerns about thrown matches, frames or shots and the influence of betting. Indeed, former world number seven and one-time BBC commentator, Willie Thorne, claims that the sport has always been corrupt, that he was offered bribes as a player and that he had suspicions about match fixing in some of the tournaments he played in.[13] Recent revelations in tennis suggest both players and officials have been involved in corrupt practices.[14]

In proposing a sports criminology, this book intends to open up friendly relations between sport, law and criminology, and to examine the resulting Venn diagram. The examples outlined here indicate some of the possibilities and more are suggested in later chapters.

This is a short book and it hopes to provoke. Readers are regularly pointed to the work of others for more information and further engagement. There is reference to criminological theory and criminal justice practice, to history and contemporary celebrity, but the intention is always to see the criminological in sport and to offer to

---

[12] Someone who bets not on the result but on the difference in points between the teams.

[13] Jonathan Liew (10 October 2011) 'Former snooker star Willie Thorne makes match-fixing claims', *Telegraph*, www.telegraph.co.uk/sport/8819193/Former-snooker-star-Willie-Thorne-makes-match-fixing-claims.html (accessed 11 October 2015). See also Higgins and Mooney v WPBSA, available at www.sportingintelligence.com/2010/09/08/in-full-the-john-higgins-match-fix-ruling-by-ian-mill-qc-080902/ (accessed 11 October 2015).

[14] BBC Sport (17 February 2016) 'Tennis corruption: Jatuporn Nalamphun banned for betting offences' http://www.bbc.co.uk/sport/tennis/35598179 and Clarey Christopher (12 February 2016) 'Tennis Umpire Suspended for Corruption Worked at U.S. Open' http://www.nytimes.com/2016/02/13/sports/tennis/tennis-umpire-suspended-for-corruption-worked-at-us-open.html?_r=0 (accessed 18 February 2016)

criminology examples from sport. Thus Chapter Two leans heavily on existing accounts of the development of sports, highlighting the criminological aspects.

Sports stars are often held up as role models, and, role models or not, are celebrities, which makes their crimes and victimisations more newsworthy. These issues are explored in Chapter Three. Having set out some of the history and given some contemporary examples, the next two chapters refer specifically to criminological theory. Just as the history chapter sought to highlight the criminological, so these chapters seek direct and indirect examples from sport of criminological theory and vice versa. There is potential for dispute over terminology, but mainstream criminological theory is covered in Chapter Four and critical criminologies in Chapter Five. Where necessary, in these and other chapters, methods and methodology are mentioned.

The metaphor of the traffic light was originally taken up in soccer and has now been reflected back into other domains including politics, where there have been suggestions to use red and yellow cards against Members of the Parliament who misbehave, with the Speaker of the House of Commons acting as referee.[15] Chapter Six looks at issues of sport criminal justice. Perhaps those errant MPs might be offered rehabilitation in the form of sport? The anecdotal and autobiographical testament of many sports stars is that without sport they would have turned to crime. Such crime prevention and desistance is explored in Chapter Seven.

The concluding chapter restates the nature and extent of sports criminology, and speculates as to its likely course. A final connecting thought brings sport and sex together and emphasises the significance of consent.

[15] Stephen Pound (25 February 2014) 'Yellow card, red card and sin bin for MPs' bad behaviour?', *Tribune*, www.tribunemagazine.org/2014/02/yellow-card-red-card-and-sin-bin-for-mps-bad-behaviour/ (accessed 11 October 2015).

TWO

A criminological history of sport

This chapter provides a general and partial history of sports affected by issues of crime, social control and criminal justice. It is illustrated by specific international examples, chiefly from the UK and the US. Examples from a variety of sports over a broad span of time illustrate the close connections between sport and crime/law. Britain often boasts of giving football to the world and cricket to many of its colonies. Attempts to bring baseball to the UK have largely been unsuccessful, but the sport has achieved a certain foothold in Cuba and Japan. The traditional Japanese sport of sumo has a long and mythic history tied up with national identity, but the money to be made from it has attracted non-Japanese participants and a degree of scandals.

No sport has been free from scandal and history should rule out any presumption of a 'Golden Age'. Here Pearson's (1983) *Hooligan: A History of Respectable Fears* is reimagined as *Cheat: A History of Entirely Anticipatable Disappointments*. To sum up, sport in the past, as now, is variously seen as 'good' or 'bad' depending on who was participating and where. Even if it seen as 'good', the attendant issues of gambling, large spectator crowds and alcohol always threaten to turn it 'bad'.

This chapter notes the illegal or unruly history of many mass participation sports and attempts by the authorities (of sport and of society) to use rules and law to exercise control. This introduces some of the discussion in later chapters of how criminological theories might be applied to sports. Sport has a history: its organisation, its relationship to wider society and the changes made to its rules/laws and internal governance. Social histories of sport often feature these matters, but sometimes gloss over the contested socio-political nature of 'folk', and even organised, sports and miss the criminological significance. Those 'men fighting', introduced in Chapter One, may be upper- and middle-class men seeking to control working-class men, while retaining the right to their own violence. Gender and race too affect one's capacity to argue that one's violence is but sport. As Huizinga notes, 'Ever since words existed for fighting and playing, men have been wont to call war a game' (1949: 89).

It is clearly not possible to give a history of all sports for all parts of the world, but here we start in Britain with field/blood sports, horse racing, boxing, soccer and cricket before moving on to the United States to take in baseball and the 'college sports' that may lead to professional sport. The chapter then looks look at athletics both in Britain and internationally before examining sumo in Japan. Hunting and other 'field sports' and even anti-hunting activity are about contesting rural space; and 'mobile games' use technology to reimagine the city.

Britain makes the rules

We start with Britain, which, as Collins says, could be described as the birthplace of modern sport:

> Although most countries have variations of folk tradition sports, which can range from hitting a ball with a bat through to mob forms of football through to maypole dancing – traditions that are very rooted in rural, agricultural lifestyles – Britain was the first place to develop what we would see today as codified, organised and commercialised sports.[1]

He continues:

> It's a story that begins in earnest in the 18th century. The reason why Britain developed these sports was it was the first nation to become an industrial, capitalist economy where people had disposable income. There was the wealth to generate both an interest in sports and also markets for sports.

While sport may be linked to criminality, this is often seen as preferable to political militancy or effeminacy. Huggins quotes a reporter from *Bell's Life*, 26 January 1840, comparing a well-attended (by 'all ranks') pugilistic exhibition with a political rally:

> … if the innocent and manly sports of the humbler classes were encouraged instead of being everywhere suppressed and hunted down by the tyrannical prejudices of puritans, we should see and hear much less of those fanatical outbreaks…. (2004: 3/4)

---

[1]   Tony Collins (6 May 2012) 'A history of British sport', *BBC HistoryExtra*, www.historyextra.com/feature/history-british-sport (accessed 11 October 2015).

Brohm (1978) would recognise the class and ideological issues here, and some of the crime prevention schemes discussed in Chapter Seven are not much more sophisticated. The Victorians and those on the political Left share something with the Puritans, as Weber noted:

> ... the Puritan aversion to sport, even for the Quakers, was by no means simply one of principle. Sport was accepted if it served a rational purpose, that of recreation necessary for physical efficiency. But as a means for spontaneous expression of undisciplined impulses, it was under suspicion; and in so far as it became purely a means of enjoyment, or awakened pride, raw instincts of the irrational gambling instinct, it was of course strictly condemned. (2012: 167)

Much of this book is concerned with the recognisably modern sports that Collins discusses, but it is also important to examine older, rural, ones too, as those traditions continue through to today (and not just for tourists or 'heritage' reasons). They show the tension around codification and commercialism and accompanying 'criminalisation' that should pique the interest of criminologists.

Holt (1990) argues for the distinctive nature of British sport: innovative in abandoning traditional, often brutal sports, and in establishing a code of 'fair play', pioneering popular sports and promoting organised spectator events. Codification largely occurred in the Victorian era partly through the efforts of energetic time- and cash-rich Victorian men (Huggins, 2004). But codification was not the only thing to impinge on sport; as Huggins notes, 'densely urban, increasingly heavily-policed areas placed far more limits on formerly mass sports like the various varieties of football' (2004: 13). The Victorian era saw a move of population and sports away from open and poorly policed country to constrained and more strictly policed urban spaces. Sports became constrained and the time and space to indulge them also became constrained by employment and policing patterns.

Field/blood sports

Fields (2014) records that cockfighting was banned in England by Edward III in 1365 to allow more time for shooting practice, then by Cromwell for Puritan reasons and then again by Charles II because of its association with immorality and dissent. It was popular in the US before being banned, first in Pennsylvania in 1830 and finally in Louisiana as recently as 2008.

In Britain, the League Against Cruel Sports (LACS) was founded in 1924 as a breakaway from what was seen as the more staid Royal Society for the Protection of Animals. The LACS website has the tagline: 'We work to expose and end the cruelty inflicted on animals in the name of sport.'[2] It is a tragic irony that the organisation's name perpetuates the very thing it is against. As we shall see, much is done in 'the name of sport'.

It is clear from Huggins (2004) and Anderson (2007) that the Victorians saw cockfighting, bull- and badger-baiting, hare coursing, fox hunting *and* bareknuckle prizefighting as blood relations. Hare coursing was not banned under the Cruelty to Animals Act 1849 like cockfighting and the baiting of dogs, bulls and bears. Bulldogs are associated with a bloody history, and while the sport of bull baiting was made illegal under the Cruelty to Animals Act 1835, many modern sports teams seem happy to include the word 'bulldog' in their names or parade the breed as their mascot. For instance, the British national Australian rules football team has the nickname 'Bulldogs' and Georgetown University's athletics team mascot is 'Jack the Bulldog'.

All these formerly rural sports could be disruptive and attract large, potentially criminal crowds and the associated nuisances of drink and betting. But much of the 'censure' (Sumner, 2005) was traditional moralising or the emerging modernist concern for rationality. These pastimes were not 'rational' and certainly not improving as the Victorians would want.

LACS says that cockfighting still exists in the UK and may even be legal in parts of Belgium under certain conditions. The website Gameness to the End hosts a petition to make cockfighting legal again in the United States.[3] Among answers to frequently asked questions on the website[4] of the American Society for the Prevention of Cruelty to Animals (ASPCA) is this: 'Cockfighting is still popular and prevalent in many other countries, such as France, Mexico, Puerto Rico, Belgium, Spain, Haiti, Italy and Malaysia.'

ASPCA admits that cockfighting still occurs widely in the United States despite being illegal. Interestingly, across the US, the nature of the criminal sanctions differs. Thus, to be a spectator at a cockfighting

[2] League Against Cruel Sports website www.league.org.uk (accessed 11 October 2015).

[3] *Gameness to the end* (nd) https://gtte.wordpress.com/legalize-cockfighting-petition/ (accessed 11 October 2015).

[4] American Society for Prevention of Cruelty to Animals (nd) www.aspca.org/fight-cruelty/cockfighting (accessed 11 October 2015).

event is illegal in 43 states, though in the District of Columbia it merely constitutes a misdemeanour charge. Fields (2014) notes that while the sport is now illegal in Texas, the raising and training of fighting birds is not. Lee and Quarles (2012) explore some of the issues surrounding cockfighting, including its 5,000 year history. They were writing in the aftermath of a scandal involving National Basketball Association (NBA) star Michael Vick in dog-fighting (Lee et al, 2010). One outcome of that case was a rise in legislative action against animal cruelty.[5]

The greatest success claimed by LACS is the banning of hunting with dogs in England and Wales under the Hunting Act 2004, though it admits that hunting of foxes with dogs still occurs. The Masters of Foxhounds Association represents 186 hunts and the patron of the associated Hunt Staff Benefit Society is His Royal Highness The Prince of Wales. This suggests that the Act has not been successful in reducing the popularity of hunts with its supporters. The rural campaigning group the Countryside Alliance backs the Act's repeal, while LACS supports its tightening or, at least, greater policing. Fox hunting remains unpopular with the majority of the population. According to an opinion poll commissioned by LACS in November 2013, 80% of respondents thought fox hunting should not become legal again.[6]

This illustrates a common theme in many sports – the thin and changing line between the legal/illegal and acceptable/unacceptable. In another context, von Essen and Allen (2015) suggest that illegal hunting in Sweden might be seen as a crime of dissent or resistance. Fear of gun crime (fanned by spree killings such as those in a Dunblane primary school in 1996 and in Hungerford in 1987) has led to increased gun control in the UK. This may cause difficulty for sports shooters, as the National Rifle Association (NRA) gleefully points out in an online article entitled 'Olympic shooting sports on the rise, but not in the UK',[7] although Squires (2015) opines that 'field' shooting has largely been unaffected by UK's tightening gun control. TV presenter Piers Morgan famously upset American viewers with his opinion that the only reason to have an assault rifle was to murder someone. Not

[5]   Anita Kumar (15 January 2008) 'After Vick Case, Dogfighting Bills Flood Va. Session', *Washington Post*, www.washingtonpost.com/wp-dyn/content/article/2008/01/14/AR2008011402419.html (accessed 11 October 2015).

[6]   Justin Parkinson (10 February 2015) 'Did fox hunting disappear?' *BBC*, www.bbc.co.uk/news/magazine-30940176 (accessed 11 October 2015).

[7]   NRA-Institute for Legislative Action (20 July 2012) 'Olympic shooting sports on the rise, but not in the UK'. www.nraila.org/articles/20120720/olympic-shooting-sports-on-the-rise-but-not-in-the-uk (accessed 11 October 2015).

everyone will find reassuring Hannaford's contention that such rifles are mostly for target shooting and shooting hogs.[8]

Fox hunting requires hounds and horses and versions of these activities continue to exist in National Hunt (NH) horse racing, and greyhounds still chase an electric hare.

Horse racing

Huggins notes that 'for much of the Victorian period the leading British sport was racing' (2004: 11). It is far less popular now and events like the Grand National are criticised by animal rights activists among others. Indeed, the Green Party might seek to ban it.[9]

Standard histories of horse racing go back 6,000 years to the domestication of the horse by the peoples of central Asia, moving on to chariot and horse racing in the Greek then Roman eras, to the significance of the Crusades in introducing English knights to Arabian horses in the 12th century, and eventually to the use of such horses in English horse racing. Such Whiggish narratives ignore the history of non-Western racing and rarely touch on crime or disorder.

It is important to recognise the centrality in horse racing of owner-to-owner wagering in the early days and generalised betting now – both legal and illegal. Such activity, if not criminogenic, could certainly be described as attracting crime, or 'criminophilic'. The similarities between horse racing and hunting are easily discerned in NH racing (over fences and hurdles) and in point-to-point racing, which recreates the idea of racing from village to village – hence the term 'steeplechase'.

Leaving aside the issue of whether hunting is cruel to the hunting and hunted animals, we have the spatial politics of class and gender to consider. Once played as an informal, rural sport, football (plebeian) was eventually confined by pitch and regulation as horse racing has been, but hunting ranges freely over the land in a way that participants in parkour might envy.

Cockfighting is seen, possibly because of its criminal connections, as a lower-class activity, yet falconry is seen as an upper-class sport

[8]   Alex Hannaford (11 March 2013) 'Why British attacks on gun culture miss their target', *GQ Magazine*, www.gq-magazine.co.uk/comment/articles/2013-03/11/american-vs-british-gun-control-laws (accessed 11 October 2015).

[9]   Kevin Rawlinson (12 April 2015) 'Green party would consider banning Grand National, suggests Natalie Bennett', *The Guardian*, www.theguardian.com/politics/2015/apr/12/green-party-would-consider-banning-grand-national-says-natalie-bennett (accessed 11 October 2015).

(though see Macdonald, 2014); fox hunting is viewed as upper class but with working-class adherents. Horse racing is now called the 'sport of kings' (a crown formerly given to hunting) and continues to enjoy royal and working-class support. Boxing, as we shall see, had upper-class adherents but lower-class performers, often from minority groups. Women jockeys, owners and trainers are becoming more common, but have yet to feature in a sporting scandal.

Boxing

It could be argued that the story of boxing also started in Britain, although Anderson acknowledges the influence of the United States' New York State Athletic Commission (NYSAC):

> In England, the predominance of the NYSAC was acknowledged by the fact that when the British Boxing Board of Control (BBBC) – the sport's private regulatory agency in the UK – was set up in 1929, it largely accepted the New York classification of the different weight categories for fighters. (2007: 55)

and

> By the early twentieth century, the United States had become the predominant boxing jurisdiction. To a very large extent, and certainly in terms of revenue, boxing was now an American sport. (2007: 61)

Fields (2014) examines the effect of the law on the popularity of a variety of American sports. Her findings are mixed and historically contingent. She notes that by the 1880s boxing was illegal in all 38 states then admitted to the Union. Wrestling remained legal but came to be frowned on, and then banned, if it occurred in a boxing match once legalised tournaments were introduced.

In *Commonwealth v Collberg* (1876) it was made clear that:

> prizefighting, boxing matches, and encounters of that kind, serve no useful purpose, tend towards breaches of the peace, and are unlawful even when entered into by agreement and without anger or mutual ill will. (Cited in Fields, 2014: 208)

Towards the end of 19th century, the Amateur Athletic Union was part of the campaign to organise legal regulated tournaments. Spectators of illegal fights were known to pay the fines of banned contestants to enable them to continue to compete, or to bribe juries to not convict, and 'exhibition' matches were allowed in some states.

Anderson looks specifically at the legal, moral and philosophical issues raised by boxing. Starting with ancient Rome, he notes that 'The gladiatorial spectacles were not sporting celebrations. They were sophisticated methods of social control and political manipulation' (2007: 6), and that 'Gladiators – typically slaves, prisoners of war or convicted criminals – were deemed *infami* under Roman law and lacked all legal status and capacity' (2006: 7), albeit half of all gladiators were free men exercising their *libertas*. In other words, they could, and did, consent to entering the arena to kill or be killed. Unintentional deaths are not uncommon in boxing today, and usually spark fresh demands to ban the sport.

Anderson (2007) suggests that early Christian views of the paganism of the early Olympics and Gladiatorial Games influenced perceptions of all sport. The need for war training saw the promotion of many sports including boxing and wrestling; 'vain, dishonest, unthrifty and idle' football (according to statute of 1365) was seen as the main threat to the 'noble and simple' archery that was essential to the defence of the realm. Elias and Dunning (1986) note that a stabilisation of English society from the Restoration onwards allowed sports to flourish.

Huggins examines the significance of sport to the Victorians, and vice versa, and notes how boxing slang became popular with young unmarried working-class males (who wore suits of 'the latest 'sporting cut' (2004: 6). Boxing also attracted the interest of Lord Lonsdale, who donated the belts for which fighters competed. He was also fond of racing and shooting, and helped found the Automobile Association, whose original aim was to confound the policing of speed limits (Groombridge, 1997).

Also famous in boxing circles is Oscar Wilde's nemesis, the Marquis of Queensbury, who sponsored the 1865 rules that bear his name. The expression 'according to Queensbury rules' has come to mean a fair contest, although the notion of 'fair play' here applies to contending gamblers, not to the contestants, as the following rules (of 12) demonstrate:

> VII. Should the contest be stopped by any unavoidable interference, the referee to name the time and place as soon as possible for finishing the contest; so that the match must

be won and lost, unless the backers of both men agree to draw the stakes.

...

X. A man on one knee is considered down, and if struck is entitled to the stakes.

The rules did, however, ensure that the glove replaced the fist – officially. Thus John L. Sullivan, a bareknuckle champion who preferred to earn a living fighting exhibition matches under Queensbury Rules, was arrested in France in 1888 for participating in a bareknuckle prizefight on the Rothschild estate, and his English opponent, Charlie Mitchell, was bound over in England to keep the peace.

Moving on in time, the Walker Law of 1920 in New York State specified 15-round contests with no grappling (the second of the Queensbury Rules bars 'hugging' too) and crucially gave protection to fights under the State Commission. This illustrates that if a sport can be seen to have proper rules and controls, it may be allowed considerable sovereignty.

We now have an 'alphabet soup' (Anderson, 2007) of 'world' governing organisations brawling over the slumped body of professional boxing. They include the World Boxing Association, the World Boxing Council, the International Boxing Federation and now the Amateur International Boxing Association (AIBA).[10] However, the money to be made is cited by some as the real reason to move into professional boxing and some fear damage to the amateur sport.[11] Anderson (2007) sets out some of the history of the alphabetisation of boxing, with money, power struggles and FBI investigations of corruption and gangsterism all playing a part.

Class need not trump all; as Wiener (2006) notes, both the duels of aristocrats and plebeian prizefighting became criminally sanctioned. Gender and sexuality are issues too, as Anderson notes from Sir Edward East's treatise *Pleas of the Crown:*

> If death ensues from such as are innocent and allowable, the case will fall within the rule of excusable homicide: but

---

[10] AIBA is the overall single authority for amateur boxing, but has recently started to promote professional fights with the intention of providing a single simple progression from amateur to professional status.

[11] James Riach (22 June 2015) 'Why English amateur boxing has been left reeling by controversial rule', *The Guardian*, www.theguardian.com/sport/2015/jun/22/amateur-boxing-aiba-coaches-ruling (accessed 11 October 2015).

> if the sport be unlawful in itself, or productive of danger,
> riot or disorder from the occasion, so as to endanger peace,
> and death ensues; the party killing is guilty of manslaughter.
> (2007: 38)

According to Anderson, activities that East deemed 'innocent and allowable' included the 'manly sports and exercises that tend to give strength and activity in the use of arms' such as 'playing at cudgels, or foils or wrestling'. In other words, they were entered into as private recreations among friends, 'though doubtless it cannot be said that such exercises are altogether free of danger yet they are very rarely attended with fatal consequences; and each party has friendly warning to be on his guard' (2006: 38).

There is no record of what Sir Edward made of women boxers of the Georgian era, but an account from the BBC HistoryExtra website gives us some indication:

> two Amazons stripped to the waist, tied up their hair.... For 20 minutes they fought fiercely, with an excited crowd cheering them on.... Savage though they were, the two females (we cannot call them women) restrained their natural inclination to tear and claw, and standing up like men punched each other with their fists till the blood ran in streams down their faces and breasts.[12]

Such events were put on by publicans as entertainments, often featuring their wives. They even paired with their wives for some fights, or pitched a number of women against a man. Georgian female boxing was a spectacle, as was much male professional boxing, then and today.

Bareknuckle boxing has not gone away; it has just moved underground, where it is unregulated. Moxon gives an example of a return of bareknuckle boxing, relating the story of how 'Danny' joined a boxing gym and found himself in illegal fights, with a suspicion that his 'promoter' had bet on him to lose.[13] Moxon wonders what the

---

[12]   Anna Freeman (25 August 2014) 'Revealed: the bloody world of Georgian female boxing', *BBC HistoryExtra*, www.historyextra.com/femaleboxers (accessed 11 October 2015)

[13]   David Moxon (15 July 2015) 'Bareknuckle prize fighter: Danny's story', *CrimeTalk*, www.crimetalk.org.uk/index.php?option=com_content&view=article&id=959:bare-knuckle-prize-fighter&catid=38&Itemid=41&hitcount=0 (accessed 11 October 2015).

All Party Parliamentary Group for Boxing might make of stories like Danny's; its laudatory report on the merits of boxing is discussed in Chapter Seven.

Football

Anderson's legal history of boxing covers the growth of (and concern about) other sports, and notes:

> Football as a team or group sport attracted the concern of the authorities and was regularly denounced and prohibited by statute. As early as 1314 the Lord Mayor of London, Nicholas Farndon, had to issue a proclamation prohibiting football as a public nuisance. (2007: 9)

And to prove that the UK is not the only country where football is associated with violence, we have events like *calcio storico* ('historic football', derived from the Roman 'harpastum'). This is still practised in Italy where teams of 27 can punch, kick (except to the head), butt and elbow each other, in accordance with rules laid down in 1580.[14] Football as antisocial behaviour is still with us. One respondent in a study on anti-social behaviour by Millie and colleagues (2005: 25) complained:

> 'Playing fields! We're not even allowed to go on there and play football. Guarantee it, if you go on that field and play football you get arrested or something. It's just used for dogs shitting on – I'm being serious.'

Off-field football violence has been the subject of much criminological and sociological enquiry, and media and political hand wringing. While crowd violence occurs in other sports, it has not been collected up for study as a named (and naming?) phenomenon quite like 'football hooliganism'. This overshadows any type of study of criminality in football, including allegations of bribery and corruption at the Fédération Internationale de Football Association, boardroom

---

[14] Jim Powell (27 June 2015) 'The Calcio Storico, the most brutal sport on earth – in pictures', *The Guardian*, www.theguardian.com/football/gallery/2015/jun/27/the-calcio-storico-the-most-brutal-sport-on-earth-in-pictures (accessed 11 October 2015).

malfeasance and 'dodgy' agents, let alone actions on the pitch to win the match or a bet.

Football has a rival in the betting stakes, however, in the form of England's summer game – cricket.

Cricket

Two recent media stories claim that the French invented cricket, with one report dating the game to late 1480s France. Both may have more to do with the tourist publicity needs of Northern France and British 'silly season' journalism than with historical accuracy.[15] The latest claim (in the *Mail Online* story) relies on a letter found in archives about a scuffle associated with the game, while the earlier account describes a death at a match and a request for the king to intervene.

Qureshi and Verma (2013) are more conventional in locating cricket's history in England as early as the 12th century and attributing the birth of betting to India in 1500 BCE. It is to be hoped that when Qureshi and Verma describe the game (to their Interpol colleagues and fellow contributors to *Match fixing in international sports*) as involving the bowler 'throwing' the ball at the batsmen, they only do so to avoid having to explain the term 'bowling'.[16] The fact that the ball is bowled is one of the features that distinguishes cricket from the related baseball and rounders.

They do their best to explain the basics of the laws of cricket before quickly moving on to point out that the vagaries of climate and pitch, and the winning of the toss, add many chance elements to success in the game. These are a boon to those who might wish to disguise corrupt practices. In some circumstances, even information about the pitch may be subject to corruption. In the Indian context, the lure of Bollywood and politics add complexity to the issue. Historically, the practice between gentlemen of wagering on a cricket match, much as they might bet on a horse race or a fight among servants, is as old as the game. Indeed, it provides the synopsis for Birley's (2013)

---

[15] Tom Payne (30 August 2015) '"Ow is that, monsieur?" Historians claim cricket was invented by the FRENCH 80 years before it was ever played in England', *Mail Online*, www.dailymail.co.uk/news/article-3216183/Cricket-invented-French-80-years-played-England-historians-say.html#ixzz3kOhhLhQS (accessed 11 October 2015) and *BBC Sport* (17 November 2002) 'France lays claim to cricket', http://news.bbc.co.uk/sport1/hi/funny_old_game/2485439.stm (accessed 11 October 2015). The word cricket has a French/Flemish origin.

[16] See Fraser (2005) on 'chucking'.

A Social History of English Cricket, which blithely trumpets 'how the game was snatched from rustic obscurity by gentlemanly gamblers'. Brookes (1974) is less colourful in his description, contending that the game assumed its importance as a means of acting out prestige rivalries between leisured elites. Clearly, changes to the game and its global reach, second only to football, have increased the chances for, and rewards of, corruption.

Birley (2013) notes that sport and games are rarely recorded in history unless they have been played by the nobility or have been censured. We have seen how football and boxing in their different ways came under legal attack and how they adapted. Birley (2013) also mentions dice, cards and tennis balls being seized during the reign of Henry VIII, and notes that in 1541 keeping a bowling alley or green for profit was banned. Cricket, if it was being played then, seems to have escaped such prohibition, either because it was insufficiently popular or sufficiently disruptive. Topography might be an issue. Cricket and football both have rural antecedents, but cricket is less easily squeezed into town spaces.

Malcolm (1999) seeks to demythologise the claims made for the absence of crowd violence in cricket. Tied up with this myth are notions of the Englishness attached to the game. Malcolm lists examples of crowd violence at cricket from 1693 – 'Thomas Reynolds, Henry Gunter and Elenor Lansford fined for their part in riot and battery' – to '1777 Crowd prevent Stowmarket winning a match, probably due to gambling interests' and '1778 Duke of Dorset, impeded by the "Hampshire people", injures one of them with his bat in attempting to play a stroke' (1999: 10).

But by 1932, an article in *The Cricketer* could claim that 'Cricket stands for law and order.... The umpire gives you out: out you must go. The man in the white coat is a symbol of constitutional government' (Williams, 2012: 12). W.G. Grace might not always agree. He played cricket right up to, and sometimes beyond, what the rules allowed, often with the collusion of the authorities blurring the line between amateur and professional (Tomlinson, 2015).

Ireland (2013) examines the fictional cricketer, and gentleman burglar, Raffles' relationship to professionalism. He is both an amateur burglar and a cricketer – that is, he does both for love. In *The Criminologists' Club* (Hornung, 1905: 324), Raffles declares that the 'criminologists' believe 'that the gladiatorial element is the curse of modern sport. They tremble especially for the professional gladiator. And they want to know whether my experience tallies with their theory.' The 'criminologists' have invited him to one of their dinners, ostensibly to talk about sport and crime such as betting and throwing matches (hence their fear of professionals), in order to catch him as a thief. In fact, he steals their research records without detection.

The 'constitutional government' that *The Cricketer*'s correspondent alludes to belies the power accorded to sports officials; the jurisdiction of the police and the criminal justice system is as nothing compared with this. Nevertheless, Fraser (2005) takes the spirit of it for the subtitle his book on cricket and the law, 'the man in white is always right'.

Like Yar (2014) and his interest in the Tour de France, Fraser (2005) only came to cricket by chance, and only when he found himself musing on the legal issues raised by 'leg before wicket' or LBW – a means of being called out (LBW gets a whole chapter to itself in his book). In this compendious tome, Fraser examines the first conviction for murder on a cricket field in 1775 (William Waterfall). But among his examination of contracts, ball tampering and sledging, he also notes: 'More importantly, however, cricket provides many useful examples of real law' (2005: xi). This book claims that all sport provides many useful examples of real law *and* crime – hence the concept of sports criminology.

Many authors back cricket's claim to being the national game of England, a view supported in a ruling by Lord Denning in 1977 (in *Miller v Jackson*) allowing an appeal by a cricket club against a complaining neighbour:

> In summertime village cricket is the delight of everyone. Nearly every village has its own cricket field where the young men play and the old men watch. In the village of Lintz in County Durham they have their own ground, where they have played these last seventy years.

He continues:

> The cricket ground will be turned to some other use. I expect for more houses or a factory. The young men will turn to other things instead of cricket. The whole village will be much the poorer. And all this because of a newcomer who has just bought a house there next to the cricket ground.

But such eulogising is nothing to that of a Supreme Court judge in a ruling on baseball, as we see in the next section.

Baseball

Like cricket, baseball has a contested history, in which the two sports are intertwined (Lewis, 1987; Majumdar and Brown, 2007). In France, both come under the same governing body as softball.[17] Just as cricket is seen to be quintessentially English, so baseball is seen to epitomise the United States.[18] Justice Blackmun of the US Supreme Court opens his judgment in *Flood v Kuhn*, 407 U.S. 258 (1972), maintaining baseball's unique exemption from anti-trust legislation, with an elegiac history of baseball:

> It is a century and a quarter since the New York Nine defeated the Knickerbockers 23 to 1 on Hoboken's Elysian Fields June 19, 1846, with Alexander Jay Cartwright as the instigator and the umpire. The teams were amateur, but the contest marked a significant date in baseball's beginnings. That early game led ultimately to the development of professional baseball and its tightly organized structure.
>
> The Cincinnati Red Stockings came into existence in 1869 upon an outpouring of local pride. [...] Shortly thereafter, on St. Patrick's Day in 1871, the National Association of Professional Baseball Players was founded and the professional league was born.

He then lists 'the many names, celebrated for one reason or another, that have sparked the diamond and its environs and that have provided tinder for recaptured thrills, for reminiscence and comparisons, and for conversation and anticipation in-season and off-season'. He lists over 70 players, including Babe Ruth and Lou Gehrig, and refers to 'all the other happenings, habits, and superstitions about and around baseball that made it the "national pastime"'.

Baseball appears to have been welcomed in the United States and given legal privileges that mark it out from other American sports as well as crucially, in its development, from the English oppressor's game, cricket. As we shall see it has been dogged by accusations of cheating and drug use. Some of its scandals are now so old they are best examined in this history chapter.

[17] Fédération Française de Baseball et Softball, www.ffbsc.org/ (accessed 11 October 2015).

[18] Henry Chadwick was born in Exeter in 1824, authored baseball's first rule book and is the only journalist to be inducted into the National Baseball Hall of Fame.

Brooks and colleagues (2013) note that on 16 June 1917 bookmakers occupied the field in the hope that a match between the Boston Red Sox and the Chicago White Sox would be cancelled. It was a more subtle and extensive incident involving betting that led to the scandal that saw the White Sox briefly being called Black Sox. The Sox of the American League were heavily backed in the 1919 World Series even though their National League opponents had a better record. They lost to the Cincinnati Reds in eight games. Large bets on the Reds fuelled speculation that the series had been fixed. A criminal investigation went on into the 1920 season, and although all players were acquitted, the commissioner banned eight of the White Sox players for life. One reason for the 'fix' might have been the poor relations, both between players and managers and within the team. Nathan (2003) argues that this event still resonates in American culture today. Kudlac (2010) reminds us that the earliest known example of crooked baseball game was in 1865 when three members of the New York Mutuals accepted $100 each to throw a game against Brooklyn Eckforts, which led to two payers being expelled from the league.

Baseball may be the US' 'national game', but it is not its most popular sport – that is probably stock-car racing. However, American football and basketball have the greater international recognition. The other sport primarily associated with this part of the world – ice hockey in the northern US states and Canada – is also played in many European countries. These sports feature extensively in following chapters and each has their complex and contested history. Their relation to crime and criminal justice is very current but some context is necessary. As professional sports, they have their roots in the American high school and college system.

College sport

Miracle and Rees (2003) explore the school sports adopted in the United States that developed in Britain and why Americans became so obsessed with them. One answer is the intimate connection with schools. Foreshadowing some of the examples in Chapter Seven of this book, these authors show how the assumption that sport is an ennobling experience is far from the truth. In their critique, they may have in mind American writers like Emerson, who believed:

> Archery, cricket, gun and fishing-rod, horse and boat are
> all liberalizers, and so are ... swimming, skating, climbing,

> fencing, riding, lessons in the art of power. (Cited in Gorn
> and Warren, 2004: 85)

Miracle and Rees found that participation has little effect on the development of positive characteristics. Far from building model citizens, competitive team sports may foster selfishness and antisocial behaviour. Students learn that 'winning isn't everything, it's the only thing', and that the end justifies the means. The only sport that they exclude from this negative discourse is cricket (albeit they only mention the five-day variety), which, they suggest somewhat naively, might encourage gentlemanly behaviour.

Athletics, meanwhile, may be at variance with educational goals: many athletes end up sacrificing opportunities for lasting self-improvement through education in the hope of achieving the short-lived glory of athletic success. As might be expected, the majority of high school team players never become successful college, let alone professional, athletes. There is a racial element to this, with Miracle and Rees (2003) noting that black students who try to emulate O.J. (Simpson), Kareem-Addul-J(abbar) or Magic J(ohnson) end up with 'no-J' (no job).

Miracle and Rees also found that school sports organisers often deceive both athletes and themselves. The real, underlying, function of sport is to provide entertainment for the community. Having winning teams is much more important than having educated and well-adjusted athletes. Clerk Kerr's aphorism is that as a university president, his job was 'providing parking for faculty, sex for the students, and athletics for the alumni'. He recalls in his memoir (2001) what was then called a 'panty raid' at Berkeley, and see Thelin (1994) for arguments about the comparability of academic and athletic corruption in universities.

Kudlac (2010) devotes a chapter to the various stages in an athlete's life before turning professional. He also notes, like Bissinger (2005), the communal significance of athletics (sport), which may lead to a sense of entitlement and privilege for leading athletes. These matters come up again with respect to professional athletes, both in his work and in this book (see Chapters Four and Five on criminological theory). There are few mentions of track athletes in Kudlac's work (2010), but those that do occur often make the contrast with 'privileged' 'jock' sports.

Fans as well as players may be drawn into crime. Eitzen (2012) tells of a 62-year-old University of Alabama football fan who poisoned two 130-year-old oaks that were traditionally 'garlanded' with toilet paper by Auburn University fans whenever Auburn beat Alabama. Leaving aside the 'green crime' of tree garlanding, we have worse:

Harvey Updyke Jr's eventual admission in 2013 to pouring herbicide around the trees. He was charged with criminal mischief, desecrating a venerated object and damaging agriculture, but pleaded guilty to criminal damage of an agricultural facility. He was sentenced to three years in prison (to serve six months) and five years' probation, with a curfew and bans on visiting university or sports facilities.[19]

Athletics

Athletics, or track and field, is increasingly in the news over allegations of performance-enhancing drugs. Once these incidents might have been dismissed as the result of a few 'bad apples' or 'fallout' from the 'Cold War', with Soviet and East European athletes being systematically 'doped'. However, allegations have also been made against athletes from Kenya and Jamaica as well as from Britain and the United States. But for much of its history, the great 'crime'/sin of athletics (shared with many other sports) concerned professional status. Founded in 1912, the International Amateur Athletic Federation only changed its name to the International Athletics Associations Federation in 2001, despite have allowed a form of professionalism with the introduction of trust funds in 1985.

The historic arc of athletics in Britain is similar to that for many of the other sports mentioned so far. Folk or traditional sports – with the added lustre of Greek Olympianism – came to be played, refined and codified by English gentlemen who could afford to be amateurs. However, Gorn and Warren (2004) note that different immigrants to the US (Scots, English and German, for instance) brought different athletic, and often associated political, traditions with them. But, as in the UK, the official embrace of amateurism required the involvement, sometimes deceptive, of professionals.

The sports considered so far have UK/US roots and international appeal. The next sport to be considered – sumo – is largely confined to one nation, and its roots go deeper than cricket or baseball.

Sumo

The title of Cuyler's (1980) book *Sumo: From Rite to Sport* summarises the mythologised history of a sport that has a deeply problematic

[19] *CBSNews* (22 March 2013) 'Alabama fan receives 3 years for Auburn tree poisoning', www.cbsnews.com/news/alabama-fan-receives-3-years-for-auburn-tree-poisoning (accessed 11 October 2015).

association with crime (and more recently with women's participation). His history only mentions crime and corruption in respect of occurrences in wider Japanese society. West (2005: 58) notes that even today sumo is more than a sport. It is 'at its heart a cultural entity', tied to Shinto, the royal family, and charged with the 'education of young persons and students' (according to the Act of Endowment of the Japan Sumo Association). This has not been sufficient to protect Japan from accusations of drug use, corruption and illegal betting (on baseball) (Manzenreiter, 2014). Amusingly, West (2005) notes that to comply with former sumo rules that fighters be five feet, eight inches or taller, one would-be fighter had implants in his head to achieve the desired height (sociology of sport's 'positive deviance' or 'overconformity' illustrated).

The round-robin nature of sumo tournaments often leads to 'dead rubbers', in which one fighter may not need to win to progress and might favour another fighter out of compassion or with the hope of future reciprocity. This has, however, led to allegations of corruption going back some time (Duggan and Levitt, 2002). Problems with the structure of tournaments will come up in Chapter Six.

End game

Between the 1940s and 1970s, pinball was banned in some US states because of claims that it was a mafia-run gambling scheme that was corrupting the youth of America. It wasn't until 1976 that an expert persuaded a court that pinball was a game of skill and not luck, after which the ban was lifted in New York City (Kent, 2010).

Huggins (2004: 2) notes how even in Scotland, its home, golf had problems with the authorities in the 1830s on moral/religious grounds. More recently, there have been allegations of corruption in golfing in China. Nylander[20] (2015) asks why China's 'illegal' golf boom is coming to an end, and notes:

> While there are no official figures for how many golf courses there are in the country, golf organization R&A estimates in a new report that there are 473. […] it could be as much as double that amount.

[20] Johan Nylander (30 March 2015) 'Why China's "illegal" golf boom is coming to an end', *Forbes*, www.forbes.com/sites/jnylander/2015/03/30/why-chinas-illegal-golf-boom-is-coming-to-an-end (accessed 11 October 2015).

When Mao Zedong took power in 1949, he branded the sport bourgeois and a lot of the existing golf courses were dug up or repurposed.[21] In 2004, the government again imposed a ban on new golf course construction in an effort to protect the country's land and water resources.

These examples of the criminalisation of sport show that criminology should be interested. As we have also seen, sometimes bans have been issued because of the connection – real or presumed – to crime, public disorder, violence, gambling and organised crime. In a New Jersey sports gambling case, the National Collegiate Athletic Association, NFL, NBA and others argued that betting violated a 1992 federal law that banned the activity in all but four states where it is currently allowed. Betting also threatens the integrity of sports games, they argued. The American Gaming Association president and CEO Geoff Freeman warned: 'With Americans betting at least $140 billion on sports illegally each year, it's clear that (the) current law is not achieving its intended result.'[22] Such things should also be of interest to criminology.

Finally, whether legal or illegal in themselves, all of these sports have some sorts of rules and 'justice systems'. It is the argument of this book that these 'crimes' should also be of interest to criminology. Chapters Four and Five respectively look at what 'mainstream' and 'critical' criminologies might make of these crimes and Chapter Six looks at the justice systems and what might be learned from them. This chapter, in giving the crimino–legal history of some sports, has mentioned various cases. The next chapter concentrates on other cases from the sports discussed above and other sports.

[21] Shanghai's premier golf club was turned into a zoo.
[22] Reuters (25 August 2015) 'US appeals court rules against New Jersey sports betting law', *Mail Online, www.dailymail.co.uk/wires/reuters/article-3210435/U-S-appeals-court-rules-against-New-Jersey-sports-betting-law.html#ixzz3mvHfk5YQ* (accessed 28 August 2015).

THREE

Celebrity and corruption: case studies of sports scandals

Kietlinski (2011) suggests that the rise in popularity of women's sports, including sumo and baseball, in Japan may be due in part to the curiosity of spectators but also to some extent in reaction to corruption in the men's games. As we shall see, the majority of the scandals examined below involve men.

Rojek (2004) looks at many aspects of celebrity, but wisely offers no definition of the term. In his work on celebrity, crime is afforded more attention than sport, although the case of O.J. Simpson involves both. According to Rojek, celebrity must at least involve notoriety and glamour. Neither does he define scandal, although Hughes and Shank (2005) examine what it might mean for commercial sponsors to invest in the celebrity of sports stars only to see their 'stock' fall when a scandal breaks.

Some scandals could be described as transient or 'local'. Hughes and Shank (2005) use American examples; only the top two in their list, the BALCO laboratory case and the accusations of sexual assault against Kobe Bryant, will be known to many. The BALCO (Bay Area Laboratory Cooperative) lab case involved the supply of a steroid, tetrahydrogestrinone (THG), nicknamed 'the clear' as it was undetectable at the time. When a test was developed to identify it, old samples were retested and 20 were found to contain THG. Those implicated in obtaining the illegal drug included baseball and American football players, track and field athletes and a cyclist. A variety of charges – legal and sporting – were made against the athletes, with various degrees of severity and success. Marion Jones had to return a number of medals and was eventually sentenced to six months in prison in 2008 for perjuring herself in respect of drug use in the 2000 Olympics and a cheque fraud carried out in 2006. She remains 'disgraced', 'fallen' (Yar, 2014). Rasmussen (2005) hints at a deeper scandal and quotes Danish scientists, Bengt Saltin and Rasmus Damsgaard, to the effect that the performance-enhancing effect of THG was unproved. 'Drugs cheats' cheated?

Notwithstanding the accusations against him, Bryant continues to play for the LA Lakers and has now regained many of the sponsors he lost at the time. The 'facts' of the case rest on the now established template of sports/celebrity rape accusations, in that the alleged victim claimed rape, and the alleged perpetrator claimed consent and admitted, with his wife by his side, to adultery. After some legal wrangling, the criminal case was dropped and a civil one settled privately. Bryant has not 'fallen'.

From a 'sociology of sport' perspective, Palmer (2011: 558) briefly attempts to analyse the ecology of a sports scandal. She opens with the Australian Crime Commission (ACC) revelation that sport in Australia is 'highly vulnerable to organised crime infiltration' through match fixing, the manipulation of sports betting markets, and the illegal sale and distribution of performance-enhancing drugs (ACC, 2013: 1). Rowe (1997) looks at how scandals reduce sport consumers' ethical expectations of stars. We have seen that cricket can be considered English, baseball American and sumo Japanese, but Rowe (2013) notes how the Australian government embraces the totality of sport as Australian. This might lead one to expect more frequent and more serious sports scandals involving Australians, but Waterhouse-Watson (2013) argues that sexual assaults by Australian rules and rugby league players are given 'narrative immunity'.

The short histories set out in the previous chapter saw concerns about general disorder (in boxing, horse racing and football in particular) and corruption (often associated with betting, and so involving boxing and horse racing again). Here the focus is on some case studies that pick up on this theme and set us up for the next two chapters on criminological theory. During the writing of the book, various scandals erupted, many of which are ongoing. Once this book has been published, new light may have been shed on some of these. The doings of FIFA and the ongoing ramifications of the Lance Armstrong case in cycling offer scope for whole libraries in themselves.

Researchers have found a 'contract' suggesting that a wrestling match between Nicantinous and Demetrius might have been fixed in Antinopolis, Egypt, in AD267. In it, the father of Nicantinous pledges to pay Demetrius 3,800 drachma if he allows Nicantinous to win. The papyrus's translator, Dominic Rathbone, is right to ponder the reasons for offering a bribe and, crucially, committing it to paper, thereby breaching the first rule of 'bribe club'.[1] Most of the cases that follow

---

[1]   Owen Jarus (16 April 2014) 'Body slam this! Ancient wrestling match was fixed', *Live Science*, www.livescience.com/44867-ancient-wrestling-match-was-fixed.html (accessed 11 October 2015).

have been equally well documented, although sometimes well after the event. This chapter features case studies of violence by individual stars on and off field as well as corporate and conspiratorial events. The latter have been accorded the suffix 'gate', which has been used to indicate scandal since Watergate, a political scandal that occurred in the US in the 1970s.

Yar (2014) examines the growing numbers of celebrity autobiographies and reflects on how the stars in question manage the crime-like stigma they live under. The key and ongoing exemplar of this is US cyclist and one-time record-breaking Tour de France winner, Lance Armstrong, although Yar also examines the cases of British sprinter, Dwain Chambers, Armstrong's antagonist Tyler Hamilton, and UK cyclist David Millar. The only woman to feature is US sprint star Marion Jones, already mentioned. We shall return to some of these cases and to sporting celebrity later in the chapter.

The Guardian recently followed the fortunes of some less high-profile ex-footballers, some of whom have since been involved in criminal activity, while others, paradoxically, have made a new career in law.[2] All of these cases resulted in reduced celebrity status for the individuals involved. Stuart Ripley, formerly a winger with various premier football league clubs, is now a sports lawyer, and Arjan De Zeeuw, once of Wigan Athletic and Portsmouth, is now a police detective in the Netherlands. Mark Ward by contrast worked as a builder and driver and now does 'ambassador' work for West Ham and occasional after-dinner speeches. He has also spent four years in prison.

As he says, in *The Guardian*'s article:

> 'I made a mistake when I was really down financially. I rented out a property: I knew it was going to be used for a stash and, knowing the people I knew, it was probably some form of drugs. It was terrible decision. What the police found – four kilos of cocaine – was down to me. I couldn't disclose who had rented the property, because of the risk of repercussions to my close ones, so I had to take the sentence on the chin. I was caught up in the cogs of it all.'

---

[2] Nigel Tassell (24 April 2015) 'They think it's all over: ex-footballers on life after the final whistle', *The Guardian*, www.theguardian.com/football/2015/apr/24/they-think-its-all-over-ex-footballers-life-after-final-whistle-premier-league (accessed 15 July 2015).

He goes on to say that he'd like to work with Xpro, an organisation of footballers looking after other footballers who have fallen on hard times, and that there are 144 ex-pros in prison, 120 of them on drug offences. *Vice News* recently asked 'Why do so many failed Premier League footballers become drug dealers?'[3] One reason is the dropping of promising youngsters expecting the big time. Football doesn't seem to have worked for them. Chapter Seven looks at claims that football might help others.

We turn now to some 'scandals' accorded the suffix 'gate'. The chapter then provides some examples of scandals in those sports covered in Chapter Two as well as others.

The 'gates'

What follows borrows from Naidoo's (2013) structure, but subjects her structure to critical engagement. Her concerns are legal and examine the extent to which more or better regulation would help. This might have been discussed in Chapter Six, but the focus here is on the scandal. Despite being an ex-CEO of the International Netball Federation and a member of several sports disciplinary panels, Naidoo recognises the difficulty of simply regulating more, or attempting to do so. However, she is prone to some naivety in her reference to, and reverence for, ethical codes, as the following quote demonstrates:

> The IOC Code of Ethics lays down the principles that 'fairness and fair play are central elements of sports competition. Fair Play is the Spirit of Sport and the values of respect and friendship shall be promoted.' (2013: 29)

Criminologists might not expect sportspeople to be 'role models'. They are sports workers and sometimes celebrities. They may attempt 'justify' or 'neutralise' their actions (Sykes and Matza, 1957), but the competitiveness of sportspeople and the structural pressures of the media and sports team owners grant them little agency save perhaps in choice of tattoo. They are in a business with a star economy and limited narratives. We expect to be entertained, to enjoy the spectacle, for them to be the circus while we scrabble for bread. The 'gates' Naidoo (2013)

---

[3] Max Daly (19 May 2015) 'Why do so many failed premier league footballers become drug dealers?', VICE News, www.vice.com/en_uk/read/ex-footballer-drug-dealer-394?utm_source=vicefbuk (accessed 11 October 2015).

discusses are 'Badmintongate', 'bountygate', 'bloodgate', 'crashgate', 'eargate' and 'skategate'.

Badmintongate

The facts of this case are that at the London Olympics 2012 the Chinese had two women's doubles pairs in the badminton competition. The players Wang and Yu (then world champions and first seeds) wanted to come second in their group and thus avoid playing the other Chinese pair, Qing and Yunlei, until the final. Their opponents, the Koreans, became aware of the manipulation, and also started to play poorly. All were disqualified.

Commenting on the case, Action Aid blogger Mike Lewis even drew parallels with tax avoidance.[4]

The Guardian's article on the case cites Lin Dan, world No 1, blaming the organisers for setting up a playing schedule that opened the door to manipulation: 'Whenever they set the rules they should take that situation into consideration,' he said. 'I don't understand why there is a group situation' (rather than a straight knockout competition).[5] This suggests that he doesn't understand the nature of sports capitalism.

Naidoo notes a number of past and contemporary examples of 'not trying' from cycling (British sprint relay team) and women's football (where Japanese women admitted drawing a match to avoid moving host city) and a case in swimming which involved a South African 100m breaststroke swimmer admitted to additional 'dolphin kicks' that went undetected by officials for want of underwater technology. Naidoo notes the 'zero tolerance' applied to drug use and wonders why such 'cheating' is not treated in the same way. It may be that the administrators in some sports know that the structure of some competitions is 'asking' to be gamed or that the practice is so common as to be seen to be 'playing the game'.

---

[4]   Mike Lewis (3 August 2012) 'Is badminton-gate the same as tax avoidance?', Action Aid, www.actionaid.org.uk/blog/campaigns/2012/08/03/is-badminton-gate-the-same-as-tax-avoidance (accessed 11 October 2015).

[5]   Rizal Hashim (1 August 2012) 'London 2012: Badmintongate throws sport's Olympic future into doubt', *The Guardian*, www.theguardian.com/sport/blog/2012/aug/01/olympics-2012-badminton-badminton (accessed 11 October 2015).

Bountygate

In 2012, National Football League (NFL) team the New Orleans Saints were found to have offered a 'bounty' in three seasons to players who deliberately injured an opponent. Naidoo's description of the events concentrates almost exclusively on the bounty, which would have breached the NFL's strict salary cap. It also raised issues of governance. As she says:

> The NFL had no clear process in place to handle this sort of allegation as it could have been dealt with as a breach of the salary cap or it could have been dealt with as an on field breach of the rules. (2013: 30)

She continues: 'The farce around how the players were disciplined and the flawed governance process actually became a bigger story than the cheating' (2013: 31).

The events she describes, involving over 20 players, coaches and manager, suggest a conspiracy to commit grievous bodily harm, so on the face of it the term 'cheating' seems mild. Luckily the only harm appears to have been to the reputation of the game not the players. Just about anything other than the targeted players appears to be of concern either to her or the NFL:

> The Bountygate case publicly played out the very interesting conflicts involving due process rights of individuals, collective bargaining agreements, and private disciplinary procedures against the highly visible tapestry of professional sports. The federal judge who heard the case questioned the fairness of the process, but chose not to rule in part because it was unclear if she had the power to do so. (2013: 31)

The arguments of Paul Tagliabue, the former NFL commissioner appointed to hear the appeals, about the use of discretion and the arguments against being over-punitive are persuasive, but again it is interesting that Naidoo gives thought not to the victims but rather to the politics and processes of the NFL.[6] Those processes and role of the courts feature again when we look at 'deflategate' in Chapter Six.

---

[6] Sean Gregory (12 December 2012) 'Reading between the lines of the bountygate ruling', *TIME*, http://keepingscore.blogs.time.com/2012/12/12/reading-between-the-lines-of-the-bountygate-ruling (accessed 11 October 2015).

Bloodgate

Historically in rugby union no substitutes were allowed, only replacements, and then only for medical reasons. At lower levels, there might be no available replacement. In 2009, in a cup quarter final, the English team the Harlequins was narrowly losing to the Irish team Leinster. The team had used all its players and had no specialist kicker on the field. With five minutes to go it needed one. Tom Williams, the last substitute, had come on carrying a fake blood capsule (and not the first occasion when he had done so) and, with the collusion of the physiotherapist and club doctor, faked an injury that allowed the specialist kicker on to replace him.

The team still lost, and was fined, and the player, coach and medics were all punished. Naidoo (2013) makes something of the different punishments – all appealed – but nothing of the reasons for the 'conspiracy'. Harlequins' director of rugby Dean Richards was banned for three years and the club fined £240,000. Stephen Brennan, the club physiotherapist, was banned from 'treating' the player for two years by the Health Professions Council. The council's sanctions policy indicates that it is not meant to be punitive, but rather, protective of the public. Brennan appealed the decision and the High Court found for him. It remitted the decision back to the panel, which replaced it with a caution order on the register. Brennan's remorse, loss of status and income, as well as the 'community service' he performed in giving ethics lectures to members of his profession, were taken into account (Connolly, 2011).

Williams had an initial ban of 12 months reduced to four months for his help in disclosing the deception. It is also interesting to note that the team doctor, Wendy Chapman, who deliberately cut the player's lip to add weight to the deception and also lied at the initial hearing, was only suspended for a year but was not struck off the medical register. So this scandal involved deception that might in real life be a crime and involved the jurisdictions of sport and two health professions, as well as the mediated court of public opinion.

In American football, offence, defence and specialist teams come on and off at the dictates of the play and the coach's strategy. In basketball and ice hockey, rolling substitutions occur. In rugby union, the number of substitutions depends on the level at which the game is being played, and the player substituted has to stay on unless replaced for blood reasons or because a specialist scrummage player is needed, for safety. In rugby league, by contrast, the squad of 17 players can be interchanged up to ten times.

So, to return to the question Naidoo poses, rugby union could prevent faking incidents, not by greater regulation but through regulating differently like other sports. Sports sometimes learn from each other. This book suggests that society might learn from sport and vice versa.

Crashgate

Naidoo (2013) baldly states that 'Nelson Piquet Junior crashed into a wall during the Singapore Grand Prix in 2008 to allow his teammate Fernando Alonso to win the race', before discussing the potential and reputational dangers involved. This was on the orders of the Renault team. The case involved both sports authorities and national courts but lawyers thrashed out an agreement that left team boss Flavio Briatore free to become involved with the sport again from 1 January 2013. Like much elite wrongdoing, it is difficult to investigate such matters and even journalists who cover the sport may be reluctant to risk their access-all-areas passes in cases such as this. This particular incident only came to light when Piquet, after Renault had dropped him, took his tale to Brazilian TV. It is not known why the Singaporean authorities laid no charges, nor made any investigation, but the prospect of bad publicity must be an issue. For that reason the Renault team lost sponsors and currently has no team.

Eargate

Naidoo (2013) refers to this case not as 'eargate', but rather 'Mike Tyson – Evander Holyfield', describing how in a 1997 fight Tyson bit off a part of Holyfield's ear. Holyfield declined to press criminal charges at the time. Naidoo opined that Tyson had been guilty of a criminal assault as the action was intentional, was not within the rules and the wound inflicted could have been described as serious. Holyfield was later inducted into the Nevada Boxing Hall of Fame in 2014 with the presentation made by Tyson. The pair also appeared in a Foot Locker TV advert that refers to the incident. In it, Tyson hands a box to Holyfield, apologising and saying and that he'd kept it in formaldehyde – public, commercial restorative justice?[7]

---

[7] Jill Martin (23 July 2014) 'Ear-biting forgiven? Tyson to present Holyfield at Hall of Fame', *CNN*, http://edition.cnn.com/2014/07/22/sport/tyson-holyfield-hall-of-fame/ (accessed 11 October 2015).

Skategate

Again, 'skategate' is not the term Naidoo (2013) uses, prosaically opting for 'Tonya Harding'. She describes an off-rink assault on ice skater Harding's rival, Nancy Kerrigan, that Harding and her husband arranged. Kerrigan recovered from her injuries and won silver at the 1994 winter Olympics. Harding took legal action to overturn the US Olympics and skating ban but could only come eighth in the subsequent championship and was eventually banned from skating for life. Harding tried both to deny and minimise the charges but received three years' probation, 500 hours of community service and a $160,000 fine for hindering the investigation.[8]

Although the assault happened off rink, not during a contest, it is still associated with the sport. As such, it is of as much interest to criminologists as it is to sports lawyers. But it is not necessarily sports criminology in the same way as a later 'skategate' incident.

In the 2002 Salt Lake City Winter Olympics, Elena Berezhnaya and Anton Sikharulidze of Russia beat Jamie Salé and David Pelletier of Canada in the pairs figure skating by a few points. The tale is complex and contested. Part of the difficulty is that the technical merit of the performance and its presentation are subjective. Some believed that the good-looking, popular Canadian pair had been 'robbed'. Attention focused on the French Judge, Marie-Reine Le Gougne. Geopolitics may be an issue too, as the Canadian and Russian judges favoured their own skaters and Germany, Japan and the US aligned with Canada against Ukraine, China, Poland and France. Le Gouge is said to have made, then withdrawn, statements confessing the fix under pressure from the French skating federation in exchange for Russian votes in another event.

Under media pressure, particularly from the US NBC network, and the International Olympics Committee (IOC), the International Skating Union investigated. Le Gougne and the French skating president received bans and Salé and Pelletier were upgraded to a joint gold medal. No action was taken against the Russians, but later that year the Italian authorities arrested, then released, a Russian gangster on a

---

[8]   James Nye (6 January 2014) 'Disgraced Tonya Harding claims the attack on Nancy Kerrigan wrecked HER chances of gold at the '94 Winter Olympics and ruined her life 20 years ago', *Mail Online*, www.dailymail.co.uk/news/article-2534732/Tonya-Harding-claims-intense-media-spotlight-Nancy-Kerrigan-attack-ruined-chances-gold-Olympics-life-20th-anniversary-infamous-assault.html (accessed 11 October 2015).

US extradition warrant for alleged involvement in the fix. Following this incident, the scoring process in skating competitions was made secret, leading to accusations that such lack of transparency was open to other forms of abuse. Nevertheless, the new scoring method does make clearer what points an athlete might expect from different skills and utilises instant video replay.[2]

More sports scandals

Not all scandals acquire the suffix 'gate', and not many necessarily last long. What follows is a selection of stories detailing other misdemeanours in a variety of sports.

Fraser's (2005) starting point for a discussion of the Hansie Cronje case is what is done within cricket that could be described as 'not cricket' – in other words, unsporting. He entitles a whole section of his book 'The jurisprudence of Hansie Cronje'. The laws of cricket allow a good deal of discretion and speak of the 'spirit of the game'. In the 2000 fifth test between South Africa (SA) and England, Cronje, the SA captain made what many thought to be a 'sporting' declaration, that is, a declaration that might give the opposition a chance to reach the South African run total and tie or win the match or force a draw. The England team went on to win that test, its only one on that tour.

Most of the first four days had been lost to rain. On the last day, Cronje proposed over breakfast (now, that *is* cricket!) to Nasser Hussein, the England captain, that Cronje would declare the SA first innings at 248-8 and that both teams should then declare their next innings, leaving England to chase a total of 249 in its second innings. Spectators and commentators are used to teams grinding out a draw in such circumstances, so this 'innovation' was welcomed as being in the 'true spirit of the game' (Lawson, 2000).[10] Fraser (2005) makes the nice point that Hussein's declaration was actually a 'forfeiture' and therefore his actions were illegal, even if in the spirit of the game. But later that summer it became clear that Cronje had made his 'sporting' offer for corrupt purposes on behalf of betting interests, and that he had taken bribes before.

[9] International Skating Union Statutes, Constitution, Regulations and Technical Rules, www.isu.org/en/about-isu/isu-statues-constitution-and-regulations (accessed 11 October 2015).

[10] Geoff Lawson (2000) 'A victory for the true spirit of the game', *Sun Herald*, 23 January.

This case turned on using the formal rules of not bowling a no ball or a wide, or deliberately getting out. In his preamble, Fraser (2005) mentions such formality too, where teams play to lose or to reduce run rates in 'dead rubbers', or for some compensating advantage later in the competition. Both captains clearly trusted that each would keep their side of the bargain in what, at least to Hussein, might be seen as a conspiracy to uphold the spirit of the game. Prisoners face similar dilemmas in game theory.

Golf is the subject of two recent scandals. One of these involved, dehydroepiandrosterone, a naturally occurring steroid precursor to testosterone production, which was recommended to golfer Scott Stallings by his doctor for chronic fatigue.[11] He reported himself to the Professional Golf Association (PGA) when he later realised that the drug was banned and received a suspension of 90 days. On the same day, Paul Fusco, caddy to Sei Young Kim who was due to compete in the US Women's' Open, was found photographing potential pin (flag) locations that would have helped him advise her.[12]

In contrast to cricket, golf and tennis, cycling has become synonymous with doping and whole books have been given over to it. Lewis reminds us, for instance, that Fausto Coppi, twice winner of the Tour de France and Giro d'Italia double (1949 and 1952):

> … was upfront about his use of drugs, particularly 'la bomba', a mix of caffeine, cola and amphetamine pills. His great rival Gino Bartali preferred more natural stimulation and would drink up to 28 espressos a day.[13]

Commenting on a report by the Cycling Independent Reform Commission (CIRC) (2015), Matt Slater (2015) followed up on the finding that amateurs were doping like professionals.[14] For instance, ex-pro rider Joe Papp (banned in 2006 for two years and losing all

[11] It is available on the internet as a 'supplement'.

[12] Emily Kay (8 July 2015) 'Golf gets scandalous with a PED suspension and a cheating caddie on the same day', *SB Nation*, www.sbnation.com/golf/2015/7/8/8909837/scott-stallings-suspension-cheating-caddie-us-womens-open-2015 (accessed 11 October 2015)

[13] Tim Lewis (31 May 2009), referring to Fotheringham (2009), http://www.theguardian.com/sport/2009/may/31/fausto-coppi

[14] Matt Slater (10 May 2015) 'Doping in cycling: Why are the amateurs "emulating the pros"?', BBC, www.bbc.co.uk/sport/0/cycling/32662773 (accessed 11 October 2015).

his results back to 2001) assisted the US anti-doping authorities with their enquiries yet he also set up as an online EPO (erythropoietin) and growth hormone supplier. This lead to an eight-year ban from sport and six months' house arrest for conspiracy to traffic drugs. He believed the majority of his 200 customers were amateur cyclists; 68 of his clients – none well known – received bans. These included a 62-year-old winner of age group masters cycling in New York. One British man whose name appeared on Papp's lists denied having used Performance Enhancing Drugs (PEDs), but also admitted that he'd never been tested. Such claims lead some to propose yet more onerous testing and surveillance of athletes.

In addition to scrutinising drug use among amateurs, Slater summarises the CIRC report as follows (a total of 174 anti-doping experts, officials, riders and other interested parties were interviewed):

- one 'respected cycling professional' believes that 90% of the peloton is still doping, another put it at 20%;
- riders are micro-dosing, taking small but regular amounts of a banned substance, to fool the latest detection methods;
- the abuse of Therapeutic Use Exemptions, sick notes, is commonplace, with one rider saying 90% of these are used to boost performance;
- the use of weight-loss drugs, experimental medicine and powerful painkillers is widespread, leading to eating disorders, depression and even crashes; and
- with doping done now on a more conservative basis, other forms of cheating are on the rise, particularly related to bikes and equipment.[15]

We return to the issue of doping and what to do about it in Chapter Six, including the issue of therapeutic use exemptions whereby drugs use is deemed necessary if a doctor signs it off. But cycling has had other scandals: all nine Festina riders were banned during the 1998 Tour de France for using EPO and some of them for using amphetamines. In the subsequent mass searches conducted by French police, other individuals on other teams were also found with drugs. The reaction of the riders was to 'strike' and 'go slow'. Other teams withdrew and only about half the peloton finished the race (Brissonneau, 2015). Some

[15] Matt Slater (8 March 2015) 'Doping culture in cycling "still exists", according to Circ report', BBC, www.bbc.co.uk/sport/0/cycling/31788505 (accessed 11 October 2015).

commentators argue that the incident also led to the establishment of the World Anti-Doping Agency (WADA) (Sefiha, 2012).

The Lance Armstrong case requires little expansion here, as the case is so well known, even among non-cycling fans. Walsh's (2013) pursuit of Lance Armstrong is recommended for more detail. Walsh's personal hurt at having initially believed in Armstrong's integrity is clear. As a sports journalist, he should have been more sceptical but he came to believe, for a while, that Armstrong was the answer to the problems that the Festina scandal posed. His subsequent disappointment led to years of detective work, which – with others – led to Armstrong's downfall.

No sports criminology can fail to mention Armstrong, but his case does not represent the 'totality' of sports criminology, which encompasses the experiences of more mundane, 'weekend warriors' taking supplements that may or may not be on the banned list, may or may not work, and may or may not contain the drugs listed on the label.

Football is often considered 'dirty' – the fouls, the simulation of being fouled ('diving'), the pay, the off-field activities of footballers and so on. Given the media's interest in sport and crime, the number of stories that might be covered is enormous and grows daily. A broad selection is presented here.

In the football magazine *Four Four Two*,[16] a survey of 123 players currently playing in the Premier Football and Scottish Premier Leagues found that 64 players thought being spat at by an opponent more offensive than racist (42) or homophobic (six) insults, or even being punched (five). Diving was only mentioned by six players as offensive. This suggests that this type of fouling has become normalised, despite some spectator and commentator concern. Strategic intentional fouls (to borrow from the title of the book by Triviño, 2012) are not mentioned, but this is another aspect of the game within a game. To 'dive' or simulate a foul to gain a penalty is one thing, but to 'book oneself' is to play the longer game. In this situation, you are carrying a penalty along with the fear that it may be compounded during an important match, so it's better get yourself sent off in an earlier match (Webb and Thelwell, 2015).

[16] *Four Four Two* (5 March 2015) 'Players' poll: spitting at another pro "the worst"', www.fourfourtwo.com/news/players-poll-spitting-another-pro-worst (accessed 11 October 2015).

Hill (2010) records massive corruption in football worldwide. This is backed up by Europol's[17] investigations, which found the following:

> A total of 425 match officials, club officials, players, and serious criminals, from more than 15 countries, are suspected of being involved in attempts to fix more than 380 professional football matches. The activities formed part of a sophisticated organised crime operation, which generated over €8 million in betting profits and involved over €2 million in corrupt payments to those involved in the matches.... In addition another 300 suspicious matches were identified outside Europe, mainly in Africa, Asia, South and Central America.

Britain and the lower leagues are not immune. Delroy Facey was found guilty at Birmingham Crown Court of conspiring to bribe non-league players. He had formerly been a Premier League player with Bolton Wanderers, West Bromwich Albion and Hull City. He was jailed for 30 months in April 2015.[18]

Other sports, other scandals

The two cases set out below illustrate the ongoing capacity of sport to enforce its specificity. Such matters are further taken up in Chapter Six, but here we focus on the case studies of individuals. The first, the case of US winter games slider, Zach Lund, is an illustration of overreaction and rough justice. Second, the very different case of tennis player Richard Gasquet illustrates the exercise of equity, but throws a fascinating light on the 'policing' of the self and others required in international sport as well as some very old-fashioned attitudes.

It may not help Lund that his case is cited by Floyd Landis[19] as an example of the deficiencies in the doping regime that saw him barred from cycling, but his story is instructive.[20] Lund is bald and from 1997

[17] Europol (6 February 2013) 'Update – results from the largest football match-fixing investigation in Europe', www.europol.europa.eu/content/results-largest-football-match-fixing-investigation-europ (accessed 11 October 2015).

[18] BBC News (29 April 2015) 'Ex-footballer Delroy Facey jailed after match fixing trial', BBC, www.bbc.co.uk/news/uk-england-32512704 (accessed 11 October 2015).

[19] Lauren Mooney (2007) 'The man', *Bicycling* (accessed 11 October 2015).

[20] Brian Alexander (29 December 2009) 'Good cop bad cop', *Outside*, www.outsideonline.com/1825536/good-cop-bad-cop (accessed 11 October 2015).

used a medical preparation containing finasteride to treat the condition. When WADA was formed in 2004, finasteride was not on its list of banned substances but he nevertheless declared his use. Finasteride was added to the list a year later as it was deemed to be a masking agent, and Lund continued to declare it. He claims to have been tested many times for illegal drug use and to have passed, but eventually failed a test for use of finasteride. He sought to argue that the substance should not be on the list, but he was thrown out of the Turin Winter Olympics, after the case was referred to the Court of Arbitration for Sport (CAS).

In 2008, WADA dropped finasteride from its list, claiming that steroid testing had moved on. As a previous offender, Lund risks a life ban for any further infraction. Some of the complaints made on behalf of Lund and others is that WADA's procedures do not meet the 'high standards' of 'due process', which are examined in Chapter Six. North American professional leagues in football, baseball, basketball and hockey are still holding out against such testing.[21] Some of the criticisms of WADA and the IOC can be seen as a proper concern with judicial procedures, but may constitute borderline xenophobia/racism or even paranoia about world government. Some of the same legal points, as well as other issues, are raised by the case of Richard Gasquet.

Gasquet is tennis player subject to the International Tennis Federation's (ITF) doping procedures. In early 2009, he was suffering shoulder injuries and playing through the pain (the sort of behaviour often deemed by sports scholars as overconforming or positive deviance) and withdrew from a tournament in Marseille in February. He travelled to Miami on 22 March to play in a tournament in which he was seeded. He had a bye that meant he was not due to play until 28 March. On the evening before the match, he discussed an MRI scan of his shoulder with his physio, coach and the tournament doctor. On his return to the hotel, he decided to withdraw but also decided to leave the formalities to the next day as he needed to return a hire car and collect an expenses cheque.

He decided to go out that night to meet up with compatriot Bob Sinclar, a DJ playing at the Winter Music Conference. They met at a restaurant with his coach, another coach and the DJ's wife. During and after the meal, they fell into conversation with a table of women, all French. Gasquet spent much, but not all, of the evening, and later at

[21] The failure of the US to sign up to the International Criminal Court is instructive and Guantanamo Bay offers its own commentary on American justice. Forman (2009) uses the example of Guantanamo to throw doubt on the claims made for the rest of the justice system.

some clubs, with 'Pamela' (her full name is never revealed) and some passionate kisses were exchanged. They parted early in the morning, and Gasquet returned to his hotel to sleep. He attended the tournament the next day to withdraw formally and took a doping test. The test contained a minute trace of cocaine and metabolites thereof.

He was punished by the ITF. At appeal the tribunal found for the ITF, but CAS recognised that he had gained no advantage and all parties accepted his explanation that the contamination had come from those kisses. It was accepted that he was not a cocaine user – or, indeed, the subject of a deliberate contamination – as the amounts one could have expected to find under such circumstances would have been larger. Gasquet kept his winnings and points from previous matches. While Smith (2011) notes a number of cases where 'zero tolerance' is shown by sporting authorities, he also gives some examples of derogation. The recent case of footballer Jake Livermore is a point in case. He tested positive for cocaine and admitted using the drug. He was suspended by his club and by the Football Association, but received no ban. The occasion of his taking the drug was the death of his newborn son.[22]

The details of Gasquet's case are fascinating, and a number of points are worth drawing out. Paragraph 16 of the ITF tribunal findings describes '… the Winter Music Conference; an event which, though the player did not know it, is notoriously associated with use of illegal recreational drugs including cocaine'. Paragraph 100 excels itself in opining: 'He proceeded to kiss a woman he had not met before who might, for all he knew, be a cocaine user.' Judges during the 1970s and 1980s were sometimes equally insensitive in dealing with rape cases.

Behind the infantilising and patronising tone of the judgment is a positivistic yet 'new penological' reliance on science and a one-size-fits-all management of crime. No proper 'policing' or evidence gathering is attempted or required (or perhaps possible, as Pamela could not be compelled to give evidence in the Gasquet case) and the player is expected to roll over and accept the strictly liability and rough justice in the name of keeping sport 'clean'. Sport may be part of an ideological state apparatus, but is often nakedly repressive. Gasquet was nearly subject to a miscarriage of justice and Lund's case might be seen in that same light, as might the case of Modahl examined in Chapter Six.

Kane (2005) notes how gloomy Huizinga was in 1938 about the lack of virtue and the triumph of commercialism in sport, but Kane himself is more conditionally optimistic:

---

[22] BBC (10 September 2015) 'Jake Livermore: Hull City midfielder avoids ban over cocaine', www.bbc.co.uk/sport/0/football/34212358 (accessed 10 September 2015).

… looking at the vast media spectacles of sport available to the Western consumer, it would be difficult to deny that the contest is, if not exactly a display of virtue, then certainly therapeutic. Figures like Tiger Woods, Venus Williams or David Beckham are exemplars of the benefits of competitive play – and this is often tied back into the modern rhetorics of play as progress, and play as selfhood, in a powerful fusion of ancient and modern traditions. Their tales are the best proof of the existence of a meritocracy. (2005: 54)

Setting aside Tiger Woods' difficulties and Beckham's embrace of commerce, might we see this chapter's tales of celebrity and sporting drama (even tragedy, if that is not too strong a word) as therapeutic too? The media often represents incidents of violence or 'cheating' involving sportspeople as scandalous, but investigative journalism and critical scholarship finds other scandals. The next two chapters attempt to see what criminology might say, and more rarely has said, about such matters.

FOUR

Game of two halves: mainstream criminological theory and sport

Everyone is entitled to an opinion on crime. Whole industries are now dedicated to discussing sport and its crimes (though they are not usually called crimes). Sports administrators, in particular, ask why people cheat. Naidoo (2013) speculates about some of the reasons – desire to win, financial reward and Tysonian 'sport rage' – but also asks 'What is the role of the sports lawyer?' From some of the examples given, we might conclude that one use for a sports lawyer is to defend 'cheating'.

Few criminologists would disagree with her conclusion where she quotes Duthie's[1] words 'regulations alone won't combat cheating', but many might baulk at the following:

> … the relevant sporting authorities need to have the necessary will to enforce them. Federations and governing bodies have to be prepared to investigate and prosecute suspected wrongdoing, even if it means some short term pain, like loss of sponsors or star teams/players being suspended or withdrawn. (2013: 34)

Not many would have the faith she places in ethics and 'sports culture'. Fewer and more rational rules might make 'getting tough' easier too.

This is not a criminology textbook, but there is a clear need to review existing criminological theory and relate it to sport. This chapter examines broadly mainstream theories of crime before Chapter Five turns to more radical and critical accounts.

As we saw in Chapter Two, rules were historically few – beyond the immediate objective of the game – and arbitrarily applied by players with no 'justice' to appeal to. But sports and games – be they individual or team sports, video games or even card and board games – need rules. Good rules make or break a sport or game and accord with modernist rationality, even if the emotions aroused by sport and gaming do not. This law making sits well enough with classicist

---

[1]   A partner in the sports group at Bird & Bird LLP. He prosecuted the misconduct complaints against Harlequins and others in the 'bloodgate' case.

conceptions in criminology, but breaches of them find explanations reaching back to pre-modern ideas of evil, biology or stereotype, or to would-be scientific positivism – for instance, attempts to explain Luis Suarez's propensity to bite opponents.[2]

Yar boldly claims that 'Criminology and allied disciplines are no strangers when it comes to sport', but recognises that 'its study remains a rather marginal and somewhat neglected area' (2014: 2-4). He sees criminological engagement in three areas: desistance (to be addressed in Chapter Seven); sport cultures or sub-cultures, specifically hyper-masculinity; and finally sport as the site of crimes of corruption and doping. These issues are unpicked throughout this book, but first a version of 'mainstream' criminological theory is set out to give this chapter structure.

There is no agreed list of criminological theories, so what follows is a partial, schematic examination that draws initially on teaching texts (Carrabine et al, 2013; Newburn, 2013). There is scope for argument as to the contents of the list and whether any particular theory should be covered in this chapter or the next. There is also the charge of 'textbookification' that Hall and Winlow (2012: 3) set out:

> The story starts with Bentham's utilitarianism and Beccaria's model for an enlightened criminal justice system, before moving on through Lombrosan 'scientific' criminology towards the early sociology of the Chicago School.... After that not much of note happens.... Left realism, postmodernism and risk theory entered the stage, but – with some notable exceptions ... were rapidly absorbed into the 'controlology' tradition.

As the next chapter and conclusion indicate, the plan is to avoid the charge of 'controlology' that might be levied against sports law and some sociology of sport, but clearly these two chapters have that 'textbook' feel. Hall and Winlow argue further that: 'The worst examples of this sort of thing can be seen in those textbooks that offer a basic description of a theory, then follow it up with bullet-point criticisms' (2012: 5). Necessarily here each theory will be briefly addressed and the relationship to sport made.

---

[2] Suarez bit Italy's Giorgio Chiellini at the 2014 World Cup, Chelsea's Ivanovic in 2013 in a premier league match and PSV Eindhoven's Otman Bakkal in 2010: BBC Sport (1 July 2014) 'Luis Suarez bite: Uruguay striker banned for four months', www. bbc.co.uk/sport/0/football/28023882 (accessed 11 October 2015).

Theories of crime can be traced back to a perspective that was common before Beccaria and throughout the growth of all the criminologies examined here, and it is an approach that is still prevalent today. This is called 'popular criminology' by Rafter (2009) and might also be termed 'commonsensical', 'theological', 'pre-modern' or 'medieval' criminology. These are not all the same, but all are rather atheoretical or un(der)theorised. This dark mish-mash suggests the architectural metaphor 'gothic' in distinction to the classical. Others (see, for example, Picart and Greek, 2004) tend to see much of criminology as 'gothic' or potentially so.

Gothic

The gruesome injuries suffered by some players, and by large numbers of fans in, for example, disasters at the Hillsborough, Ibrox, Heysall and Valley Parade football stadiums, might be seen as gothic in Picart and Greek's terms. Explanations of player (or fan or administrator) behaviour in terms of 'evil' or moral deficiencies come closer to the usage intended here. In the gothic, crime and sin are often fused in theocratic fashion. It doesn't have theorists so much as spokespeople, and in sport they may be administrators or commentators (some of whom might be ex-players with a history of sport crime or 'sin' to be joshed about). The condemnation of gothic action and injury may require the extensive and extended replaying of slow-mo highlights from all angles for our edification.

Classicism

The 'written constitutions' and rule base of sport are clearly classical. You set out what the game is and what the penalties are for infractions. Such criminology can be virtually indistinguishable from the concerns of law. The celerity that Beccaria demanded for punishment can be seen in the speed with which most decisions are made in sport. Even the delays occasioned by reference to a television match official are nothing compared with the law's delays. There might be more dispute about the quality of such speedy justice and its proportionality. Sending off a player and awarding a penalty in football can have a disproportionate effect on the result, but time in the 'sin bin' seems fairer, more proportionate, in rugby union and ice hockey.

As Chapter Two showed, slowly but surely a proper set of tribunals has come to rule sport. Yet 'gothic' corners can be found in the 'alphabet soup' of world boxing (Anderson, 2007). The work of thinkers like Beccaria and Bentham and modern followers and the law of the land – and of sport – seeks to keep the darkness at bay with its straight lines and classical proportions. Every game or match offers opportunities for contest between these tendencies. Within criminology, the contest is more often simplistically posed as being between classicism and positivism. The emphasis on rational law in classicism is picked up in administrative criminology with its emphasis on the rational, dissuadable, offender.

Administrative criminology

Administrative criminology is also quite strong in sport. Its thinking is that we don't know why people are disposed towards breaking the rules of sport, but we will attempt to stop them anyway. A line will be drawn, or, sometimes, redrawn. Some rules changes and the uneven pace of technological assistance for officials might be seen in this light. It might be stretching a point to suggest that the line of scrimmage in American football is meant to be a capable guardian of the quarterback victim that the outside linebacker or defensive end aims to 'sack'. Felson's routine activity theory (1998) can be applied to non-criminal acts like this, though he has little say about sport, save that, for crime prevention reasons, coaches should tell parents when football practice is cancelled, lest students use the spare time to get into trouble. Situational crime prevention owes much to observations of the sometimes serendipitous prevention of accidents or incidents when implementing policies. The authorities of American football did not decide to ask or tell players to be less rough, but allowed helmets from the 1920s. Initially leather, these helmets are now capable of advanced protection and indicate when a player may be concussed.[3]

Learning from sport, perhaps all pedestrians ought to wear full body armour instead of relying on policing speed limits. More seriously, Bricknell (2015) completes her review of corruption in sport in Australia by setting out a table of situational crime prevention measures from randomising allocation of officials, to requiring multiple person sign-offs, and operating due diligence on betting accounts that economists would recognise as 'rationally efficient' (Maennig, 2005). She also recommends morality clauses, education and training, and encouragement of media coverage. Here we might see the media as a

---

[3]   NFL (14 November 2012) 'History of the NFL football helmet', www.nfl.com/news/story/0ap1000000095139/article/history-of-the-nfl-football-helmet (accessed 11 October 2015).

form of CCTV/surveillance. Nothing about past media coverage of these issues backs her confidence that this is the answer. Neither can we be convinced that morality and education are situational measures. Administrative criminology might be described as neo-classical in that it shares the belief of classicism in the rational offender, but it uses more empirical and pragmatic methods akin to positivism.

Positivism

Traditionally, as Hall and Winlow (2012) sportingly skewer, criminology modules or texts might start by comparing the armchair freewill rationality of the classicists with the empiricism of the positivists. Leading light, and dark secret, of positivist criminology is Lombroso. He had a fascination with tattoos that seems to be shared by modern sports people. Lombroso collected tattoos as pieces of skin, as pictures and photographs. David Beckham is often taken as an exemplar of the sporting tattoo collector – his are on his own skin. Does this mean he should be seen to be a criminal?

Journalist Sarah Vine raises the issue of criminality in her criticism of tattoos in terms of taste and class:

> These footballers' tattoos are a similar thing, only in reverse. They are a way for young men who feel disorientated by their huge paypackets and lavish lifestyles to anchor themselves to what they still consider to be their class.... David Beckham was one of the first. A Leytonstone boy, he grew up to become eye-poppingly rich. But his tattoos and accent are a perennial reminder of his working class roots.[4]

Tattooed sportspeople can continue to find non-criminal work unlike the subjects of Timming's (2014) work. There is a 'modest' flow of 'tatistical' (Groombridge, 2015) criminological work, but none specifically on sport and tattoos, save mentions of fans' tattoos. Several of the contributors to Perryman's collection (2001) largely uncritically use tattoos metonymically to mean 'hooligan'. Poulton's (2001) chapter on 'framing' the hooligan references tattoos in its title.

Lombroso's work on tattoos marks a turn in his work that might (Groombridge, 2015) be seen as a tendency towards the cultural and

---

[4]   Sarah Vine (11 June 2014) 'Body art? No, tattoos are hideous self-harm', *Mail Online*, www.dailymail.co.uk/debate/article-2654596/SARAH-VINE-Body-art-No-tattoos-hideous-self-harm.html (accessed 11 October 2015).

social even though he retained his biologism in arguing for the lower pain threshold of criminals (and sportspeople?).

Positivism in criminology is often foundationally linked to Lombroso; it has an ongoing presence whether mentioning his work or not. As we have seen, Lombroso mixed the social and biological in his studies of tattoos. For analytical purposes, biological, psychological (and psycho-analytical) and sociological positivism will be discussed separately in turn.

Biological positivism

Newburn (2013) covers biological positivism in a chapter and confines Lombroso, the eugenicists and somatypists to an earlier discussion of the contrast with the classicism of Beccaria and Bentham. At the fundamental level, Lombroso believed in the 'born criminal', an approach that also chimes with the popular belief in the natural abilities of successful athletes. It also chimes with racist assumptions about the criminality of black men. The criminalisation and punishment of Jack Johnson discussed in Chapter Seven might be seen in this light. Hylton (2009) notes the attribution of natural talent to successful black athletes, but hard work and team play to the success of white athletes.

To the eugenicist, the high-minded Victorian sportsman might be seen as the opposite of the low thief or prostitute; they might seek to breed the one and eliminate the other. The rigorous positivism of Goring led him to conclude after his 13-year study of 3,000 English convicts:

> In fact, both with regard to measurements and the presence of physical anomalies in criminals, our statistics present a startling conformity with similar statistics of the law-abiding classes.... our inevitable conclusion must be that there is no such thing as a physical criminal type. (1913: 173)

Such is Goring's attention to detail, he explores the definition of left-handedness and it is here that his only mention of sport occurs – how a man might hold a golf club or cricket bat! Despite arguing 'There is no such thing as an anthropological criminal type' (1913: 370), he continues:

> the criminal of English prisons is markedly differentiated by defective physique – as measured by stature and body weight; by defective mental capacity – as measured by

general intelligence; and by an increased possession of wilful anti-social proclivities. (1913: 370)

To him, criminals are smaller and weaker – 'puny' (1913: 8) – yet Lombroso found the opposite. Kudlac quotes the work of Sheldon on somatypes in asserting:

> Criminals tend to be more mesomorphs than ectomorphs. Obviously, there are differences even among criminals with this depending on what type of criminal behaviour you are discussing, for example, violent crimes versus tax fraud. (2010: xv)

It should also be noted that not all sports require or favour the muscular mesomorph body, yet many explanations around the body, sport and crime come down to violent sports being associated with violent crime (participants and fans).

The terms endomorph (soft, round), mesomorph (muscular) and ectomorph (lean, delicate) derive from the work of Sheldon (1949), but an earlier somatype by Kretschmer (1921) uses the term 'athletic' for mesomorph. Kretschmer related physical type to personality, as does Sheldon, but he went further in suggesting a link to delinquency. In the same vein, Eleanor and Sheldon Glueck (1950) found male delinquents to have bigger chests, forearms and so on. While some might find these crude body typologies meaningful in broad terms, they probably have most relevance for sport.

These body types presume (like phrenology and physiognomy before) to reveal the psychic type, and we shall examine this shortly. Newburn (2013) divides biological positivism broadly into genetic and biochemical factors influencing or associated with crime. Starting with the genetic, we have already noted Goring's eugenist take on the issue. The most extreme take on eugenics is Nazism (though liberal and democratic states explored it too), and we can see it in their desire to promote sport and eliminate those deemed feeble. Genetic studies with twins and adopted children have proved inconclusive on the heritability of criminality. We hear less about XYY 'supermale syndrome' as applying to criminals now but it is sometimes used in the context of sportspeople.[5] A line might be drawn from Goring (1913) and his like

[5]   David Runciman (10 January 2010) 'Is the rise of the super-athlete ruining sport?', *The Guardian*, www.theguardian.com/sport/2010/jan/10/future-of-sport-runciman (accessed 11 October 2015).

to Herrnstein and Murray's (1994) work linking IQ to criminality. The stereotype of the sportsman as brawn over brain might fit with the criminal as a feeble-minded type. It might be interesting to test the IQs and criminality of the Oxford and Cambridge boat race crews.

Epilepsy, attention deficit hyperactivity disorder, brain damage, neurotransmitter imbalances, left-handedness and problems with 'slow' autonomous nervous system have all been suggested in the past as being associated with crime. The evidence in all such cases is mixed and contested. Clearly, all these conditions have consequences for sport, with, perhaps, only left-handedness providing an advantage in some sports.

Closer still to sports are hormonal-based explanations for crime, particularly with regard to testosterone. Newburn (2013) assesses these explanations in terms of mixed validity. Interestingly, in the first edition of the book, the picture illustrating the chapter on testosterone features boxing while in the second it features cage fighting, yet Newburn makes no explicit link to sport in the text. What should be noted is that all these biological explanations relate to men, even though the criminality of women is often associated with their biology.

Sportspeople are increasingly concerned about their nutrition. But might nutritional supplements be a gateway to the use of performance-enhancing drugs? Contaminated supplements are sometimes blamed for positive drug tests, while aspects of nutrition are cited by others as criminogenic – examples being low blood sugar, food allergies or vitamin and mineral deficiencies. The sheer emphasis on the body in sport lends itself to biological explanations of criminality, but sport now looks equally to the mind. We examine the 'psy' positivisms next.

Psychological positivism

Newburn (2013) broadly offers learning and cognitive theories, but starts with Freud quoting Valiér (1998) on the little direct influence that psychoanalysis has had on criminology, as the whole of psychoanalysis is about antisocial behaviour and therefore broadly criminological. It might be argued that much sport is related to the sort of instinctive pleasurable behaviours associated with the id and that the rules of the sport might be likened to the ego insisting on socially realistic ways of playing the game. Clearly, the supervising superego of some sportspeople is faulty. Might a psychoanalytical sports criminology examine the early childhoods of those who dive in football, take a dive in boxing or fix matches?

Skinnerian 'operant conditioning', or in commonsensical terms 'carrot and stick' rewards and punishments, might be allied to Darwinian natural selection whereby the footballer who accidentally falls down but is rewarded with a free quick or penalty might, if it happens again, 'learn' to do it to order. This might fit with Jeffery's (1965) application of operant conditioning to Sutherland's work. Adding Bandura's cognitive learning theory, we might expect our footballer not to need to experience the rewards of feigning a foul, but merely see others benefit from such a tactic. Such theories undermine the demand that criminal activity requires a special explanation. Crime is learned, sport is learned and life is learned. The work of Akers (1998) is similar and Kudlac (2010) quotes him on the 'good' influence of sport on potential delinquents, though his whole book is more about the bad effects of sporting peers.

Moving now to cognitive theories, we find the sort of work that underpins 'rehabilitative' tools that underlie attempts to increase criminals' capacity to think' so even the bounded rationality imagined by rational choice theory might apply. While Yochelson and Samenow (1976) concentrate on cognitive development, Piaget and, particularly, Kohlberg (1963) concentrate on moral development. Perhaps a sportsperson who has reached Kohlberg's sixth stage of 'principled' or 'post-conventional' moral development might refuse to take to the pitch?

Clearly, some biological theories shade into psychological ones and others still into the sociological, so before turning fully to the sociological we look at Eysenck's (2013) 'biosocial' theory. This adds some sociology and psychology – particularly scales of extroversion, neuroticism and psychoticism – to somatyping. Eysenck associates criminal bodies with 'athleticism' following Kretschmer. Interestingly, one of the studies that supports his work derived from research into personality and sport and his work features strongly in books of sports psychology. Thus Beashel and colleagues note Eysenck's contention that:

> Extroverts and high psychotics scorers are more likely to take up sports and excel in them, because their low arousal levels lead them to seek sensory stimulation … and they are more tolerant of the pain associated with sport. (1996: 262)

More of the same can be found in Eysenck and colleagues' work on sport and personality (1982), and it is amusing to note that Eysenck has this to say about his own involvement in sport:

I was well developed for my years, and always good at sport, so I could hold my own. (1997: 18)

I was in the rowing team, in the handball team ... ice-hockey and field hockey; *Schlagball* (a rather rudimentary kind of baseball widely played in German schools); football. (1997: 20)

I took up boxing while an undergraduate ... I was a 'middleweight' ... this last fight [against a heavyweight] I lost on a technical KO, and came home with two black eyes and a bloody nose. (1997: 51-52)[6]

Sociological positivism

Sociological positivism is less 'hard' or 'determining' than biological or psychological versions, and, as we shall see, sociology takes up non-positivist positions and (in Chapter Five) anti-positivist positions.

Durkheim is often a starting point in criminological texts where his radical relativism leads swiftly into discussion of Merton and strain theory. We might pause here to note that Birrell (1981) argues from a Durkheimian perspective for the religious/ritual nature of sport. She makes no mention of crime, but one can see why sport crime might take on such significance for some as striking at deep socio-cultural roots, for instance, with reference to sumo. Nearer to our concerns, we find Atkinson and Young (2008) using Durkheim to think about 'wanted deviance' – wanted by fans and administrators, sometimes explicitly sometimes more shame-facedly – from fights in ice hockey to the home run breaking season only later found to have been fuelled by steroids. It is also 'wanted' by administrators and the media to demonstrate moral or regulations limits. Sportspeople provide for these 'wants'.

Furthermore, Atkinson and Young (2008) see the use of performance-enhancing drugs as Mertonian 'innovation' (Goode, 2011 would agree), not the 'retreatism' that other drug use is often seen as in criminology. They are critical of sports sociology for taking up Hughes and Coakley's (1991) notion of 'positive deviance', which, they argue, overlaps with Merton's extant concept of 'innovation'. Sefiha (2012) explicitly links use of performance-enhancing drugs to Mertonian notions of innovation. Merton himself noted:

---

[6]   He also mentions skiing and tennis.

> In competitive athletics, when the aim of victory is shorn
> of its institutional trappings and success in contests becomes
> construed as 'winning the game' rather than 'winning
> through circumscribed modes of activity' a premium is
> implicitly set upon the use of illegitimate but technically
> efficient means. (1938: 675)

He lists some of those illegitimacies, such as 'the star of the opposing
football team is surreptitiously slugged' (1938: 675) and then more
opaquely, 'the wrestler furtively incapacitates his opponent through
ingenious but illicit techniques' (1938: 675), which suggests he has
little experience of the ring, in contrast to Eysenck's (1997) prowess
or Wacquant's (1995) pugnacity. Merton's first suggestion would be
criminal in itself and the second, while possibly criminal, is clearly in
breach of the rules of wrestling, although it does not fulfil the 'wanted
deviance' of the modern professional wrestling crowd (Corteen and
Corteen, 2012). Merton's third suggestion is that 'university alumni
covertly subsidize "students" whose talents are largely confined to the
athletic field' (1938: 675). There is nothing 'covert' about the assistance
given to US college athletes today. Merton even finds examples in
the area of card games, for instance, dealing oneself four aces in poker
or even 'sagaciously shuffling' (1938: 675) to win (against oneself) at
solitaire.

Giulianotti (2005: 10) illustrates Merton's concepts by reference to
football for young American males thus:

- *conformism* ... eg playing American football in college
  in an aggressive, highly competitive manner
- *innovation* ... eg playing other sports outside college in
  an aggressive highly competitive manner
- *ritualism* ... eg routine football team involvement and
  an intense knowledge of its rules and procedures
- *retreatism* ... eg abandon the sport entirely
- *rebellion* ... eg playing sports without competitive
  emphasis outside of educational institutions.

Under such a scheme, might 'jogging' or playing frisbee be seen
to be rebellious and 'aggressive' track and field for a non-college
club innovative? Generally, cheating within a sport might be seen as
innovation; that is, you want to win at football or poker and accept
the convention that scoring more goals than the opposition or holding
(and retaining) better cards are the desirable legitimate ends but use

devious illegitimate means to achieve them. In other words, one is so competitive that one exceeds the demands of conformity and innovates. It is here some of the argument between Atkinson and Young (2008) and Hughes and Coakley's (1991) arises.

Hughes and Coakley specifically attempt to delineate their 'positive deviance' from Merton's innovation:

> We are not arguing that athletes engage in what Merton (1957) has identified as 'innovation' grounded in the acceptance of cultural goals and the concomitant rejection of accepted means to those goals. Merton's framework renders athletes as mere opportunists. This is inappropriate since athletes who engage in positive deviance accept goals as well as means to an extreme degree and without critical examination of either. Both goals and means are 'overdetermined' and extended to an excessive degree. Instead of innovation, positive deviance in sport reflects more the notion of the hero's quest, or the extraordinary, rather than mere utilitarianism. Therefore if Merton's framework is applicable in any way, the behavior we are describing would best fit into an extension of the conformity category. (1991: 316)

Many criminologists will have no problem with the slippage between conformity and deviance – we might say 'drift' (Matza, 1964) – and sports fans and criminology know the founding myth of rugby union is that William Webb Ellis innovated by picking up the ball and running. In 1906, the rules of American football were changed to allow the one forward pass per down, which might now be seen as the distinguishing feature of the game. Some teams saw it as 'sissy' or too likely to cede possession, so not all adopted it immediately.[7]

Rugby still outlaws the forward pass, but rugby union's law 12 now states: 'A throw forward occurs when a player throws or passes the ball forward. "Forward" means towards the opposition's dead ball line', which means that a ball can travel forward provided it is due to the

---

[7]   Jim Morrison (28 December 2010) 'The early history of football's forward pass', *Smithsonian.com*, www.smithsonianmag.com/history/the-early-history-of-footballs-forward-pass-78015237/?no-ist (accessed 11 October 2015).

momentum of the passing player imparting the forward motion, not his or passing hands.[8]

In the amateur days of rugby union, the lifting of those jumping for the ball in the lineout was illegal but surreptitiously practised. Now it has been decriminalised and is legal (for over-16s) and a crucial part of the game. It was only fully incorporated into the international game in 2009, although 'supporting' was allowed before that. That might be called innovation, while the use of drugs and over-rigorous training regimes are seen as 'positive deviance'.

Much of the work deriving from Durkheim through Merton is termed 'strain theory'. Agnew (1992) is seen to have brought this up to date. In his work, he seeks to differentiate between strain theory (emphasis on the negative drivers towards delinquency), control theory (absence of the positive drivers towards conformity) and differential association (presence of positive drivers towards delinquency). In other words, 'strain' is caused by the failure to achieve positively valued goals. These are not literal goals as in sport, but the same strain is true of most sports. One's way to goal is blocked – by the rules, the opposition and even one's own position on the team (goalies rarely get to score). In a discussion of youth sub-cultures, Agnew mentions 'athletic ability' as a factor, along with intelligence, physical attractiveness and personality, but otherwise makes no other sporting references (1992: 51).

DuBois is only now being given some due mention in criminology textbooks (see Carrabine et al, 2013). Unlike Eysenck and his sporting college life, DuBois thankfully talks of how 'the absence of distractions, either in athletics of society, enable me to re-arrange and rebuild my program for freedom and progress' (1944: section 17) and unlike many of the sociologists already quoted seems not to use sport as a metaphor (Girdwood, 2009 attempts to use DuBois in a reconsideration of sports sociology). Better known in sociology/criminology circles, but similar to that of DuBois is the work of the Chicago school.

Chicago school

Very broadly, the Chicago school might be seen to comprise qualitative and quantitative aspects, that is, the ethnographic, 'appreciative' work and the cartographic 'ecology' of the city. A simple route is from Burgess's (1925) suggestion of different criminal zones in the city

[8] Paul Rees (5 December 2013) 'Confusion reigns as the forward pass rule continues to baffle everyone', *The Guardian*, www.theguardian.com/sport/2013/dec/05/the-breakdown-rugby-union-forward-pass (accessed 11 October 2015).

to Shaw and McKay's (1942) test of it and suggestion of 'cultural transmission', which in turn influenced Sutherland's differential association.

Burgess notes that 'there are no playgrounds in the city in which a boy can find ... "real sport".'(1925: 109) and in the same edited volume, Park (1925: 43), citing Aristotle and Freud, notes the catharsis provided by sport and art. He concludes too that 'music or a sport, like horse-racing' (1925: 45) might be 'moral regions' for 'eccentric and exceptional people' (1925: 43).

Shaw and McKay (1942: 175) use baseball in an analogy of their theory:

> ... comparable to that which might be established among baseball players through their appearance in official line-ups or regularly scheduled games. In baseball it is known that the techniques are transmitted through practice in back yards, play ground, sand lots and in other places where boys congregate.

Shaw took his concerns to practical levels and founded the Chicago area project in the 1930s, which continues today[9] – a model, if not always acknowledged, for many similar schemes like those examined in Chapter Seven.

Differential association

Sutherland's work is seen to develop that of Shaw and McKay but also Gabriel Tarde and George Herbert Mead (Newburn, 2013) and Thrasher's (1927) *The Gang*. Sefiha (2012) makes mention of Sutherland and criminology specifically in a study of cyclists attitudes to doping, in that individuals learn criminal techniques and attitudes that favour deviance. The Festina affair revealed that the team was seen very much to be the place where one learned to 'dope'.

Thrasher (1927) is very fond of using the word sport (20 times in the book). Sometimes the use is literal and sometimes metaphorical; some references might be seen as provocative. Thus a gang of pickpockets is said to 'find excellent opportunity for sport' (1927: 12) at a local market, and he also asserts that 'the great majority of athletic clubs, however, which are usually conventionalised gangs, must have subsidies

---

[9]   Chicago Area Project (nd) www.chicagoareaproject.org (accessed 11 October 2015); this belies Newburn's claim (2013:193) that it was closed.

from saloonkeepers or politicians in order to make a go of it financially' (1927: 67). Thresher even lists (1927: 88) the games that the gangs play, like 'hide and seek' or 'cops and robbers'. Dice games ('indoor golf') are a 'favourite sport' (1927: 90), but stealing 'is as much a result of the sport motive as of a desire for revenue' (1927: 92). This is reminiscent of Katz's work (1988), which we examine in the next chapter under cultural criminology.

The familiar refrain of sport as 'good' is also seen in Thresher's work, as the following extract shows:

> In the realm of sports the gang boy is most completely assimilated to the dominant social order. He knows the standing of the big ball clubs, follows the world-series and has special admiration for the wrestlers and 'pugs' (pugilists).... Sports and athletics provide the gang one quite wholesome and very popular form of new experience and escape from ennui. They are the mechanisms through which secondary conflict is substituted for the primary type. (1927: 98)

He talks of the baseball leagues set up to engage gangs and the popularity of all sports including 'swimming, skating, fishing, football, basket-ball, wrestling and boxing' (1927: 9). But boxing is particularly popular and gangs have their own 'pugs' whose cauliflower ears are as much marks of distinction as duelling scars. But gang life offers opportunities for real fights that might be seen as 'sport'. Thus, 'fighting a gang of indians or bandits is Tom's favourite sport' (1927: 104). Robbing or abusing drunks and beggars might also be 'sport' (1927: 315), as might snowballing a new cop on the block (1927: 357).

Some commentators relate theories of cultural spillover to those of differential association, or suggest scenarios that combine the two (Straus, 1994). The suggestion is that the violence within sport spills over into life. This would accord with Stansfield's (2015) findings. Bloom and Smith (1996) looked at violence in ice hockey. They associated the 'approval of violence' and willingness to use violence by older players in competitive leagues. Some work in this tradition looks at whole societies; for instance, Baron, L., Straus, M.A., and Jaffe, D. (1988) relate the levels of support for the use of violence across all 50 states of America to rates of rape in those states. Perhaps Bloom and Smith (1996) should have tried to relate support for violence in the area to supporting an ice hockey team?

Yar touches lightly on the possibility that Sutherland and colleagues' (1995) social learning theory might suggest sport as promoting the pro-social, but spillover and other theories may also suggest the opposite. Zamanian and colleagues (2012) specifically locate their work on using sports participation to reduce 'social delinquency' in Tehran in a differential association framework, but still warn against overestimating the role of sports in tackling social problems.

Sub-culture

Yar mentions cultures or sub-cultures in his discussion of sport and crime, specifically 'hyper-masculinity' (2014: 4), which is discussed in Chapter Five. There are few mentions of sub-culture in Cohen's (1955) *Delinquent Boys*, although this includes a reference to Thrasher. Cloward and Ohlin have fewer still but instructively comment that 'studies have shown that some lower-class persons orient themselves toward occupations in the field of entertainment and sports' (2013: 104) and 'sports, hell raising, and gang fights become "kids' stuff" and are given up' (2013: 185). In this construct, sport is a childish activity equivalent to crime and only fit as an occupation for the lower classes.

Neutralisation

Sefiha's (2012) work on cycle racing specifically addresses the issue of neutralization. Sykes and Matza's (1957) work is cited throughout, and, given the emphasis on stigma in Yar's (2014) book, it is no surprise to find that he leans heavily on these authors too. In his sole-authored work, Matza likened the skills of the athlete to those of the criminal: 'Any reasonably good athlete can *behaviorally*, be an excellent delinquent' (1964: 186, emphasis in original). In cycling in particular, research often finds claims that, to paraphrase, 'everyone is at it'. This is often depicted as neutralisation, but in some cases may reflect fact.

Harding (2014) makes considerable mention of when dog-fighting was not a criminalised sport and discusses its continued existence with 'rules'. Citing Sykes and Matza (1957), he notes that dog fighters deny the dog's status as victim; duck responsibility by insisting the dog 'loves to fight'; more improbably deny evidence of injury to dogs; and appeal to the higher authority of the glory of the sport's history; and condemn the extremism of animal rights activists.

Control theories

Hirschi's (1969) only mention of sport is in the inclusion of a couple of questions to this effect in his questionnaires. Yar, however, makes the connection to sport, which can be seen as the sort of activity that might bolster an individual's 'investment in conventional social values by imparting a belief in fair play, cooperation, persistence and rule-following' (Yar, 2014: 3). Such investment and involvement in sport is clearly behind the schemes examined in Chapter Seven. Stansfield (2015) addresses a number of these matters specifically in respect of sports participation and 'delinquency'. Included in his definition of delinquency is 'violence', marijuana use, and beer and spirit consumption. Violence, whether 'serious' or 'minor', was measured on a yes/no basis over a year and drink and drugs over the previous month. He found that higher levels of sports involvement did increase the incidence of violence and moderate participation in sport increased drug and alcohol use, although this declined with greater participation. Hirschi's (1969) social bonds (belief, attachment, commitment and involvement) were seen to increase with sports participation, although Stansfield found that such involvement, even for girls, was associated with 'delinquency'. This clearly has consequences for the many schemes examined in Chapter Seven.

Right realism

Smith (2011) identifies the practices of the Court of Arbitration for Sport (CAS) and national and international sports governing bodies as following principles of 'zero tolerance'; for instance, the upholding of a ban on a Ukrainian referee (Mr Oriekhov), who was found not to be corrupt but to have failed to report an approach that might have been deemed corrupt. The condemnatory language in respect of drugs use and corruption fits easily within this school. This is examined in Chapter Six. Some of the demands for more, and more onerous, drugs testing in the face of recent scandals might also be seen as falling within this school of thought. People will cheat; we must stop them. The feudalism of the 'amateur' era has passed and sport as business is firmly in the grasp of neoliberalism.

Labelling

Tattoos, mentioned earlier, can be a form of self-labelling that marks you out as a criminal. The athlete's body indicates his or her sporting capacities. For some, that body indicates a lack of intelligence that may be associated with criminality. Criminologists, and the sociologists of deviance who coined the term 'labelling' usually mean more subtle or individualised markers of deviance or criminality, but the more critically inclined might note also take it to mean labels of race and gender. Becker's *Outsiders* (1963) makes no mention of sport, the jazz and drug taking described being recreation enough.

Cohen (2011) only touches on sport in passing, but Goode (2011) sees anti-doping as a 'moral panic'. He may be right, but his analysis pays no attention to 'folk devils', unlike Cohen and his adherents.

The labelling perspective was aware that labels were not applied randomly but the full extent of structural inequalities and extensive theorising around that had to await the 'new' and radical/critical criminologies discussed in the next chapter.

This chapter has made some connections between criminological theory and sport. These connections have sometimes been metaphorical, but the references to sport in the work of the criminologists cited might be a way into sports criminology for some.

FIVE

The second half: critical criminological theory and sport

Chapter Four set out what might be called mainstream criminological theories. This chapter examines broadly radical/critical theories, some of which, as we shall see, may relate back to mainstream ones and all of which may relate to each other.

The scheme is to carry on from the discussion of labelling in Chapter Four to examine the emergence of new and radical criminologies. This requires an examination of Marxist and conflict theories that underpin some of these, and which, along with other strands from sociology, have been woven into left realism. Feminism has its own roots outside of and within criminology, but left realism's concern with the victim makes a link to the various feminisms. Some of those feminisms blamed men for the victimisation of women but studied women. Feminists and gay men were behind the development of an interest in masculinities that also found its way into criminology. We also see how sub-cultural and anarchist approaches link in to mainstream cultural criminological theories. Finally, the chapter considers green and rural criminologies.

New criminology/radical criminology

Chronologically, we might tackle the work of Taylor and colleagues (1973) after Marx and American radical criminology, but their arguments condense much of that theorising. We turn to those antecedents later, as Young noted it was labelling perspectives 'which set the creaking chariot of radical criminology off on its course' (1988: 163). This wonky, and certainly unintended, sporting metaphor might be extended by noting that the performance-enhancing drug of the time for young theorists was Marxism, with perhaps a side order of feminism or critical race theory. The only brushing mention of sport in Taylor et al's (1973) book *The New Criminology* relates to work on football hooliganism by one of the authors, Taylor, who then saw it in terms of 'resistance'.

This work was swiftly followed by an edited collection on critical criminology (Taylor et al, 1975), which progressed the debate on radical criminology and contained a spat between the editors and Paul Hirst about Marxism. Hirst contended: 'There is no "Marxist theory of deviance"…. Crime and deviance are no more a scientific field of for Marxism than education, the family or sport' (1975: 204). In defending themselves against his charge of 'revisionism', Taylor and Walton (1975) came back to this very passage. It is the only mention of sport, and aleatory at that. Interestingly, in a memoir-like contribution, Brown places sport first in a list of subject matters of radical deviancy theory, before 'crime thrillers, mental illness, music, demonstrations and drugs' (2013: 75). It is the only mention of sport in that book, save a repeat of the quote from Hirst (1975), all of which brings us to Marx.

Marxism

Marx famously wrote little about crime, yet a Marxist criminology came into being. Biographies of Marx by Wheen (2012) and Berlin (1978) make no mention of any interest in sport, yet Marxist sports sociology exists. T.R. Young argues forcefully that:

> A Marxian theory of sport has two major dimensions: a political economy in which one weighs the degree to which sports serve the accumulation problems of advanced monopoly capital and a cultural-Marxist dimension in which one examines the ways in which sports solve the problems of legitimacy and help produce alienated consciousness in self and society. (1986: 3)

Some of the same sentiment can be found in Vincent Hanna's critique:

> Suppose someone told you there was a regime in Europe where agents scoured the country looking for talented young boys, who are taken from their homes and brought to camps to do menial jobs and train constantly for whom, because of the intense competition for places, education is cursory. The lucky ones are kept on, bound under a contract system where they can be bought and sold by employers. The successful and the bright do very well. But many of the second raters will find themselves, in their 30s, on the scrap heap and unemployed. (Cited in Kuhn, 2011: 82)

In a collection of Marxism, sport and cultural studies by Ifekwunige (2009), the only mention of crime involves an account of the theft of some Air Jordans trainers. The introduction to that book (Carrington and McDonald, 2009) acknowledges the work of Marxist C.L.R. James (1963), whose book *Beyond a Boundary* discusses cricket, albeit not from a conspicuously Marxist position.

In his work on sport in the Victorian era, Huggins notes how people like the Prince of Wales (the future Edward VII):

> ... with no need to work and ample private means, could enjoy conspicuous, self-indulgent leisure. They were looked up to as 'true sportsmen', with 'less vice', who could run horses, play games honestly and bet for fun. (2004, 22)

Bonger was a committed Marxist and criminologist but makes only three passing mentions of sport in *Race and Crime* (1969), relating to the gaining of self-control in education, the phlegm of the English and the rising popularity of sport. In the *Introduction to Criminology* (2015), he notes how others, including Bentham, propound the theory that sport is preventative of crime.

Vold writes in the 1950s from a non-Marxist pluralistic perspective of various conflicts between capital and labour, between parties and within unions, and between ethnic groups. Conflicts arise over what and/ or who is to be criminalised. Turk's work saw conflict not in Marxist terms but in terms of domination, subjection and typified crimes on a matrix of organised/disorganised and sophisticated/unsophisticated designations. Chambliss noted the use of crime to divert the attention of the poor from the crimes of the powerful. A parallel might be seen in the attention paid to the wrongdoings of individual sportspeople without due regard to the responsibilities of the relevant national and international governing bodies.

We wait to see how diverted people are by the recent allegations of widespread corruption in FIFA, official guardians of the 'people's game'. Quinney's work eventually moved towards 'peace-making criminology', which Zaksaite (2013) uses to counter the 'zero tolerance' and classical deterrence theories of sports authorities' attempts to scare participants into line. Without any reference to criminology, let alone of a peacemaking variety, Russell and Mustonen (1998) show in a study on sports rioting that 26.2% of Finnish ice hockey fans (n=129) would seek to make peace if a fight broke out near them. They turned out to be less aggressive (though taller) and no less impulsive than the 2.4% who would join in. Jock Young and his colleagues were also influenced by Marx, but they also sought to counter some of the arguments of the right that crime had some reality and affected the working class, women and other victims

Left realist theories

The teleological idealism and unacknowledged positivism of much radical criminology lead Young and others such as John Lea and Roger Matthews to espouse a left realism. This countered the right's argument that poverty could not be blamed for crime (a rhetorical simplification of the left's position) by focusing on 'relative deprivation' (Runciman, 1966) and marginalisation. The proponents of left realism were also critical of the tendency for much criminology to focus on only one aspect of crime. The Marxism they had previously embraced focused on the state's capacity to criminalise and to act criminally yet 'within' the law. Society had obviously been the focus of the sociologists, and offenders the focus of many criminologists, while feminism and anti-racist campaigners had raised the issue of victimisation by offenders, state and society.

The geometric metaphor of the square of crime might seem positivist, and for our purposes we might imagine it as a squash court where the ball might be found in one of the corners. In explaining some aspects of sport crime, the corner given to 'state' might be replaced by the relevant governing body, but at other times the state may see the governing body as the victim or the offender.

Feminist criminological theories

Once upon a time, criminology felt it could ignore women because 'they weren't criminal'; or, if criminal, clearly 'manlike' (meaning lesbian) or at variance with the theory. Similar attitudes are to be found in sport, so it is no surprise that women's crime in sport tends also to be ignored. In his work on sports and criminal behaviour in the US, Kudlac (2010) mentions women 27 times, yet there is no associated index item. Like the criminologists of old, he might claim he is looking largely at male sport and that one should therefore not be surprised. When he does turn his attention to the issue, it is to dismiss it thus: 'with more male athletes committing crime than female athletes' (2010: xv). Women are most frequently mentioned as victims.

Some, from a right-wing or moralistic base, might blame the victim, but feminists would want to understand the victim. Indeed, they may prefer the term 'survivor' (Alcoff and Gray, 1993), although Lamb (1991) problematises the word 'survivor' as both too 'grand' and too deterrent a term. Waterhouse-Watson (2013) settles for 'complainant', since most of the cases of sexual assault by players she examined were at the allegation/pre-charge phase.[1]

This terminological point should make clear that being, or having sympathy with, a woman may make you a feminist but does not determine what sort of feminist. Very broadly, feminists may fall into the liberal/equal opportunities or radical/separatist camps. Carol Smart (1990), before she left criminology, argued strongly for a postmodern epistemology, which she posed against the empirical and standpoint epistemologies of liberal and radical feminisms. Postmodernism has waned and even radical feminists might now use the tools of the positivists once dubbed 'malestream'.

Early engagement with crime by feminists like Adler and Adler (1975) and Simon (1975) broadly argued that women's crime would increase as woman became more like men or at least had the same opportunities as men. Forty years later, women's lot has improved but still lags far behind that of men and any increase in female 'criminality' is more likely to do with increased criminalisation than 'emancipation', let alone 'feminism'. Neither Adler and Adler nor Simon had anything to say about sport, but women's increased participation in sport and media recognition of their success might fit their theories better than crime. When might we have our first 'diving' or 'betting scandal' in women's soccer? Will Kudlac (2010) then be interested? Would Pollak (1950) argue that women were as good at simulating fouls on the pitch as they were in feigning orgasm or hiding menstrual blood?

Later feminism concentrated on the structural evils of the patriarchy (sometimes mixed with a broad socialism or a more narrow Marxism). For liberal feminists, that might mean campaigning for equal opportunities backed by law. A comparative example from sport would be equal prize money in tennis or track and field events. Radical feminists might dismiss sport (Theberge, 1981) as masculinist, echoing Sabo and Runfola's assertion that:

> sport and masculinity are virtually synonymous in American culture ... a primary function of sports is the dissemination and reinforcement of such traditional American values as male superiority, competition, work, and success. (1980: x–xi)

---

[1] Krien (2013) offers an embedded journalistic view of one rape allegation.

In other words, just as socialists should see sport as a snare and a delusion, so should women. There is a clear feminist interest in crimes against women in and around sport. The next section, on masculinity, examines the considerable media interest in on- and off-field violence committed by sports stars, but there are further issues to consider from a feminist perspective, including the human trafficking and prostitution sometimes associated with sport.

Clearly the trafficking of people is a serious issue, but it is not always easy analytically or practically to distinguish it from people smuggling and illegal immigration. It is an issue around which groups campaign for money and prestige as well as action. A report for the Future Group's on prospects for the Vancouver Winter Olympics is typical:

> According to analysis of comparative statistical data from the Greek Ministry of Public Safety, there was a 95% increase in the number of human trafficking victims identified by Greek authorities in 2004. In other words, the number of known human trafficking victims almost doubled in the year of the Athens Olympics. In 2005, the year after the Olympics, the number of known trafficking victims declined by 24%, but was still up 47% from the 2003 figure. (Perrin, 2007: 4)

Slightly more cautiously, the report notes: 'While numerous factors come into play, a certain correlation between the Olympics and an increase in human trafficking cannot be discounted' (Perrin, 2007: 4). Sikka (2014), on the other hand, examined the Canadian experience and is more critical. She sees the associated discourse and policies as looking for a 'victim' who then gets no meaningful redress.

In the run-up to the London Olympics, Palmer (2011) looked at violence against women related to sport. She reviews the literature on all violence by men against women in the context of sport, and tends towards viewing it as proved. On the matter of trafficking, she concludes:

> Human trafficking for the purpose of sexual exploitation remains difficult to quantify, with the research evidence frequently being contradictory, but literature suggests that events such as London 2012 may well provide a context in which women and girls could be trafficked. (2011: 3)

By contrast, London Councils/GLE (2011) concluded:

> In most cases the media spread fear over huge numbers of predicted trafficking victims, which is not based on evidence ... impossible to measure the extent to which different factors that fuel trafficking have contributed to the case of each trafficked individual. (2011: 20)

Different countries offer different contexts; sex trafficking in some is a long-term problem that should not be targeted for action just during sporting events. Any mass event – from the Edinburgh Festival, to a pilgrimage or the five-yearly meeting of the National Congress of the Chinese Communist Party – might be a context in which women are trafficked.

The Global Alliance Against Traffic in Women (2011) takes a sceptical perspective, noting claims, for example, that 40,000 foreign sex workers/trafficked women would arrive in South Africa in the run-up to the 2010 World Cup. In fact, these claims were unfounded, and the report suggests that business fell for sex workers during this period. It should be noted that a distinction should be made between women who respond to the market signal, to use an economic term, and freely go where they believe there is money, and those who are tricked/forced into going, either with or without the promise of money for sex work. Furthermore, any criminologist would be reluctant to place too much emphasis on the police finding no trace of trafficking in such circumstances.

A more direct relation between sport and trafficking can be seen in the case of Al Bangura, a former Premier League footballer who says he was trafficked into Britain for sex.[2] Always interested in football, he claimed asylum and eventually played for Watford FC. He now campaigns to raise awareness about the scamming of boys from Africa whose dreams of football glory are used to lure them into forced labour and more (see also Hawkins, 2015).

Some feminists would see the violence of men both in the home and on the field of play as all of a piece. Such cultural spillover might better explain the case of Hope Solo, goalkeeper of the US women's soccer team, who in 2014 faced charges of assaulting her sister and 17-year-old nephew in a drunken, violent outburst. Clear gender issues arise,

---

[2] Sima Kotecha and Sarah Bell (20 November 2015) 'Former premier league footballer "was trafficked for sex"', BBC, www.bbc.co.uk/news/uk-34849619 (accessed 27 November 2015).

particularly in respect of Solo's alleged taunts of her nephew (6 feet, 8 inches tall, and weighing in at 270lbs) that he was a 'pussy' and of one of the arresting officers that he was 'a 14-year-old boy'. It should also be noted that in the US media the incident was deemed to constitute 'domestic violence'.[3] Others have sought to link it to the Ray Rice case (discussed in Chapter Six) and argue for greater action against her by the soccer authorities.[4] Clearly influenced by feminism but worthy of a separate section, we now consider sporting masculinities.

Masculinities

Following Connell (1995) and Messerschmidt (1993), the term masculinities is preferred to a singular 'masculinity'. Are sportsmen more violent? If so, which men and which sports? Is it worse if men are in gangs? And what of male spectators (the Super Bowl effect)?

Huggins (2004: 23) notes: 'A billiard room, smoking room and gun room were increasingly part of a masculine suite within country houses from the 1860s.' That assured, 'sporting' masculine stance has come under fire. Zero-sum masculinists believe that feminism is to blame for the problems in their lives and many would have taken as vindication of their views the news story that England Rugby Union fly half Danny Cipriani had been punched by his then partner, the celebrity model Kelly Brook. In her autobiography, Brook mentions punching Cipriani in the face; when challenged about it on daytime TV, she made light of it and giggled.[5]

While violence against men is acknowledged to occur, it is an under-researched area. Given the preponderance and disproportional impact of male violence against women, it is no surprise that most attention and campaigning activity has focused on male-on-female violence,

[3] Mark Fainaru-Wada (7 June 2015) 'Documents reveal new details about Hope Solo's actions last June', ESPN, http://espn.go.com/espn/otl/story/_/id/12976615/detailed-look-hope-solo-domestic-violence-case-includes-reports-being-belligerent-jail (accessed 11 October 2015).

[4] Ta-Nehisi Coates (23 September 2014) 'No, Hope Solo is not "like" Ray Rice', *The Atlantic*, www.theatlantic.com/entertainment/archive/2014/09/no-hope-solo-is-not-like-ray-rice/380626/ (accessed 11 October 2015).

[5] Jessica Earnshaw (8 September 2014) '"Domestic violence isn't funny": Kelly Brook branded "disgusting" after "giggling" through interview on "punching exes Jason Statham and Danny Cipriani"', *Mail Online*, www.dailymail.co.uk/tvshowbiz/article-2747786/Kelly-Brook-branded-disgusting-giggling-interview-punching-exes-Jason-Statham-Danny-Cipriani.html (accessed 11 October 2015).

but female-on-male and same-sex violence both need examining too. They may also assist in understanding the larger problem. Research on men's reluctance to report violence suggests some of women face similar issues. Tsui (2014) found considerable gender symmetry in her study of uses of services by male victims of intimate partner abuse. But as Newburn and Stanko (1994: 164) argue:

> All men will not experience violence or respond to violence in the same way…. Some, perhaps even the large majority, will remain largely unconcerned or lastingly affected by such experiences, whilst others may suffer long-term trauma not just as victims of crime, but as *male* victims of crime. (emphasis in original)

Messner's pro-feminist work suggests that it is not all sportsmen or all sports that are culpable of violence against women. He argues that the 'athletes most likely to engage in sexual and other violent assaults off the field are those participating in the sports I define as at the institutional center of sport' (2002: 26). This might account for the apparent preponderance of African-American athletes in such statistics (for instance, 80% of National Basketball Association athletes are black), but in Canada, whose central, or national, sport is ice hockey, white players are most often accused of violence against women. The notion of 'central' sports will recur, but it should be remembered that these are studies carried out in the US by American scholars and cannot readily be transplanted.

In his discussion of the potential for sub-cultural explanations of crime in sport, Yar (2014) concentrates on the wrongdoing of a number of sports stars. Some of these are mentioned in Chapter Three but Yar's list covers: John Daly (golfer charged with assaulting wife); Mike Tyson (boxer, rape); O.J. Simpson (American National Football League [NFL] player, charged with murder and later convicted of armed robbery and kidnapping); Michael Vick (NFL player, interstate dog-fighting); Mickey Thomas (soccer player, counterfeiting); Graham Rix (soccer player, indecent assault and unlawful sex); and Wolfgang Schwarz (figure skater, kidnapping and human trafficking).

Yar notes from Forbes and colleagues (2006) the suggestion that 'the valorisation of aggression in competitive sports spills over to "off the field" behaviour', predisposing male athletes to sexual aggression and violence towards women' (2014: 4) and draws on Welch (1997) to suggest that the 'hypermasculinity' of such athletes 'may be bolstered by a sense of superiority and entitlement conferred by the broader cultural esteem accorded to sports stars' (2014: 4).

Forbes and colleagues (2006) may be splitting hairs when they argue:

> There does not appear to be any clear empirical evidence of a relationship between participation in professional sports and violence against women (Blumstein and Benedict, 1999). However, there is empirical evidence of a relationship between participation in college athletics and dating aggression or sexual coercion.

Their work reveals many associations between aggressive sport (which they define as football, basketball, wrestling and soccer) and negative attitudes towards women and gays among the 147 college athletes they surveyed. These attitudes, however, were not necessarily formed in college or through sport, and the authors note that the retrospective nature of their survey cannot address issues of causality. Moreover, basketball and soccer are strictly speaking non-contact sports, and the Greco-Roman wrestling favoured in American colleges should not be mistaken for the professional sport shown on TV. Jenkins and Ellis (2011) tackle the issue of what constitutes a violent sport. In Forbes et al's (2006) survey, 115 respondents reported having participated in one or more sports in high school and the study covered baseball, basketball, soccer, golf, cross-country, football, swimming, track and field, wrestling, tennis, and other sports.

It is just such diversity of sport that leads Palmer (2011: 7) in her review of the literature to emphasise the following:

> The gendered nature of sport, and the differing requirements of aggression in certain sports needs to recognised, alongside other contributing factors such as those described here, in the context of VAW [violence against women] by male athletes.

Her review is full of the necessary academic caution, but tends to an acceptance of an underlying causal association between sport and male violence. It is, perhaps, telling that she does quote Forbes et al (2006) but not Blumstein and Benedict, who compared arrest rates for NFL players against the general population of young men weighted for race and found that 'even though our initial assessment was that the NFL rates looked very high we found them well below the rates for the general population' (1999: 14).

In other words, demographics are a major factor: NFL players tend to be young, mostly black, men. Blumstein and Benedict speculated, like others, about whether the elevated status of the respondents in their sample meant that any wrongdoing would attract immunity rather than greater scrutiny (by sports authorities at that time, but more likely by the media today). They were unable to compare the incomes of their respondents with those of similarly wealthy individuals (those earning $200,000 a year) and thus most likely corporate executives. Perhaps they should also have sought to investigate levels of violence among that group. Interestingly, Lewis's (2014) study of the crimes of high-frequency traders makes no mention of 'sex', 'violence', 'rape' or 'sexual assault'.

With a nod to the diversity of sports as a whole, some writers have sought to classify the distinctions between sport (in Chapter Seven we see similar attempts to identify which sports might promote desistance) and even within sport. Gage (2008) uses Messner's (2004) idea of 'central' sports and Welch (1997) even attempts to explain different rates of violence within an American football team.

Welch (1997) admits in a footnote that he was standby place kicker for his college team. Other than this personal note, he makes no attempt to address issues of ethnography or reflexivity, but, using newspaper reports (neither the NFL nor the players' union cooperated with him), he traced 100 (to June 1996) NFL players known to have committed violence against women (domestic violence, rape and sexual assault). Of these 100 players, 51 played in defensive and 49 in offensive positions, and 38 of the total were 'scorers' (wide receivers or running backs).

It is unclear from this why both offensive and defensive players should be violent off field, and the study raises a number of issues for other sports. Welch presumes scorers get more attention, and therefore opportunities, but might they also be more attractive to women, less physically intimidating? In a study of sexual deviance among male college students, Jackson and colleagues (2006) found opportunity and previous behaviours more likely indicators of sexual violence than sport or other issues. It is interesting to speculate about comparable levels of violence among British soccer players.

Welch (1997) also recognises that as the 30 NFL teams number 1,590 players between them in a year, his sample is relatively small. Only one placekicker and no punters in his study were associated with an incident of violence against women. Although Welch does not use the phrase 'hegemonic masculinity', it might be said that the hegemonic masculinity of the team is the scorer or denier of scores, whereas specialist players (like placekickers and punters) are seen as marginal (and, he notes, likened to soccer players). This does suggest that not even all 'jocks' are the same.

Although she fails to mention Welch (1997), Gage (2008) addresses the issue of marginality too, but applies it to sports and non-sports participants, finding differences between college athletes and men who do not participate in college sports, as well as between men who play different sports. In her study, athletes in central sports scored significantly higher on hyper-masculinity scales, had poorer attitudes towards women, and displayed more sexual aggression and more sexual activity than men who competed in marginal sports (for example, track and field) or no sport at all. But like others, Gage could only find associations between her variables (religiosity appeared to offer some amelioration and fraternity membership to exacerbate poor attitudes) and she admits that her sample is small and the university in question unrepresentative in terms of high levels of athletic achievement. A considerably larger study is that by Stansfield (2015), who used data from the second International Self-Report Delinquency Study of 12- to 15-year-old students (n=67,883) to suggest that sport was bad for both genders.

Crosset and colleagues (1995) examined 20 athletic institutions during the 1992–93 school year and the records of 10 judicial affairs offices over a three-year period from 1991 through 1993. Male student-athletes were overrepresented in reports of sexual assault in both locations; the differences between student-athletes and other male students are statistically significant only when it comes to the number of incidents reported to judicial affairs offices. In terms of sports centrality, the authors found that football and basketball players comprised 30% of the student-athlete population but 68% of reports of sexual assaults.

Gage posits one potential confounding issue:

> There may be a recruitment effect. Different sports may have recruitment processes that favor men with systematic pre-existing differences in acceptance of hegemonic masculinity and aggression. Perhaps men who are aggressive are more attracted to sports in which the game is built around aggressively dominating one's opponent. (2008: 1029)

Craig (2000) examines the perception of violence by athletes. Her study asked 31 men and 32 women aged 18-33 and reflecting the diversity of Southern California about their perception of assault by sportsmen. The hypothetical scenarios examined involved different sports (basketball and ice hockey), different levels of violence, whether drink and drugs were a factor, and so on. The assault by the basketball player was perceived as being most typical, with respondents possibly influenced by race and by real-life cases involving black basketball stars. Respondents were unlikely to apportion blame for assaults to victims, but where victim blaming did occur, male respondents were more likely to make such an accusation. Both men and women were more in favour of imprisonment for the basketball player. The notion of provocation by the victim as a trigger was more prevalent than that of drink or drugs being to blame, but neither type of provocation was seen as significant. While the study is largely inconclusive, it does add to the debate about the extent to which different sports, and how they are perceived, are related to crime and victimisation. Thus basketball is seen to be black and ice hockey white, but ice hockey is the more violent.

Gangs in sport

Having considered violence among sportsmen and whether particular sports or player positions are more violent than others, we now turn to the issue of gangs in sport. Recruitment is a factor in this respect. In their 2001 study on the presence of gangs in US colleges, Alpert and colleagues surveyed 130 university athletic directors and campus police chiefs, and interviewed student athletes at two universities. Two thirds of directors and campus chiefs thought gang members were participating in athletic programmes, and both groups knew of crimes committed on campus by athletes, although the question of whether these were gang-related is moot. It was thought that gang membership was most prevalent among male football players, and both male and female basketball players. Case studies show that some athletics departments have turned a blind eye to the gang affiliations of recruits in revenue-generating central sports participation, with continued ties to family, friends and community cited as justification for gang membership.

Gang-affiliated athletes may be cut some slack by sports authorities, criminal justice systems and the media, but Atencio and Wright (2008) note that gangs also may respect the talents of their athletic members and athletes more generally. A respected athlete might move between gang territories to compete, for example. The authors conclude that despite the simplistic duality of the 'sport versus gangs' narrative:

the young men could create spaces of meaning and value in their lives in neighborhoods where they had extremely constricted social and educational opportunities because of poverty. (2008: 277)

This is a long way from the notion that sport prevents crime or aids desistance. In other words, sports programmes neither created sports superstars nor prevented criminals, but, less quantifiably, 'the discourse created a space from which the young men could also pursue more diversified and socially democratic masculinities' (2008: 277). We return to these issues in Chapter Seven.

Super Bowl effect

What of the Super Bowl effect in the US or the 'Old Firm' derby effect in Scotland? It is alleged and frequently repeated by the media that domestic violence rises on the occasion of these matches. The Super Bowl is played annually between the winners of the two conferences of the National Football League (NFL) – the American Football Conference and the National Football Conference. The 'Old Firm' derby is played between Glasgow Rangers and Glasgow Celtic, the two most successful Scottish football teams, who have played each other about 400 times. When Rangers Football Club was liquidated (for tax offences) at the end of the 2011/12 season and demoted to the fourth tier of the league, another three years were to pass before the two teams met again in a cup match.

Crowley and colleagues (2014) were commissioned by the Scottish government to explore the correlation between 'certain matches football and domestic abuse'. Their research, based on incidents reported to the police, found that relative to various comparators, there was an increase in recorded domestic abuse incidents on the day the fixtures were played of between 13% and 138.8%, depending on a number of variables: the day of the week the match took place; the comparator day/event; and the salience/outcome of a match. Such nuance and recognition of confounding variables is rare. The authors are critical of Williams and colleagues (2013) for failing to take into account the comparators they use; for instance, Scotland international matches took place during the week not at weekends. There are also differences between studies about which time period around the match is covered. Although Williams et al (2013) only claim their analysis to be preliminary, they confirm the association between Old Firm matches and an increase in levels of domestic violence. It would be interesting to investigate the effect of a gap in tournaments of this kind – such as that which occurred during the three-year demotion of Rangers – on levels of domestic violence.

Both Crowley et al (2014) and Williams et al (2013) cite Gantz et al (2009), who examined police records relating to domestic violence incidents in 15 cities with NFL teams over a six-year period. The analysis suggested that domestic violence in a city increased both when the local team played during the season, and during the Super Bowl (whether or not there was local allegiance to the competing teams). The Super Bowl was seen to result in an average increase of 244 domestic violence incidents per city, representing 6.5% of incidents that day. Influencing factors are that the Super Bowl is the last game of the season and a public holiday, so it may be assumed that, it being winter, spectators are cooped up together indoors consuming large amounts of alcohol.

As with emotive issues such as human trafficking, there is a danger of the significance of high-profile public events being inflated by the media or by campaigning groups. Thus Snopes' investigative website claims that the alleged rise of domestic violence on Super Bowl Sunday is 'false'.[6] Following Gantz et al (2009) and others (uncited), the website found Christmas to the busiest time for domestic violence shelters. This raises the issue of whether we should ban Christmas because of this.

Snopes also mentions the work of Kirby et al (2014), although this does not appear to further its argument with its claim that: 'Every time England loses the World Cup, domestic violence against women raises 38%.' But Crowley et al (2014) argue much of this effect might be attributed to other factors, particularly alcohol. Kirby et al (2014) note the deficiencies of their own study, and conclude with an account of where and when the violence occurred; the precipitating factors; the levels of violence; the associated consumption of drugs or alcohol; and a comparison of the game's expected and final result.

This latter issue is taken up by Card and Dahl (2011), who, as economists, discuss 'family violence' in the somewhat surprising terms of 'intra-family incentives'. They illustrated this with respect to police reports of domestic violence on Sundays associated with American football matches. Controlling for variables like weather, time and 'pre-game point spread', they found that if the home team was expected to win by more than three points but lost there was an 8% increase in male-on-female violence..

[6] snopes.com (nd) 'Super Bull Sunday', www.snopes.com/crime/statistics/ superbowl.asp (accessed 11 October 2015).

Cultural criminology

In cultural criminology, we see a return to the earliest concerns of Jock Young (1969) when he published in *Anarchy* on the 'zookeepers of deviance'. Newburn (2013), meanwhile, tackles cultural criminology in the same chapter as sub-cultures. He notes the tendency of cultural criminology to criticise the unthinking use of statistics (Young, 2004) and situational prevention, and to focus on failures of social control. For our purposes, it is interesting to note the following judgement from Hallsworth:

> Cultural criminologists need to study the culture and edgework of the state and its workers with the same diligence and verve they extend towards studying the edgework of those who engage in extreme sports. (2006: 149)

It is notable that Hayward's attack on rational choice theory (2007) discusses 'expressive' and sensation-gathering crimes. Farrell's rejoinder usefully lists these as follows:

> Joyriding; Drug use; Football hooliganism; Fire-setting; Street robbery; Binge drinking; Gang-related crime, gang membership; Peer-group fighting; Child molestation; Rape; Drunken assault; Happy slapping; Graffiti; Skateboarding; Illegal BASE jumping; Train surfing; Parkour 'tree runners'; 'Street protesters' and 'Other urban-adventurer criminals'. (2010: 42)

This backs up Hallsworth's barb about the place of extreme sports in cultural criminology and some of these sports will be discussed in later chapters. Sefiha (2012) carried out cultural criminological 'edgework' – embedded with a low level cycling team in Belgium. It is attractive to consider attempting an 'edgework' (Lyng, 2005) of FIFA or the International Olympic Committee, but lack of budget and the unlikelihood of gaining access prevent it. So back to those 'men fighting', and necessarily, to masculinities too.

In a cultural criminology collection, Curtis Jackson-Jacobs (2004) writes about the 'brawling' culture of some young men in Tucson. There is a very rough continuum from brawling through prizefighting to boxing, where the lines between illegality and legality, and respectability and disreputability, may be drawn in different places, at different times and in different jurisdictions. Jackson-Jacobs sets out his dissatisfaction with theories of failed self-control, psychic or status frustration to assert: 'All patently fail to account for violence looked at in the context of spectatorship, performance, and participatory attractions' (2004: 232) – as good a definition of sport as any.

In his former hometown, Jackson-Jacobs hung out with and interviewed a loose group of 85 young people, mostly men and mostly white but reflecting some of the ethnic diversity of the local population?. Many were from economically comfortable families, most had jobs and some were doing military service. The group included current and ex-girlfriends. Some of the women had brawled, but not all of the men had. Jackson-Jacobs concentrates on one brawl in March 2000 that had entered the group's joint narrative.

Essentially, the group went looking for brawls. Parties to which they had not formally been invited presented opportunities for brawling as well as for picking up girls. Jackson-Jacobs' account hints at the relationship between the two – 'the brawl is intended to be a one-time affair.... Strangers entice by promising a non-committal relationship' (2004: 234) – and makes reference to 'a brawl experienced through the metaphor of the sexual "pick up"' (2004: 236). Reminiscent of Groombridge's (1997) joyriders, the terms 'joyfighting' or 'one-night fight' could be alternative descriptions for their activities.

Jackson-Jacobs tells of the group's attempts to get into a fight with some University of Arizona footballers, in which they eventually succeed. They expect that they will get beaten, as indeed they are, but they claim victory on the basis of getting in some taunts and not suffering as many injuries as they expected. Moreover, 'Rick' fantasises about seeing 'Dukey' being beaten up and coming to his rescue. Psychodynamic or queer explanations might be appropriate here for such homosocial sadism and chivalry. The invitation to fight even has a 'flirtatiousness' about it that reminds of the 'party girls' that some athletes claim swarm around them. Redhead describes the performance of hyper-masculinity given by the football fans he studies as 'camp' (2015: 23). Camp might also describe much professional wrestling, although Corteen and Corteen (2012) focus on the real pain involved even in 'scripted' fights.

Tomsen (1997) might call such a scenario a 'top night', so it is surprising that Jackson-Jacobs (2014) does not reference him. His Australian ethnography involved witnessing tales of fights rather than merely listening to subsequent accounts. Like Jackson-Jacobs, alcohol features in his account, although it is central in neither. But speaking of alcohol, he:

rejects the conventional left view that popular expresses elements of social control or false consciousness, to argue instead that it frequently embodies collective cultural resistance to efforts to regulate the 'dangerous classes' or the 'lower orders' in different societies. (1997: 90)

Alcohol is often associated with sport but both are often seen in the same way by both left and right. Tomsen (1997) witnessed 37 assaults (including seven in one visit, including violence by bouncers) over 300 hours of observation at 36 visits to pubs or discos. He classified five of the visits as 'highly dangerous', involving broken bones and weapons. He 'was sometimes abused and challenged, and on a few occasions assaulted without real harm' (1997: 93). The amounts of alcohol consumed appeared to make no difference to the severity or frequency of assaults.

Tomsen (1997) spoke to some of the fighters and found that being beaten up was less shaming than refusing the fight. Those spoiling for a fight could always rely on doorstaff to give them one. He noted much of the behaviour that Jackson-Jacobs notes. He seems puzzled by the randomness of much of the violence, although the 'protest masculinity' (Connell, 1995) he ascribes to the heavy drinking would appear to be a factor. Tomsen cites Katz (1988) on the sensual attractions of such crimes and warns against a moral panic or cultural snobbery, as it 'too simple either to romanticise or straightforwardly denounce this behaviour' (1997: 100). Tomsen's own experience was fairly 'edgy' and raises the issue of masculinity again. Is all this edgework a macho sport?

Lyng's (1990) academic expansion of Hunter S. Thompson's work was based on the sport of sky diving, and in it he talks of marathon runners and endurance runners as possessing 'edgework skills'. He notes the 'illusory sense of control' and risk underestimation of young men. Such confidence in their own abilities recalls Groombridge's (1997) joyriders; it could even be argued that most drivers (AA, 1992) participate in a form of 'everyday edgework'.

Jefferson's (1998) work is ostensibly about boxing, engaged through the figure of Mike Tyson, but it also examines other sports (including motor racing and Tour de France cycling) and masculinities. It is black masculinity that is the focus – that masculinity where crime and sport contend or combine to lead an individual out of the ghetto and into jail or the Hall of Fame or both. Jefferson also adds in the psychosocial. A bullied 'little fairy boy', Tyson eventually ends up in a reformatory where he is taught boxing. Jefferson discusses not only bodybuilding but also the necessity for Tyson to build his body (and the mind to use it) – and indeed the need for all men to do so.

Wacquant (1995) actually stepped into the ring for his four-year ethnography on the South Side of Chicago, which involved entering a tournament and sparring with professional fighters. Clearly looking at some of the same black masculinities as Jefferson (1998), and keen to bring the body back into sociological accounts, his 'beef' is with theory. He is pugilistic. He has Marx, Weber, Foucault and Bourdieu in his corner. He details the demands of the boxers' lives, which contrast strongly with the lives of the men described by Jackson-Jacobs and Tomsen. There is no sex or violence. It is, perhaps, this discipline that leads to the presumption that sport cures rather than causes crime.

In his paean of praise for the city, Hayward talks about various disruptions of 'the smooth functionalist flows of modernist space' (2004: 156) that situational crime prevention and administrative criminology seek to control/patrol. Though his work is not about urban sports per se, he specifically mentions skateboarding and the smooth, albeit 'against the grain', flows of parkour. Parkour, or free running, is an urban recreation, which, like skateboarding and roller blading, is popular with young people. It is more problematic for the authorities, however, and is the subject of crime prevention measure through environmental design and antisocial behaviour orders. Tim Shieff, 2009 Barclays World Freerun Champion, was warned by a police community support officer that his behaviour was 'antisocial'.[7] Hartley notes the potential parkour raises for negligence and public liability claims and rightly argues that it is 'a site ripe for socio-legal analysis of law and popular culture' (2010: 278). In other contexts, free runners, or *traceurs*, have been heralded as high-speed 'flaneurs' (Atkinson, 2009), and parkour has attracted the attention of cultural geographers (Saville, 2008) and the concern of medical practitioners, in terms of the potential for injury. Clearly there is an interest for cultural criminology and youth justice specialists where this analysis might commence.

Atkinson aligns parkour with an anarcho-environmentalism that contrasts with his normal experience of running:

> ... rationally calculating and environmentally detached
> wheel of athletes concerned predominantly with externally

---

[7] Tony Bushby (14 March 2010) 'Nosy parkour faces ASBO', *Daily Star*, www.dailystar.co.uk/posts/view/126273 (accessed 23 July 2015)

defined, preset, and tightly policed time and distance running goals. (2009: 171)

Parkour could be described as a 'postsport' (Pronger, 1998), and indeed is recognised by Sport UK as a legitimate sporting activity, associated with coaching awards and international competitions, and often featuring in exhibitions alongside other 'extreme' sports.

The practice of parkour implicitly transgresses, and may even trespass; as Atkinson says: 'Lines separating roads, buildings, cultures, selves, and bodies disappeared. I had never experienced the city, or running for that matter, in this way' (2009: 171). Saville's (2008) article on parkour is illustrated (figure 2: 901) by a picture of a man attempting to look over a wall while a friend looks on. It is captioned 'Getting to know space', but might equally come from a crime prevention manual about defensible space. A later diagram (figure 4: 906) might be captioned 'usable space'. Kidder says of the respondents in his study on parkour: 'Whether it is testing their athleticism, tempting arrest, or simply touring unknown environs, *traceurs* are engaged in the fatefulness of action' (2013: 237). He also mentions flirting with women and shoplifting as other 'adventures' his respondents might have.

For all Atkinson's (2009) hippy poetics, he notes the origin of parkour in the work of George Hébert, a naval officer whose 'natural' methods were eventually espoused by the French military. One soldier taught Hébert's son, David Belle, who, with his friend, Sébastien Foucan, developed a more urban style of parkour that required no access to forests. They fell out with, Belle aiming to keep to the natural, spiritual side of parkour holding out against the 'sportization process' (Dunning, 1999). Atkinson is right to link this to divisions that occur in sub-cultures, but it also mirrors the proliferation of governing bodies in some sports, notably but not exclusively boxing and martial arts, as well as darts. This can lead to jurisdictional issues that sports law might address.

The greatest freedom of movement afforded to most of us is in online, where we can be who we want to be, or playing video games, where we can fly, drive badly, kill, steal or maim. From tearing up the virtual landscape, we now turn to consider we now turn to reality and consider the environment in relation to criminology.

Green criminology and rural criminology

Green criminology is widely considered to comprise crimes against the environment. Even the activities of farmers might be considered by some to be environmental crimes. Indeed, a vegan green criminologist might consider the raising and slaughtering of cattle or other animals to be criminal acts. A mainstream rural criminology might examine crimes that occur in the country – theft of tractors, fuel or livestock – but a more radical one (Donnermeyer and DeKeseredy, 2013) might look at the deficiencies of the rural policing of domestic violence or the particularities of rural pornography or drug use. So the definitions of both rural and green criminology are contested and there is some overlap that cannot be examined here, but, just as the previous sections have concentrated on urban land use in relation to sport, so we turn to rural (or suburban) land use with the examples of golfing and hunting.

An article by Pearce (1993) asked 'How green is your golf?'. In China, the game is under scrutiny; once banned as bourgeois, it is now the focus of environmental concerns and, not for the first time, an anti-corruption drive. One Ministry of Commerce official recently came under fire for allegedly playing golf on an illegal course.[8]

As we saw in Chapter Two, 'field' or 'blood' sports form part of our discussion and foxhunting in the UK may well be seen by some as an environmental concern. In other countries, hunting with guns is a contested rural/green issue. Landscape and land use is historically shaped by such practices. An irony of the debate is that sporting interests might trump economic ones and result in a monoculture. The cover currently left for foxes or pheasants is pleasing to the eye and breaks up the big fields of industrial agriculture.

The largest collection on green criminology pays no attention to sport, but the editors note in their introduction the corruption and lack of accountability in horse racing in the United States – 'a blood sport in which wonderful animals are volunteered, indeed bred, to participate in a sport that, any way you look at it, grinds them up' (Rhoden, cited in South and Brisman, 2013: 19), so clearly a green criminology of sport is possible. For instance, the 2015 progress report of the Committee on Climate Change to parliament notes:

> Wetland habitats, including the majority of upland areas with carbon-rich peat soils, are in poor condition. The damaging practice of burning peat to increase grouse yields continues, including on internationally protected sites.

[8] Adam Minter (7 April 2015) 'Beijing declares war on illegal golf courses', Bloomberg, www.japantimes.co.jp/opinion/2015/04/07/commentary/world-commentary/beijing-declares-war-on-illegal-golf-courses/#.VXWjBGA6Vm0 (accessed 11 October 2015).

Albeit not canonically 'cultural' or 'green', criminology studies of joyriding are relevant here. In her discussion of joyriding, Campbell (1993) provocatively links the events on Blackbird Leys Estate in Oxford in the summer of 1991 to the presence of the nearby, then British Leyland, car plant, which now turns out Minis for BMW. She posited that the workless sons of the workers were engaged in 'autodressage', that is, likening joyriding to the upper-class equine sport of dressage. Equally, joyriding might be placed within a 'car culture' in which our desire for freedom trumps any environmental concerns (Groombridge, 1997). As the Blackbird Leys Estate incidents showed, there are clearly rules for the game of joyriding, particularly goading the local police.

Indeed, all car use, not just that for 'sporting' purposes, might be seen from a green perspective to constitute a harm that might be criminalised. Agnew suggests that 'ordinary harms have been neglected not only by mainstream criminologists, but by many green criminologists as well – who more often focus on the environmental harms committed by states, corporations, and organised criminal groups' (2012: 58). To counter criticism that the sport causes environmental damage, executives behind the launch of Formula E motor racing lay claim to its green credentials:

> Formula E chief executive, Alejandro Agag … claims lofty ambitions for the zero-emission race series: to make electric cars sexy, accelerate improvements in the technology and tackle city-choking air pollution and, ultimately, climate change.[9]

But the same article also notes: 'Agag, like most of those involved, have roots in Formula One and are reluctant to criticise the brash, gas-guzzling F1 circus seen by some as an eco-horror show.' No green himself, even former champion Mario Andretti told *The Guardian*:[10]

[9]   Damian Carrington (7 July 2014) 'Formula E: do the guilt-free thrills of electric car racing herald a new era for motor sport?', *The Guardian*, www.theguardian.com/environment/2014/jul/07/-sp-formula-e-electric-car-racing-motor-sport?CMP=fb_gu (accessed 11 October 2015).

[10]   Paul Weaver (27 October 2014) 'US sounds warning to Formula One, a sport teetering on the brink of crisis', *The Guardian*, www.theguardian.com/sport/blog/2014/oct/27/us-grand-prix-formula-one-mario-andretti-f1 (accessed 11 October 2015).

Formula One should loosen up a bit. I think they've gone slightly overboard with the technical side of the engine. And we saw in Sochi, teams backing off for fuel reasons, just to make it to the end.

Thoreau would have been against motor sport, but he supported sports that immersed people in nature like walking, running, sailing and rowing (Gorn and Warren, 2004). To this list we might now add the original parkour. So a green perspective might see access to the countryside as an issue, and argue that rural land interests are tilted towards field/blood sports (objectionable in their own right) over human sport in nature. Such denial of access could be seen to be a harm or crime. Gorn and Warren (2004) note that Fletcher's *A Few Notes of Cruelty to Animals* (1846) favoured gymnastics as a 'manly' substitute for blood sports. In the spirit of the activities discussed in Chapter Seven, a green criminologist might therefore recommend gymnastics for illegal badger-baiting offenders, and note that although the sport of badger baiting is illegal, badger culling may be compulsory.

Some of the theories discussed in this chapter relate to, or interact with, each other, or link back to mainstream theories. While this chapter has explored why athletes might commit crime, the next chapter focuses on efforts within sporting circles to try to prevent criminality and on-field infractions.

SIX

Red card: sport, justice and social control

Mahiedine Mekhissi-Benabbad is a 3,000-metre steeplechaser, whose 'crime' was to remove his shirt during the last part of a race, with one hurdle to go, in the final of the European Championships in 2014.[1] Unlike Tommie Smith and John Carlos, who gave the Black power salute on the podium at the 1968 Mexico Olympics (Hartman, 2003), Mekhissi-Benabbad was not making a political point; rather, he was prematurely celebrating his success in winning the race, much like a footballer. He was initially shown a yellow card by stewards before being disqualified when the Spanish team protested on behalf of their fourth-placed man. One reason for the rule of retaining one's shirt is the need to correctly identify the runner, as the shirt carries the number.

It would be nice to think the rules of the International Association of Athletics Federations (IAAF) were a nod to feminism, ensuring that men be subject to the same restrictions as women. When Brandi Chastain took off her top to celebrate scoring the winning goal in the 1999 Women's World Cup for the US, however, the incident became 'iconic'. Now it is routine for such celebrations by both men and women to receive a yellow card, which might be seen as indicative of the zero tolerance or zero humour on the part of sports administrators.

The Queen's racehorse, Estimate, tested positive for morphine after winning the 2013 Ascot Gold Cup. The test result was eventually blamed on poppy seed contamination at a milling plant on the continent. Horse racing has long been associated with betting scams, and therefore with the potential to manipulate outcomes by impairing horses' performance through doping, and the fact that the Queen's horse was suspected added to the incident's newsworthiness. This chapter discusses some of the issues such incidents raise for the policing/ justice systems of sport.

---

[1] Oliver Brown (14 August 2014) 'Mahiedine Mekhissi-Benabbad stripped of steeplechase gold after stripping off at European Championship', *Telegraph*, www. telegraph.co.uk/sport/othersports/athletics/11035554/Mahiedine-Mekhissi-Benabbad-stripped-of-steeplechase-gold-after-stripping-off-at-European-Championship.html (accessed 11 October 2015).

The PGA Tour, the organiser of the main professional golf tours played in the US and North America, has its own anti-doping programme, which some claim is not as stringent as the World Anti-Doping Agency (WADA) code.[2] For the 2016 Olympic Games in Rio (the first Olympic golf competition since 1904), participants will automatically be required to comply with the WADA code under the International Golf Federation's (IGF) anti-doping policy. So we see that the land of sport has multiple jurisdictions and that WADA has been granted some transnational policing powers.

The global nature of crime indicates to some that transnational crime might require transnational policing (Reichel and Albanese, 2013). For these scholars, transnational crime generally constitutes the trafficking of people, prohibited items and money, and more recently, even concerns pollution. Transnational policing is generally a tale of police cooperation and sport is rarely mentioned in this context (an exception is the reference by Bowling and Sheptycki (2012) of sport as a generator of 'mega events' that require policing) and even then the concern is often related to terrorism rather than to the potential for corruption in decision making around bids for hosting lucrative tournaments.

In a blog for the Sport and Recreation Alliance, Thompson floats the idea of 'a global body – similar to WADA – to tackle match-fixing and corruption'.[3] He cautions:

> This may sound attractive but the obvious questions of funding (how much and by whom?), responsibilities (for what?) and accountability (to whom?) would take up even more scarce time and resources to answer.

Criminologists and policing scholars will recognise these questions. More intriguingly for criminologists should be the two sources of Thompson's reflections: first, cuts to police budgets in the UK under the banner of austerity; and second, the claim by the director general of WADA, David Howman, that '25 per cent of sport is controlled

---

[2] James Riach (18 July 2015) 'IOC president urges PGA Tour to comply with Wada code before Olympics', *The Guardian*, www.theguardian.com/sport/2015/jul/18/ioc-president-pga-tour-golf-wada-olympics (accessed 11 October 2015).

[3] Leigh Thompson (nd) 'Match-fixing: why sport needs to use brains as well as brawn to protect integrity', Sports and Recreation Alliance, www.sportandrecreation.org.uk/blog/leigh-thompson/09-10-2014/match-fixing-why-sport-needs-use-brains-well-brawn-protect-integrity (accessed 11 October 2015)

by organised crime'.[4] Howman said these figures came from Interpol; he was speaking at a conference of the International Centre for Sport Security where he suggested a World Sport Integrity Agency modelled on WADA, which does rather assume that WADA has been successful.[5]

These vignettes introduce the question of how various sports detect/deter/punish or even rehabilitate their 'criminals' on field and off. The structure of the next section follows Kraska and Brent's (2011) attempts to theorise criminal justice. They approach the task metaphorically; thus criminal justice can be seen as follows:

- as rational/legal;
- as a system;
- as crime control versus due process;
- as politics;
- as socially constructed reality;
- as growth complex;
- as oppression;
- as late modernity.

The first thing to note is that Kraska and Brent's book contains no discussion of sport. It sticks closely to 'black letter' definitions of law and criminal justice, so we might look at Abel's discussion of informal justice to see if sport should be considered there. Abel does not mention sports in his book either, but notes that informal justice is 'dissociated from state power', 'dependent upon rhetoric rather than force', 'nonbureaucratic, decentralised, relatively undifferentiated, and non-professional ...' (1982: 2). That might have been true of some sports in the past, but also of much 'justice' still played out in the courts, off the pitch and on field where the 'formal' informality of mediation and arbitration is used.

[4] Ben Rumsby (6 October 2014) 'Organised crime controls 25 per cent of world sport, warns Wada chief David Howman', *Telegraph*, www.telegraph.co.uk/sport/othersports/11144807/Organised-crime-controls-25-per-cent-of-world-sport-warns-Wada-chief-David-Howman.html (accessed 11 October 2015).
[5] Nick Harris (23 February 2011) 'Head of WADA calls for global anti-corruption body', Sportingintelligence, www.sportingintelligence.com/2011/02/23/head-ofwada-calls-for-global-anti-corruption-body-230201 (accessed 11 October 2015).

Criminal justice as rational/legal

Hopkins–Burke (2013: 278) sketches the orthodox social progress model, which:

> ... claims that the development of modern societies, their laws, and criminal justice systems are the product of enlightenment, benevolence, and a consensual society where the great majority of the population shares the same core values.

Similarly changes in the rules of sport might be taken as reforms, although this rather glosses over the view that rugby football came into being in trying to formulate and reform the playing of association football, and that later rugby also split into union and league. The rules are set out and the punishments delineated and applied as necessary, with the expectation that this process will act as a deterrent, or failing that, result in retribution. This often happens more quickly in sport than in other areas of life. Justice was never so summary as in sport, and yet the cheat, the fouler and the simulator are rarely deterred and much retribution is hardly restorative. Webb and Thelwell (2015) found that referees may tailor their style to the perceived cultures in European football, preferring to keep flow in England but recognising a greater tolerance of stop/start in Italy, where the finer points of play might be argued.

Criminal justice as a system

It is generally accepted that the criminal justice system is not particularly systematic, has many bottlenecks and lacks adequate mechanisms for feedback. Moreover, there are turf and resource wars between the agents and apparatus of the criminal justice system. Sports justice systems sit uneasily beside those for criminal justice, although sports law operates adequately in both areas. Most sports have referees or umpires, some both, and many rely increasingly on technological aids akin to CCTV to monitor contests. These agents often combine the powers of police, prosecutor, judge, jury, first appellate body, gaoler and probation/parole officer. The juridification of sport has not led to the full separation of those powers.

Balanced precariously at the top of the system is the Court of Arbitration for Sport (CAS). A current challenge for CAS is the case of Claudia Pechstein, a speed skater who was banned for two years in 2009 because of irregular blood results, although she never failed a drugs test. CAS rejected her appeal against the charge. But in January 2015, a Munich court ruled that Pechstein could go ahead with a lawsuit demanding more than £2.8m in damages over lost earnings. She will get backing from the world footballers' union (Fifpro), which was concerned that CAS lacked 'independence, equal representation and accessibility'.[6] The human rights of Caster Semenya were widely seen to be breached in her brush with sporting authorities in 2009 (as mentioned in the Preface).

Criminal justice as crime control versus due process

Packer (1964) sets out seemingly contrasting models of criminal justice that are often conjoined in the expression 'law and order'. In the law and order formulation, 'law' can be seen as Packer's 'due process' and 'order' the 'crime control':

> The Crime Control Model is based on the proposition that the repression of criminal conduct is by far the most important function to be performed by the criminal process. The failure of law enforcement to bring criminal conduct under tight control is viewed as leading to the breakdown of public order and thence to the disappearance of an important condition of human freedom. (1964: 9)

There are clear elements of this in much sport where the presumption is that without the authority of the referee the freedom of action of some would curtail the freedom of others. But as we saw in discussion of Mertonian innovation in Chapter Four, the goal of sport is not challenged by cheats. Stepping on to the field of play is to sign the social contract of political theory more obviously than being born into a society. Even if you only 'have jumpers for goalposts', you can still play football without a referee, even if it means you have to drop the offside rule.

Due process is more difficult in the hurly burly of live sport, but the National Football League's (NFL) officiating command centre

---

[6] BBC (14 July 2015) 'Claudia Pechstein: speed skater gets Fifpro funding in CAS case', www.bbc.co.uk/sport/0/winter-sports/33517639 (accessed 11 October 2015).

Gameday Central can 'correct decisions from on high and far away'[7] and the increased use of technology can ensure a degree of fairness. *The Economist* predicts that technology will enter sport to the extent that 'the referee's a robot'.[8] It details the use of camera and software to determine offside incidents and to track the exact position of the ball. It even mentions an innovation by a British company, Smallfry –accelerometers in shin pads that can determine a 'dive' where the player simulates a foul.

Some sports decisions take longer and the 'deflategate' case in the NFL is a case in point. NFL officials found that Tom Brady, the New England Patriots quarterback, had colluded with team staff to deflate footballs below the allowable limit during a playoff game (deflated footballs are considered easier to throw and catch). In September 2015, a US judge overturned a four-game suspension of Brady. According to the BBC:[9]

> U.S. District Judge Richard M. Berman found that NFL Commissioner Roger Goodell's penalty suffered from 'several significant legal deficiencies' including failing to notify Mr Brady about the possibility of a punishment against him.

The decision is being appealed, but there is clearly a tension between the on-field need for order and off-field obligation to pay due heed to law. Such legal formalism may be coming more common. Yet in play many referees use discretion, informal dispute resolution and even forms of restorative justice.

[7] Andrew Anthony (19 October 2014) 'NFL officials can correct decisions from on high and far away', *The Guardian*, www.theguardian.com/sport/blog/2014/oct/18/ nfl-decisions-faw-away-atlanta-falcons-detroit-lions-wembley (accessed 11 October 2015).

[8] *The Economist* (7 September 2013) 'The referee's a robot', www.economist.com/ news/technology-quarterly/21584440-technology-and-sport-deployment-goal-line-technology-assist-football (accessed 11 October 2015).

[9] BBC (3 September 2015) 'Tom Brady case: judge overturns "deflategate" suspension', www.bbc.co.uk/news/world-us-canada-34143081 (accessed 11 October 2015).

Criminal justice as politics

Seb Coe was elected over rival Sergey Bubka, the Ukrainian ex-pole vaulter, as president of the International Association of Athletics Federations (IAAF), after a campaign centring on promises of money (for development, not corruption) and being tough on drugs. This could be seen as an example of sport mirroring politics, in its use of the discourse of 'crime' to gain and hold positions of government (Feeley and Simon, 1992). Following Feeley and Simon, we might argue that a renewed 'war on drugs' in sport will lead to more banned athletes but not necessarily an 'cleaner' sport; rather, we risk a clear loss of human rights and privacy and greater surveillance of those athletes and those associated with them.

Criminal justice as socially constructed reality

Kraska and Brent argue that the social construction of reality lies 'in opposition, for the most part, to rational legal or systems thinking' (2011: 155).

Clearly some of the politics of criminal justice are socially constructed and the same is true of sports justice. Thus, as drugs are construed to be a problem in sport, so in politics the justice system is brought to bear on that problem.

Kraska and Brent (2011) use the work of Kappeler (2004), Rafter (1990) and Zatz (1987) to discuss this issue. Kappeler covers many myths about criminal justice, where 'smoke and mirrors' (not his term) and particularly the media distract. None of Kraska and Brent's contributors mentions sport, so they don't claim, like Brohm (1987), that sport is the 'circus' that works with 'bread' to placate the masses. But clearly sport frequently trades on its myths, claiming all along to be real. One myth of law is impartiality and claims of this nature are often made in sports. But as every fan knows, 'There is now overwhelming evidence that referee decisions favor the home team' (Pollard, 2008: 12) and football fans will doubtless all be familiar with the term 'Fergie time'.[10]

Rafter (1990) argued for the examination of the social construction of criminal justice as a practice and as a discipline. She makes no mention of sport, but does argue for a sociology of knowledge within

[10] The idea that under Sir Alec Ferguson's management Manchester United received additional time to equalise or win matches. See Charlotte Pritchard (23 November 2012) 'Fergie time: does it really exist?', BBC, www.bbc.co.uk/news/magazine-20464371 (accessed 11 October 2015).

criminology and other disciplines. Within the sociology of sport we find Malcolm doing just that. He argues against sports sociology's embrace of the sociological 'mainstream' and closeness to 'physical education'. He notes the 'political dynamics and consequences of the social construction of the field' (2014: 1). It should be clear that sports criminology will seek to recognise the social construction of sport and crimes within it.

Zatz's (1987) work on Chicano gangs shows how the social construction of gangs as a 'social problem' helped the local police to acquire federal funding to deal with it. Again, sport's 'war on drugs' might be seen in the same way. Empires are constructed to deal with problems in real, virtual and sporting life. Whether such problems constitute 'moral panics' is debatable. On the one hand, 'drug cheats' could be construed as 'folk devils' (Cohen, 2011), but on the other, it seems more likely that any increase in the numbers of wrongdoers or levels of 'deviancy' are the result of rational calculation than scaremongering.

Criminal justice as growth complex

In criminology and criminal justice, the term 'prison–industrial complex' (Donziger, 1996) is well known; Christie (2000) calls it 'crime-control industry'. The only mention of sport in Donziger's work is a reference to a newspaper article demanding TV and sport be withdrawn in prisons to make punishment tougher. What complexes might we find in sport? The idea of such complexes is well established, but Lefever (2012) also notes other formulations: 'sports/media complex' (Jhally, 1989), 'media–sport–cultural complex' (Rowe, 1997) or 'media–sport–production complex' (Maguire, 1991).

One strand of the discussion in this book is the extent to which sport has always been close to gambling and is now close to media, so it should be no surprise that crime arises and connection made and remade. The kidnap of a 16-year-old in Honduras in October 2007 might not have been reported by *Daily Telegraph* had the youngster's brother, Wilson Palacios, not been a Tottenham Hotspur footballer.[11] Jhally (1989), Rowe (1997) and Maguire (1991) make no mention of crime specifically, but their formulations, particularly where they

[11] Julie Henry (9 May 2009) 'Edwin Palacio's kidnap: body of Tottenham footballer Wilson's brother 'found', *Telegraph*, www.telegraph.co.uk/news/worldnews/centralamericaandthecaribbean/honduras/5300651/Edwin-Palacios-kidnap-body-of-Tottenham-footballer-Wilsons-brother-found.html (accessed 11 October 2015).

include the 'cultural', are capable of embracing the suggestions of sports criminology.

Criminal justice as oppression

For Kraska and Brent (2011), the extensive literature on criminal justice as oppression largely boils down to left and feminist arguments. One reason why athletes don't attract the sympathy of critical scholars is that they often seem to embrace their servitude and demand that they and their colleagues are held to even more strict regimes of policing and punishment. Cyclist and Tour de France winner Chris Froome and Olympic athlete Mo Farah have provided more details about their bodies that most of us know about ourselves and might be reluctant to share. Farah is reported to have told the *Sunday Times,* 'I'm happy to do what it takes to prove I'm a clean athlete.'[12] He wants his anti-doping blood test data to be made public, while Froome has released his 'power data'.[13]

Lawyers have started to get to work on the rights of 'oppressed' sports stars, and academics have also started to show some interest. Froome and Farah's openness can be seen as 'transparency'. Henne (2015) argues that it is sports governance that should be transparent and this is examined in the next section.

Criminal justice as late modernity

Kraska and Brent (2011) point us in the direction of Loader's (2008) extensive review of Ericson (2007), Simon (2007) and Garland (2002) for work on late modernity. Of these, only Simon makes any mention of sport. His choice of the descriptor 'jazzy' and his mention of 'media attention' suggest that he is not persuaded by 'midnight basketball' (2007: 103; see also Chapter Seven below) as a method of crime prevention. Chapter Seven examines why he might be right, but why should such high theory books mention sport? Loader does not have sport in mind when he says of Simon that 'crime inhabits the

---

[12]   Press Association (9 August 2015) 'Mo Farah calls for his anti-doping blood test data to be made public', *The Guardian,* www.theguardian.com/sport/2015/aug/09/mo-farah-anti-doping-blood-test-data-public (accessed 11 October 2015).

[13]   Michael Hutchinson (21 July 2015) 'What can we learn from Chris Froome's power data?', *Cycling Weekly,* www.cyclingweekly.co.uk/racing/tour-de-france/what-can-we-learn-from-chris-froomes-power-data-183677#6wKrILWzRJkadARz.99 (accessed 11 October 2015).

habitus of US citizens and becomes a structuring feature of mundane culture' (2008: 401), but sport is part of that mundane culture. Is it now governed through crime?

Ericson was not talking about sport's 'war on drugs', but he identifies authority's continued contention 'that more will work where less has not' (2007: 12). So it is in sport. Where these cultures of control (Garland, 2002), crime governance (Simon, 2007) and concern for security (Ericson, 2007) most impinge on sport is at mega-events like the World Cup or the Olympics. Thus, in similar vein, Fussey et al (2012) pick up such issues and quote Ericson's frequent writing partner Haggerty (Boyle and Haggerty, 2009) on issues of surveillance, adding notions of cleansing from the work of Douglas (1966). A similar analysis of sport's 'war on drugs' might prove useful. Pappa and Kennedy (2012) found that their athlete respondents spoke the language of anti-doping, but that drug use was normal practice. They use Foucault's work on 'governmentality' to suggest that athletes often dope with the knowledge or connivance of coaches or authorities but still they took individual responsibility.

> In this way, athletes' internalization of responsibility for doping can be seen as part of the art of governing competitive sport. By not acknowledging the 'networked athlete' explanation of doping, WADA minimizes the influence of the pressures and norms of the sports environment and encourages athletes to take responsibility for altering their own behaviour. (2012: 290)

Without using the same terminology, Rasmussen (2005) comes to a similar conclusion: that anti-doping represents the quest for an imaginary evil, a quest that never ends but leaves individual 'cheats' condemned and the mechanisms of surveillance further tightened and extended to the rest of us.

Loader (2008) notes the resistance to governance by crime (Simon, 2007) shown by individual states and institutions within the US. Such resistance in the field of sports is often not for political but for commercial reasons. Thus unscrupulous boxing promoters may exploit the different licensing requirements of individual states, and major league baseball is unique, even among US sports, in being exempted from anti-trust legislation (Grow, 2012). This position has enabled these sports to control the working conditions and opportunities of players and 'protect' them from intrusive drug testing.

Henne (2015) does not reference these late modern theorists, but does examine corporate sports governance from a socio-legal perspective. Consideration of her work also paves the way for the next two sections of this chapter. Part of the problem of dealing with global sport governance is the hybrid legal nature of national and international sports bodies. Henne deploys the work of Braithwaite and Drahos (2000) on regulation to argue for moving beyond accountability by audit. She outlines:

> .... five areas of sport that are core targets of transparency agendas: concerns around match-fixing and money laundering, the bidding process for sport mega-events, the infrastructure contracts for those events, human rights violations, and performance-enhancing drug use among athletes. (2015: 2)

Having looked at different metaphors for criminal justice and relating them to sport, we might consider some specifics of the operation of the criminal justice systems of sport. The main problems seen to beset sport might broadly be seen as use of performance-enhancing drugs (PEDs) and corruption. Use of PEDs is seen as a form of corruption by some. In addition, one noticeable development has been the extent to which sports now seek to control the off-field activities of their players. In keeping with the book's argument about the sovereignty often exercised by sport, this section treats sport like a foreign country, and so talks of 'extra-territoriality'. Included in this final section are supra-national matters such as human rights, which perhaps should be higher up sport's list of concerns.

Performance-enhancing drugs

The 2015 film *The Program* focuses on Lance Armstrong, the Tour de France cyclist forced to admit to taking drugs. In publicity for the film, the actor Ben Foster described taking part in a rigorous training regime and spending time on the US Pro Challenge cycle tour in preparation for playing the lead role. Foster also admitted to having taken PEDs,[14] a confession that was treated as indicative of his commitment to his art. Such behaviour is not necessarily healthy or beneficial to an actor's

---

[14] Ryan Gilbey (10 September 2015) 'Ben Foster on playing Lance Armstrong: "doping affects your mind"', *The Guardian*, www.theguardian.com/film/2015/sep/10/ben-foster-the-programme-lance-armstrong-interview (accessed 11 October 2015).

art, but it is not seen as cheating. In sport, by contrast, drug taking is seen to be cheating of the worst order. In the recent Athletics World Championship, Justin Gatlin was routinely referred to in the British media as 'Justin Gatlin, drugs cheat'.[15] If he could ensure that his lane was only 95 metres long or managed to fool the reaction timers in his blocks, that would be cheating.

Over the summer of 2015, Alberto Salazaar, coach to Britain's multi-medal-winning long-distance runner Mo Farah, was accused of encouraging doping among athletes in his care in the past.[16] Following a Department of Culture, Media and Sport (DCMS) Select Committee[17] hearing about doping, particularly in the London Marathon, the British world marathon record holder Paula Radcliffe, has been forced into a passionate defence of her record and the right to keep the results of her blood tests private, likening demands to release them to 'abuse'.[18] The DCMS committee also released a report by the University of Tubingen for WADA that had been blocked by IAAF, which suggested that 29%-45% of athletes under examination (not of all athletes) may have been doping.

Diane Modahl's case raises issues in respect of the testing procedures and the contractual relationship of athletes (Hartley, 2013). In 1994, Modahl failed a drug test for the presence of testosterone; she was sent home from the Commonwealth Games in Victoria and subsequently banned. That ban was initially upheld by the British Athletics Federation (BAF). It was later accepted on appeal, with the help of the science of bacterial degradation of urine samples, that she had not been guilty of doping. The original test had been carried out in a Portuguese laboratory. There were delays in the testing of the second

[15] A Google search (11 September 2015) for the terms 'drugs cheat' plus 'Justin Gatlin' found 20,900 news items although Gatlin maintains he did not knowingly take banned substances.

[16] Matt Lawton (19 August 2015) 'Drug chief refuses to rule out bringing charges against Mo Farah as part of ongoing investigations into Alberto Salazar', *Mail Online*, www.dailymail.co.uk/sport/sportsnews/article-3203981/Drug-chief-refuses-rule-bringing-charges-against-Mo-Farah-ongoing-investigations-Alberto-Salazar.html (accessed 11 October 2015).

[17] House of Commons (8 September 2015) 'Committee publishes "blocked" study on doping', www.parliament.uk/business/committees/committees-a-z/commons-select/culture-media-and-sport-committee/news-parliament-2015/chairs-statement-blood-doping-15-16/ (accessed 11 October 2015).

[18] BBC (10 September 2015) 'Paula Radcliffe: pressure to release blood data "almost abuse"', www.bbc.co.uk/sport/0/athletics/34204775 (accessed 11 October 2015).

sample and in informing her of the positive test for the first one. Her various attempts to sue for loss of earnings and so forth failed, but the costs of the legal proceedings led to the winding up of the BAF. Despite this nearly ruinous engagement with sports law, Modahl demanded in 2012 that WADA:

> ... has to get tougher on their penalties. Because let's face it, two years [banned] is not a deterrent. I don't think it sends out any sort of message that if you cheat at the highest level you will be severely punished. Two years is nothing.[19]

Henne (2015) notes that transparency is itself an invasive surveillance of athletes' bodies and is sceptical of its shortcomings. In earlier work with others (Henne et al, 2013), she notes that WADA also has responsibility for tracing use of non-performance-enhancing drugs (that is, 'recreational' drugs) as well as PEDs (for which 'occupational' drugs might be a better term). Sefiha's ethnographic study among cyclists found that 'it unsurprising that PED use is further characterized as nearly an occupational necessity for professional riders and those existing on the margins of the sport' (2012: 228). Henne (2015) reveals inconsistencies in what is prohibited and suggests reform rather than simply the removal of illicit drugs from the list.

Lund's problems with drugs for his baldness (Chapter Three) are indicative, but so is the United States Anti-Doping Agency's (USADA) ongoing 'war on drugs attitudes':

> While the use of medical marijuana may be decriminalized or legalized in some states, it is still illegal under federal law. Currently, USADA will only consider TUE [therapeutic use exemptions] applications for legal, FDA-approved uses of THC, such as the drug Dronabinol, to manage some of the symptoms of AIDS, or to treat nausea and vomiting caused by cancer chemotherapy. USADA will not accept any applications for 'medical marijuana'.[20]

---

[19] *Evening Standard* (30 April 2012) 'Diane Modahl happy for drug cheats to compete', www.standard.co.uk/sport/other-sports/diane-modahl-happy-for-drug-cheats-to-compete-7696792.html (accessed 11 October 2015).
[20] USADA (nd) 'Athlete guide to the 2015 prohibited list', www.usada.org/substances/prohibited-list/athlete-guide (accessed 11 October 2015).

Modahl's case centred on medical evidence, which, in the context of USADA's statement above, raises the issue of TUEs applied to synthetics such as THC. A TUE might allow an athlete who has asthma, or a diagnosis thereof, to use an inhaler barred to other athletes on the principle of the levelling of playing fields (see Moller et al, 2015). But it can get more complex than that. For example, different countries set different allowable blood alcohol levels in drink-driving legislation. This indicates differences of opinion on where impairment occurs.

Endocrinologists do not agree on how low an individual's levels of the thyroid hormones thyroxine (T4) and liothyronine (T3) should be before a diagnosis of hypothyroidism can be made. Most, however, would not set it at the level determined by Dr Jeffrey S. Brown, endocrinologist to some of Salazaar's athletes. The TUE test does not apply here, as thyroid hormone treatment is not banned, on the grounds that it is believed to have no performance enhancing-effect. This is despite the fact that the athletes under Brown's regime have won 15 Olympic gold medals between them.[21] Is it possible here to draw a comparison with vitamins that are widely taken and advertised by athletes but are of dubious value beyond a placebo effect? If vitamins or unnecessary treatments for thyroid did work, they would be banned. So who is being fooled? Are athletes the victims of a con? Or practitioners? Such contradictions are a staple of criminology.

Dimeo (2007) goes further than Henne et al (2013) seeking to go 'beyond good and evil' but is damning. He notes:

> many sports inherently contain health risks, and many less risky sports still have unhealthy practices. The question then becomes: why the panicky, anxiety-ridden fuss over drugs? (2007: xi)

Anderson is clearer still; he 'contends that, as an alternative, harm reductionist measures should be promoted, including consideration of the medically supervised use of certain PEDs' (2013: 135). His work is interesting because he refers to Garland (2002) and Simon (2007) among other criminologists and reminds us of discussions of 'right realism'. He argues against WADA policies, which, he states:

---

[21] Sara Germano and Kevin Clark (10 April 2013) 'US track's unconventional physician', *Wall Street Journal*, www.wsj.com/news/articles/SB10001424127887323 5506045784129131490430 72?tesla=y&mg=reno64-wsj (accessed 11 October 2015).

many criminologists would see as the third and arguably most important elemental flaw in a zero tolerance approach: it reflects and is invariably accompanied by a 'populist punitiveness'. (2013: 147)

Anderson (2013) also picks up on Simon's example of 'governance through crime' as a means of recruitment through drug testing. He persuasively applies four more of Simon's examples to sport, clearly qualifying this as a work of sports criminology *avant la lettre*.

First, Anderson notes Simon's appeal to the 'vulnerabilities and needs' (2007: 76) of victims, suggesting that WADA deploys 'the spirit of sport' (2013: 147) in the way that victims' rights are often seen to trump those of defendants – an example of Ericson's 'counter-law' (2007) – who are subjected to vengeance and ritual rage.

Second, Anderson notes Simon's contention that mandatory sentencing, non-discretionary 'zero-tolerance' policing and the prosecution of 'drug cheats' are 'blunt' instruments. Rough justice might also be an appropriate epithet. His 'lawyerliness' finds him concerned about issues of intentionality (*mens rea*) where the deliberate and serial cheat may be treated in the same way as the inadvertent offender. The third point is legal too, in highlighting Simon's related concern about the neutering of judges, which has the effect of turning them into 'judgment machines' (Simon, 2007: 140). International law experts might want to judge whether CAS has more freedom than the supreme courts of the US or the UK.

Finally, Anderson suggests that sports authorities have been 'governing through doping' (2013: 148). Like Simon (2007), he suggests that there has been some push-back against the frenzy of laws, 'wars' and technological initiatives that contribute to the public's 'doping lassitude', that is indifference 'to doping-related sports stories in the media (2013: 148, emphasis in original). More research is needed to confirm that just as public opinion has changed on the 'war on drugs' so it has on 'drugs cheats'.[22]

He recognises that no current sports body or administrator is currently proposing to adopt, let alone tentatively suggest, his harm-reduction, health-related proposals. *The Sunday Times* recently reported that between 2001 and 2012 one third of medals in endurance events had been won by athletes who had recorded 'suspicious' tests. Former Olympian and former Member of Parliament, Lord Coe, then an

[22] A search on Lexis Library for the term found 948 mentions in the year to 15 August 2015.

IAAF presidential candidate, responded 'that this is not a war we can allow ourselves to lose', which indicates he learned little in his time as a politician.[23]

The presumption is often that such policies are aimed at elite sportspeople competing at national or international level, ignoring concerns about drug taking among other groups such as amateur rugby union players and cyclists (although it should be noted that the UK drugs testing agency only found 22 positive tests out of 5,000 in 2014).[24] Back to transparency and surveillance, Henning (2014) found that non-elite road runners 'disciplined', in a Foucauldian sense, themselves. They had some awareness of drug-testing regimes and complied with them, but their lack of knowledge of the precise rules and use of supplements in pursuit of better performances placed them in danger. The danger might lie in the athlete failing a test applied in a non-elite event such as a fun run, or, more likely, in damaging their health. They may also be buying ineffective, bogus or contaminated supplements, much as any illegal drugs user.

Henning found:

> interviewees shared a view of doping as cheating and athletes who use banned substances as morally corrupt, interviewees would not view their friends as 'bad' people or 'cheaters' who deserved to be banned from competition if they were caught doping. (2014: 501)

They did not see the use of supplements as akin to doping, but in the same way as they might see 'legal highs' – that is, because they are legal, or not banned, they are safe and appropriate. An argument against going down the doping route, however, can be found in Graham et al (2009: 142), which cites a study by WADA indicating that 53% of injectable steroids and 23% of oral tablets found on the black market are counterfeit.

[23] Motez Bishara and Amanda Davies (18 August 2015) 'Sebastian Coe: "queasy" at idea of Justin Gatlin beating Usain Bolt', CNN, http://edition.cnn.com/2015/08/13/sport/sebastian-coe-doping-iaaf/ (accessed 11 October 2015).

[24] Paul Gallagher (8 February 2015) 'Anti-doping experts concerned at rise in number of amateur athletes turning to drugs to get ahead', Independent, www.independent.co.uk/sport/general/others/antidoping-experts-concerned-at-rise-in-number-of-amateur-athletes-turning-to-drugs-to-get-ahead-10031430.html (accessed 11 October 2015).

You don't need to be an Eliasian or figurational sociologist to agree with Dunning and Malcolm when they look at 'anti-doping' to argue against 'judgementalism': 'drugs and sports policies to date have tended primarily to involve an emphasis on detection and deterrence, and yet the use of performance-enhancing drugs continues to grow apace' (2003: 2). Atkinson and Young (2008) set out some possible directions for a 'criminological' study of sports deviance. Under their 'victimology' strand in the doping area we might add and investigate 'miscarriages of justice', 'abuse of process' and 'human rights'.

It would be tempting to make a comparison here with other forms of assistance that are not seen to be 'cheating', from natural biological differences through high altitude training to the sort of technological and psychological advances made by UK's Olympic cycling team. Our emphasis must be on drugs, however, because they feature so strongly in law and sociological accounts and in media coverage, as well as within criminology, albeit usually in different circumstances. To make a crude distinction, sports law and sports sociology usually deal with legal, allegedly performance-enhancing, drugs (doping), whereas criminology deals with illegal often performance-impeding drugs (that is, dope). Much of the martial and maximalist discourse is shared. Similarly, much of the argument in Waddington and Smith (2009) on drugs in sport is congruent with criminological understanding.

Stewart and Smith (2008: 279) suggest:

> The implication of this argument is that drugs-in-sport policies dominated by testing, coercion, and escalating penalties are flawed and should be supplanted by harm-reduction models that give greater focus to the health and well-being of athletes.

Many criminologists would agree, arguing the same about drugs in society. There is a further cross-over in that steroid use, as the Advisory Council on the Misuse of Drugs (2009: 7) has it, has now:

> become increasingly concerned at the use of anabolic steroids by the general public, and in particular young people. These substances have become 'popular' in relation to body building and image enhancement. Data from the British Crime Survey (2006/07) estimate that 32,000

people had used them in the last year and 14,000 in the last month.[25]

Corruption

Brooks et al helpfully set out 15 types of fraud and corruption that illustrate some of the issues and many of the problems inherent in modern sport. The list is not jointly exhaustive or mutually exclusive and issues of definition arise, but it covers:

> bribery; collusion; conflict of interest; embezzlement; extortion; cronyism/nepotism; fraud; gifts and hospitality; lobbying; money-laundering; revolving door; abuse of authority; trading in influence; illegal disclosure of information and vote-rigging. (2013: 5-7)

If only on the face of it, criminologists should be interested in these areas, but while some relevant studies exist, there are many grey areas. Take the example of collusion in terms of teams playing for a draw. We have already noted Naidoo's (2013) concern with 'dead rubbers', although many would consider this mere gamesmanship (and indeed many articles in the journal *Sport, Ethics and Philosophy* wrestle with this; see, for instance, Triviño, 2012). Good management of one's championship aimed at securing the long-term prize may make a strategic draw or even a loss sensible – a gambit in chess. Such 'collusion' or temporary alliances are a feature in Tour de France cycling tactics. Moreover, such strategies may require no collusion. In Naidoo's (2013) example involving badminton players, it was obvious what the players' best strategy was even if it was impossible for them both to draw in the same way as in football (by score) or chess (by agreement).

One of the most notorious cases involves a game of football between Germany and Austria in the 1982 World Cup that led to the elimination of Algeria. Because of earlier results in group matches, a win by Germany by one or two goals would have seen both teams through. In the 10th minute, Germany scored and thereafter neither side tried very hard. Some angry fans claimed that this was a clear case of corruption, but a common language and shared culture (footballing and societal) probably explain much. Chaabane Merzekane, Algeria's full back and 'man–of–the–match', said:

[25] Bunsell (2014) found in her ethnography of female bodybuilders that they often used steroids.

We weren't angry, we were cool.... To see two big powers debasing themselves in order to eliminate us was a tribute to Algeria. They progressed with dishonour, we went out with our heads held high.[26]

Brooks et al (2013) discuss fraud and corruption in sport with separate chapters on football, cricket, horse racing, basketball, baseball and boxing. Each sport is seen to have different problems and very different methods for dealing with them. It is worth examining some of them in greater detail. Thus the chapter on football covers ticket sales, money laundering, agents' fees, and 'questionable' player transfers. All these might addressed through criminology, but the main focus here on match fixing falls clearly within sports criminology, as it requires in-game action even if it is prompted by off-field bets.

International cricket is beset by claims of gambling-related corruption; see, for example, the case involving Hansie Cronje discussed in Chapter Three. Such corruption usually involves spot fixing (a bet that a wide or no ball will be bowled at a certain time).[27] Even so, the number of imponderables cannot guarantee a result; Cronje engineered the circumstances in the hope of achieving a certain result, but England could still have failed to secure it. In horse racing, variables such as the state of the racecourse (known as the 'going') and the performance of the jockey on the day make it difficult to guarantee a win. It often easier to guarantee a loss.

That said, there is always scope for corruption, as the Gay Future case shows. The story involves such complexity and so vast an array of characters that it warranted a film – *Murphy's Stroke* (1980), starring Pierce Brosnan). A substitute horse, near identical to Gay Future but far better, was trained in Ireland. It was entered into a race in Cartmel, Cumbria, in place of Gay Future, and won by 15 lengths. Multiple bets on the substitute horse by an Irish gang led by millionaire builder, Tony Murphy, were disguised in the sort of combined bets that 'mug punters' might typically make. The starting price odds were artificially raised by declaring a poor amateur rider – substituted for the fake horse's usual rider – and rubbing soap powder on the horse so that he

[26] Paul Doyle (13 June 2010) 'The day in 1982 when the world wept for Algeria', *The Guardian*, www.theguardian.com/football/2010/jun/13/1982-world-cup-algeria (accessed 11 October 2015).

[27] Mike Selvey (15 April 2010) 'Spotting spot-fixing is harder than ever in era of Twenty20', *The Guardian*, www.guardian.co.uk/sport/blog/2010/apr/15/spot-fixing-cricket-mike-selvey (accessed 11 October 2015).

appeared to be sweating up in the ring. Some bookmakers paid out on the winning bets, but not all, and the plot unravelled when a journalist discovered that other horses named in the bets had never left the yard. In other words, these horses were never intended to run and were only entered as a cover. Their withdrawal turned a combined bet into single one on Gay Future to win at 10-1, which, if successful, would have been worth about £300,000 (more than £3m now). At Preston Crown Court, Murphy and the trainer were fined. The Jockey Club (then the disciplinary authority) also issued a fine and banned them for 10 years.[28] The story has a coda.

Forty years on, the trainer most involved, old Harrovian Tony Collins, was welcomed to the Cartmel racecourse, wined and dined, and invited to regale the crowd.[29] He was also introduced to Michael Caulfield, an ex-chief executive of the Jockey Club. Furthermore In a further twist, Caulfield's late father was the judge Collins had faced at Preston Crown Court. It transpired that the Gay Future case was the only one his father had ever discussed with him as a boy. This 'heart-warming' tale of bygone roguery says much about the sort of admiration for 'capers' that movies tap into, as well as the English class system and ideas of victimhood. Because the bookmakers were the victims in this case, many racing aficionadas would forgive the plotters, forgetting that they themselves are at the mercy of those bookmakers every time they place a bet. Incidentally, Collins' golf club expelled him as a result of the case, and has not readmitted him to this day.

Such punishment may seem absurdly light, although other cases have been treated more harshly. Smith (2011) notes the case of Leighton Brookes, a racehorse owner disqualified from competition for three years by the disciplinary panel of the British Horseracing Authority on 3 December 2009 for betting on his own horses to lose. He failed to attend the hearing and claimed he shared the betting account with a friend who had placed the bets.

For Brooks et al (2014), the issues in basketball focus on 'point shaving' by college and National Basketball Association teams, whereby you win the match but limit your victory to a 'spread' that favours a gambling interest. Obviously, sympathy for the loser might also stay

[28] Neil Clark (25 August 2014) 'The boldest betting scam ever? Story behind a plot to trick the bookies 40 years ago', *Express*, www.express.co.uk/news/uk/503092/ Story-behind-the-plot-to-trick-a-bookies-40-years-ago (accessed 11 October 2015).
[29] Chris Cook (25 August 2014) 'Gay Future betting plot still holds fascination at Cartmel, 40 years on', *The Guardian*, www.theguardian.com/sport/2014/aug/25/ gay-future-betting-plot-cartmel-40-years-on (accessed 11 October 2015).

your hand, as might a lack of motivation. It is difficult to deal with 'not trying' in sport, although many sports seek to.

The problems of corruption in boxing go well beyond individual fixed fights, and Brooks et al (2014) look at more the structural issues that face fighters. Baseball has many of the same problems as other sports, but Brooks et al (2014) spotlight the manipulation of American little league baseball by Taiwanese interests to boost national prestige. It is in their chapter on baseball that they also look at the use of PEDs.

Brooks et al (2014) look to the wider business world to find solutions and argue that sponsorship is key. Modern sport is governed, formally if not substantively, by sponsorship, and the regulatory requirements placed on business should also be placed on sport. Brooks et al (2014) note the very different patterns of club ownership in England, Germany and Italy, which all change the landscape for business and sporting fraud. As betting is behind much of the corruption found in a variety of sports, this presents problems in itself. Where betting is legal, it often falls behind the criminals in an information and technology arms race and in countries or circumstances where it is illegal, no regulation is possible.

Maennig (2005) discusses the early history of sports corruption, when the fist fighter Eupolos bribed three of his opponents in the Olympic Games of 388 BCE, and concludes that reducing the 'economic rents' (rewards) of sport, increasing transparency and providing monetary disincentives are 'efficient'. In later work, Maenning (2008) compares the anti-corruption policies and practices of the Amateur International Boxing Association (AIBA) and the German Football Association (DFB). Helpfully he lists many suspicious and scandalous events in sport and, unsurprisingly for an economist, favours rational market-driven choice making as his major explanatory tool.

He notes that following a bribery scandal in the Seoul Olympics 1988 where a Korean boxer was corruptly favoured by the referee, AIBA was forced by the International Olympic Committee to monitor the performance of referees. In the resulting system, five referees placed around the boxing ring register each hit, and a hit only counts if it is registered by at least three of the five referees within a second. Video recording makes it possible to check the accuracy of each given hit retrospectively. All of the activities of the referees are subjected to statistical analysis and the protocol for obtaining the result is immediately and unalterably available at the end of the contest. The DFB case in 2005 involved a number of corrupt referees, for which there was no technical solution, so an extensive ban on betting was implemented instead. But might similar technological solutions in football help, such as the robot refs or linesmen briefly mentioned in Chapter Five?

We have seen some of the actions, efforts and policy statements on the part of sports authorities to tackle these issues, but what about nation states? The UK government released a 60-page Anti-Corruption Plan in December 2014.[30] The one page devoted to sport specifically concentrates on sports betting and Europe-wide initiatives. Analysing this, and past initiatives, Carpenter (a sports lawyer[31]) finds:

> in the past 15 years, despite there often being ostensibly strong evidence in favour of a conviction, there have been only a small number of successful investigations and convictions brought for match-fixing offences.

He lists failed cases brought against snooker player, Stephen Lee, and 13 footballers for match fixing as well as the few recent successful prosecutions against Pakistani cricketers and semi-professional footballers, which relied on long-extant conspiracy laws. Both Carpenter and betting industry lawyers believe that the Gambling Act 2005 does not sufficiently clearly define match or spot fixing to allow the Crown Prosecution Service to act.

Henne (2015) argued for the need for transparency against corruption in match fixing, money laundering and the bidding process for sport mega-events, and kicks of her article by looking at the corruption alleged against FIFA. Paoli and Donati (2014) have edited a book on the topic, and a special edition of the journal *Trends in Organized Crime* (Volume 18, Issue 3, September 2015) indicates a growing awareness of the issue, which should trigger further criminological work.

---

[30] UK Government (nd) 'UK Anti-Corruption Plan', www.gov.uk/government/uploads/system/uploads/attachment_data/file/388894/UKantiCorruptionPlan.pdf (accessed 11 October 2015).

[31] Kevin Carpenter (13 February 2015) 'Tackling match-fixing: a look at the UK's new Anti-Corruption Plan', LawInSport, www.lawinsport.com/blog/item/tackling-match-fixing-a-look-at-the-uk-s-new-anti-corruption-plan?category_id=139 (accessed 9 September 2015).

'Extra-territoriality' versus globalisation

Journalist Marina Hyde[32] imagines FIFA as a country. In a column on the many accusations and complaints about FIFA, she opines:

> With each passing year, Blatter's outfit has felt less a sporting governing body than a quasi-state, with its ability to ride roughshod over the constitutions of the satellite nations which host its tournaments – establishing its own courts, setting its own tax rates at an enticing 0%, making strategic alliances with emerging powers and oppressive regimes.

When faced with the task of tracking developments at FIFA, she throws her hands up and asks, 'Who the hell should have jurisdiction over its activities? The Hague? The Pentaverate?' She even imagines a 'war on FIFA', its invasion or the condemnation of Switzerland by the United Nations for harbouring it. Her darkly comic imaginings are borne out of frustration that although much suspicion – heightened by recent events – surrounds the activities of FIFA, nobody is in a position to do anything about it.

Sports have their own on- and off-field 'justice systems' (Colucci and Jones, 2013). These normally apply to the actions of sportspeople in sport. In the US, Ray Rice, a Baltimore Ravens running back, was indefinitely suspended by the NFL under its personal conduct provisions after a video of a violent assault on his partner was put online. Most commentary on the case has focused on the insufficiency of the NFL's original two-game ban. Rice admits to the violence, but is challenging the ban on 'due process' grounds. In this the NFL could be seen to be acting 'extra-territorially' in that the assault occurred in a public place; if it had been in a private place, it would have been a matter for the local state criminal justice system.

In other respects sport is becoming increasingly global. NFL matches are often played in London and there are regular global tournaments in tennis and golf. Each sport seeks to act like a nation state even while nation states face further pressures from the neoliberal demands of capital, the feudal demands of terrorism and the apolitical, but politicised, threat of global environmental issues. These tensions sometimes play out through their justice systems. The isolated nature

---

[32] Marina Hyde (19 November 2014) 'Ethics report shows war on Fifa is as futile as 'war on terror', *The Guardian*, www.theguardian.com/football/blog/2014/nov/19/fifa-ethics-report-fiasco-war-futile-sepp-blatter (accessed 11 October 2015).

of much US sport has insulated the country from some issues. Some sports have been able to retain control over their own jurisdiction but doping/corruption scandals in cycling and more recently in athletics have weakened their power to resist external pressures. In athletics, Russia has recently been accused of widespread and corrupt doping violations and the fall-out has forced Kenya to clean up its act.[33] Still resisting is the Board of Control for Cricket in India, which does not comply with anti-doping measures because its ethics code prevents the imposition of the whereabouts rule on its players.[34] Could any of these bodies be recommended to run crime prevention schemes?

As we have seen, sport has been given considerable latitude in setting the rules of the game and even standards of players' behaviour in wider society. That is frequently challenged. Both sport and society might benefit from proper consideration of the contradictions that arise. Criminology should contribute to that, and indeed, sports criminology provides a way in. We turn now to consideration of sport as a 'solution' to problems in society, that is, crime.

[33] AFP (2015) 'Kenya establishes anti-doping agency', Mail Online, www.mailonsunday.co.uk/wires/afp/article-3318458/Kenya-establishes-anti-doping-agency.html (accessed 25 November 2015).

[34] Mike Selves (28 October 2015) 'Olympic Games and cricket are a difficult match to make', *The Guardian*, www.theguardian.com/sport/blog/2015/oct/28/cricket-olympic-games-tokyo-2020 (accessed 15 November 2015).

SEVEN

Retraining: crime prevention and desistance through sport

In her examination of the place of psychoanalysis in the history of British criminology, Valiér mentions the Boy Scouts movement and sporting activities as having found favour among the therapists who founded the body that gave rise to the British Society of Criminology. Such activities were seen as providing 'a more wholesome sphere for the expression of youthful energies' (1998: 3). Kelly (2008) notes that such 'moral improvement' has now fallen out of favour. But great claims are still made for sport as a means of broader development; see, for instance, the claims for the significance of sport in 'peacebuilding' made by the United Nations (nd). In previous chapters, suggestions, even from Bentham, have been made for the benefits of sport as well as the disbenefits. Here we assess some of the growing literature around the role of sport in crime prevention.

First we examine boxing, which is well represented in academic, popular media and cultural representations of the use of sport to prevent crime, aid to rehabilitation or encourage desistance. After boxing we consider joyriding, which does not involve direct physical violence but raises some of the same issues of masculinity and the close relationship between sport and crime. The next section considers football, rugby, basketball and other sports. The question has to be asked whether such crime prevention measures might also work for women's sport. It should be noted that this chapter takes a largely uncritical approach, although Blackshaw and Crabbe (2004) discuss the 'social control' aspects of sports schemes, while Stansfield (2015) suggests that sport fails in this regard.

Boxing

A former prison officer at Her Majesty's Youth Offender Institution Feltham broke the first rule of Fight Club[1] when he blew the whistle

---

[1]   A reference to the 1999 American film based on the 1996 novel of the same name by Chuck Palahniuk.

about illegal fights organised by officers among inmates.[2] In fact, the ill-advised action of allowing antagonists to settle scores among themselves might owe more to public school or Borstal than the complex meditation on masculinity of Fight Club.

In Bring Back Borstal[3] (2015), the 'boys' play a game of rugby union against a local team and go on cross-country runs – shades of the book and subsequent film *The Loneliness of the Long Distance Runner* (Sillitoe, 1959) – but they do not box. Several fights break out and a punch ball takes a hammering in episode 3 to allow one young man to 'let off some steam'.

Boxing has three mentions in Meek's (2014) book on sport in prison. Her survey found that boxing was the activity inmates favoured, even when it was banned (p 109); that it had recently been approved for use with non-violent offenders (p 33); and that it was now being offered in a number of establishments (p28). Elsewhere Meek (2012) asked 75 inmates who had not participated in football and rugby programmes what they wanted: 45 said boxing.

In Meek's work (2012, 2014), and more generally in the literature, it is not always clear whether boxing means boxing training – that is, pad work, speed ball, skipping or running – or more serious sparring or even boxing matches, with headguards and gumshields. Equally unclear are the terms used by organisations like the Boxing Academy (based in Tottenham and offering an 'alternative to mainstream school, combining basic education and mentoring with the discipline and culture of boxing and other sport training to re-engage the most difficult-to-reach young people') and Fight for Peace (London and Rio de Janiero), which speak of 'boxing', 'martial arts' or 'boxing training' without necessarily meaning fighting. They also offer, as part of their packages, education and other interventions, which complicates attempts to identify sport as the successful element in such programmes.

[2]   David Collins (11 April 2015) 'Prison officers "organised Fight Club among rival inmate gangs" in Britain's most violent jail', *Mirror*, www.mirror.co.uk/news/uk-news/prison-officers-organised-fight-club-5502230?utm_content=buffer76779&utm_medium=social&utm_source=facebook.com&utm_campaign=buffer (accessed 11 October 2015).

[3]   ITV (2015) Bring Back Borstal, www.itv.com/presscentre/ep1week2/bring-back-borstal (accessed 11 October 2015).

For every boxer who claims that without the sport he would have ended in prison (for instance, Luis Collazo),[4] we might find 'the 10 best boxers who ended up in prison'.[5] The list by Aaron King was prompted by the case of Floyd Mayweather, who served a 90-day sentence in a county jail rather than a federal or state prison. The offence is not mentioned and the writer is 'thankful' that an upcoming fight with Paquiano can go ahead as scheduled. You need to look elsewhere to discover that Mayweather was sentenced for 'domestic violence and battery' against the mother of three of his four children.[6] The media have covered incidents of violence against five different women over 14 years by Mayweather.

In King's list of the 10 best boxers who went to prison are: Jack Johnson; Carlos Monzon; Pernell Whitaker; Charles 'Kid' McCoy; Bernard Hopkins; Sonny Liston; Mike Tyson; Dwight Muhammad Qawi; Diego Corrales; and Edwin Valero.

There are doubtless many other boxers who could be included, but for the purposes of this book the significant details are that all those on King's list went to prison, whether before, after or during their career. Poverty and troubled early life are often mentioned as influencing factors, as are fast living and substance abuse on achieving success.

Jack Johnson's conviction in 1912 for interstate trafficking of a prostitute should be known to radical and critical criminologists and should serve as a warning to naive interventions in the area of 'human trafficking'. The Mann Act was inspired by panic about 'white slavery' and Gaskew (2012) is clear that racism was behind the first ever use of the Act, in a case against Johnson. Johnson's popularity with white women was deemed to be immoral and arguments relating to the women's consent were set aside. He served a year in prison in 1920, having surrendered to Federal authorities after time in Canada and Europe. Campaigns for his pardon continue; most recently the US

[4]   Gareth A. Davies (30 April 2014) '"Without boxing, I would have gone to prison, no question", says Amir Khan's opponent Luis Collazo', *Telegraph*, www.telegraph. co.uk/sport/othersports/boxing/10798626/Without-boxing-I-would-have-gone-to-prison-no-question-says-Amir-Khans-opponent-Luis-Collazo.html (accessed 11 October 2015).

[5]   Aaron King (6 January 2012) '10 best boxers who went to prison', Bleacher Report http://bleacherreport.com/articles/1013180-10-best-boxers-who-went-to-prison (accessed 11 October 2015).

[6]   Kevin Mitchell (28 April 2015) 'Storm grows over Mayweather's violent past', *The Guardian*, www.theguardian.com/sport/blog/2015/apr/26/floyd-mayweather-espn-report-violence (accessed 11 October 2015).

Senate passed an amendment urging a presidential pardon sponsored by Republican senator and one-time presidential candidate John McCain.[7]

More like the stereotype of the out-of-control celebrity athlete is Carlos Monzon, who took up film roles in Europe after he retired and in 1988 threw his wife from a balcony. But King adds:

> One legacy of Monzon's unfortunate history has been the influence on the commendable work of fellow Argentinian middleweight champion Sergio Martinez, who has been a strong advocate for victims of domestic abuse.

That 'commendable' work has given Martinez the opportunity to meet Pope Francis for a private conversation to discuss the Pope's work on violence against women and anti-bullying; Muhammed Ali was the last boxer to be granted such an honour.[8]

Pernell Whitaker had trouble with cocaine use in retirement, while Charles 'Kid' McCoy was notorious for playing mind tricks before fights and shot a woman he was living with. Bernard Hopkins' 18-year sentence for armed robbery (five of which he served) came before his boxing career. Liston's story follows a similar narrative arc, while Qawi learned to box in prison. Corrales fought Mayweather in 2001. He lost the fight, but has the dishonour of having served longer sentences for domestic violence than Mayweather.

Mike Tyson's career is so well known that it requires no further mention. Edwin Valero's trajectory illustrates the issue of poor regulation in boxing as he entered the sport suffering from bleeding on the brain and with a skull fractured in a motorbike accident. He murdered his wife in 2010 and killed himself a day later in jail. He had been under psychiatric treatment since being arrested for abusing his wife.

This anecdotal material is illustrative but far from conclusive. Qawi's case brings us to Prison Fight, a charity whose website claims world connections but seems to have little reach outside of Thailand, where it

[7] *Sports Illustrated* (16 July 2015) 'US Senate passes amendment urging pardon for boxer Jack Johnson', www.si.com/boxing/2015/07/16/jack-johnson-boxer-us-senate-amendment-mccain-reid# (accessed 11 October 2015).

[8] Stoyan Zaimov (9 October 2013) 'Pope Francis to meet boxing champion Sergio Martinez; talk anti-bullying, violence against women', Christian Post, www.christianpost.com/news/pope-francis-to-meet-boxing-champion-sergio-martinez-talk-anti-bullying-violence-against-women-106321/#qSXGC862T68UouCS.99 (accessed 11 October 2015).

is based.[9] It uses Muay Thai (Thai boxing) as a method of rehabilitation and holds out the possibility of amnesty to offending fighters. To the untutored eye, the videos hosted on its website look exploitative, and the World Prison Fight Association, to which it claims to be affiliated, does not appear to be an independent body. The website also makes reference to the Thai Department of Corrections. In a photo essay on Thai fighters, the *Daily Telegraph* attributes the amnesties to:

> … a quirk in Thai law, all inmates have a chance at an amnesty if they achieve a great sporting achievement. The law dates back to 1767 when the Burmese took thousands of Thai soldiers prisoner after the capture of the country's then-capital Ayutthaya. During their time in prison, the soldiers took part in organised fights against their captors, with the greatest fighter purportedly being granted his freedom.[10]

Amnesty requires abstinence from drugs and includes agricultural work as part of its rehabilitation programme. No evaluation is offered beyond the website's following claim:

> First Prison Fight event has take [*sic*] place on January 2013 and from the first moments has shown good results and was highly appreciated by the Department of Corrections and inmates.

So some officially sanctioned fighting is occurring in prisons in Thailand. Prison fighting was legal in the US in the 1970s, but brought to an end when a prisoner on furlough (temporary parole/home leave) died in a fight in January 1980.[11] The prisoner, Charles Newell, died nine days after being knocked out in a welterweight contest at Hartford Civic Center. Previously, the lifting of an eight-year ban in

---

[9]   prisonfight.com (nd) http://prisonfight.com/prison-fight/ (accessed 11 October 2015).

[10]   Borja Sanchez Trillo/Getty Images (nd) 'Thailand's prison fight clubs – in pictures', *Telegraph*, www.telegraph.co.uk/news/picturegalleries/worldnews/10966417/Thailands-prison-fight-clubs-In-pictures.html?frame=2974410 (accessed 11 October 2015).

[11]   John Cavanaugh (23 August 1981) 'Boxing programs held in prisons are halted', *New York Times*, www.nytimes.com/1981/08/23/nyregion/boxing-programs-held-in-prisons-are-halted.html (accessed 11 October 2015).

1973 allowed two prisoners to fight on a professional bill at Westbury Armory. In 1978, 13 prisoners were given furlough specifically to box (Milling, nd) at the Connecticut state prison in Enfield. From 1973 to 1980 about two dozen prison inmates fought in matches throughout the state and, very occasionally, in other states. One even fought an eventual champion, Sugar Ray Leonard, but none excelled as professionals on release (might this be considered an output measure?). But Miller says that the programme drew praise from prison officials.

There is no mention of any formal evaluation of the programme, and nor does Milling (nd) attempt one. We may have moved on from the era of 'nothing works' (see Sarre, 1999 on the work of Martinson, 1974) to some acknowledgment that all manner of things might work some of the time for some people, but lack of evaluation of rehabilitation programmes continues to be an issue. We also have to take on cynical trust Cavanaugh's note that:

> It was also supported by the state's boxing promoters, who have found professional fighters in short supply in a state where boxing has failed to capture the attention of the sporting public.

What of Britain? The All Party Parliamentary Group for Boxing (APPGB) reports that:

> The first example of boxing's role in the prison system was at Ashfield Prison and YOI in the West Country, which ran a boxing academy for its young offenders from 2005 until the prison's closure in March 2013. The Ashfield programme engaged 18 people at a time and offered a 3 month, non-contact boxing programme focusing on health and fitness, run by local boxing clubs. (2015: 17)

Since then HMP Doncaster has used boxing as part of its rehabilitation programme, focusing on boxing coaching and training others rather than teaching prisoners to box. However, the APPGB notes that the prison and it partner, the Police Community Clubs of Great Britain[11] (wrongly referred to by the APPGB as Policy Community Clubs of Great Britain), has temporarily suspended the programme, as those they feel are most likely to benefit from it – violent offenders – are disbarred by the Ministry of Justice. It might be that the Ministry of Justice fears that such programmes will incur the wrath of the British tabloid press. Interestingly, a UK TV comedy from the 1970s, Porridge, features boxing in prison, although this cannot be taken to be a true reflection of reality. In the episode entitled 'The Harder They Fall' (1975), two prisoners are matched up for a fight. Both are bribed to take a 'fall', which they do in the first round. This result pleases only the protagonist Fletcher, who had bet on a draw.[12]

It is difficult to believe that the modern US prison system would now countenance the events that brought Dwight Muhammad Qawi (the eighth boxer on King's list) together with James Scott in Rahway State Prison, New Jersey, on 5 September 1981 in a televised contest. Butler and Emhoff (nd) set out the whole tale but highlights are as follows.

Both fighters were prisoners at Rahway. Qawi was then known as Dwight Braxton and had been taught to box by Scott. Scott had had a promising career as a lightweight when he was convicted in late 1975 of a violent armed robbery. He was cleared of murder, but was given a sentence of 30-40 years. In late 1978, he challenged Eddie Gregory (now known as Eddie Mustafa Muhammad) to a boxing match in prison. Gregory, himself an ex-prisoner, was a contender for a title shot, but with the promise of an easy purse, and with Home Box Office offering TV coverage, he agreed to the challenge. Scott had learned his craft in the juvenile and prison systems. He had even gone rounds with Rubin 'Hurricane' Carter[13] and had become the New Jersey prison champion – so clearly fighting in prison had been allowed previously. Scott beat several lesser fighters before the bout with Gregory, winning on points. In his last fight, he lost to Qawi. He was given hopes that his success might win him early parole. Whether this was true was never tested, as the warden, Robert S. Hatrak, was moved on.[14]

Morris et al (2003) examine 600 programmes in Australia that use sport to tackle antisocial behaviour and it is this sort of programme that is more typical than the prison examples already discussed. Also typical is the finding about the evaluation data supplied by one project, described as 'Informal feedback from the project coordinator and program participants' (2003: 68).

---

[12]   Porridge: The Harder They Fall (1975) IMDB, www.imdb.com/title/tt0676974/plotsummary?ref_=tt_ov_pl (accessed 11 October 2015).

[13]   Twice convicted of a triple murder, twice released, middleweight boxer. Admitted criminal, campaigner for the wrongly convicted and subject of Bob Dylan song and biopic starring Denzel Washington, *Carter* (2011).

[14]   Controversially he promoted 'Scared Straight' programmes (Wilson and Groombridge, 2009) but also education and rehabilitation, and, perhaps fatal for his career, favoured self-promotion and publicity.

Turning to contemporary Britain, we have the APPGB making the following bold claims in a foreword by Olympic flyweight gold medalist, Nicola Adams:

> As the case studies in this report show, boxing has the power to transform lives. It has an almost unmatched capability to engage some of the most disaffected young people and help to combat a massive range of social problems, covering crime, educational underachievement, health and fitness and community cohesion. (2015: 3)

The APPGB chair, Charlotte Leslie MP,[15] continues:

> Talk to some of our Olympians, and some of our superb Olympic boxers in particular, and they will tell you how, in a parallel universe, it could have been them on those London streets in 2011, were it not for boxing and the transformations that can happen in a boxing club. (2015: 4)

Anecdote tells the story, but some figures given in the APPGB report claim that attendees are less likely to commit crime – though this a survey of attitudes, not of actual (re)offending) – and even that 175 crimes have been avoided, with a saving to society of £1,059,471. Contrary to Morris et al's (2003) claims, the APPGB recognises that any activity – not just boxing specifically – might be at the heart of any success. The APPGB give five reasons given by boxers for the programme's success:

1. 'It's like a family to me.'
2. 'People respect you if you go to the boxing club.'
3. 'It's a way to let go of my frustration.'
4. 'He's like the dad I never had.'
5. 'I've learned to walk away from a fight.'

Appeals to family are common in popular and moral discourse around crime, but can also be found in (self-)control theories of crime and differential association. But what marks out boxing clubs in particular? No evidence is given for the APPGB's claim that:

---

[15] Leslie admits that she too was an 'angry young person' and claims attending a boxing gym was an outlet for her 'energy and frustration'.

> Boxing often appeals to those who have been bullied and victimised, including girls who have suffered sexual or physical abuse, as well as those with tougher personalities or issues with aggression. (2015: 10)

'Respect' can be a big issue on the street (Anderson, 2001) and APPGB's (2015: 10) claim that boxing can engage because it is seen as 'anti-establishment' and has 'street cred' may tap into that, but this raises other issues. How is that respect won? Is it gendered and gendering? Thus Jump (2015) in an article based on her doctoral ethnography in a boxing gym concludes:

> Diversionary activities and sport-based programmes that incapacitate are only one element in the theory of change. In conclusion, I have argued that boxing actually traps men in an attendant culture of respect that requires them to respond in aggressive ways to maintain an image of both masculinity and respect. This attendant culture, that is transposable between gym and street, can override the pro-social incapacitating elements that the gym can offer, and reinforces the logic and discourses that evokes and traps men in habits of responding to violence. Therefore, in terms of future policy and practice, new directions need to be sought.

Jump's boxing training did not lead her to become a supporter of boxing as a means of crime prevention/desistance, but her work suggests that troubling and troublesome masculinities can be ameliorated by working with that masculinity in schemes like boxing. She is rightly concerned that the men become trapped in their masculinity. Perhaps boxing might be supported if long-term work on masculinity was done. There may be worse traps than particular masculinities. Thus the APPGB quotes Jovan, a former gang member and Commonwealth Games boxer:

> Boxing Is The Only Thing That's Acceptable From The Gang's Point Of View. When I Got Involved In Boxing, The Gang Members Said To Me 'Leave Us Behind, Jovan. Go And Get A Future For Yourself'. (2015: 15)

This reminds us of Atencio and Wright's (2008) finding about basketball in the US mentioned in Chapter Five.

In the same section of the APPGB report, the diversionary/incapacity argument is made – ie too tired or doing other things, for crime. But again boxing is not unique in this.

The presence/absence of fathers is a component of popular, right-wing criminologies, particularly in explanations of black criminality (Herrnstein and Murray, 1994). APPBG also mentions positive role models and credible authority figures. This clearly overlaps with issues of family and masculinity more generally.

No example is given by APPGB of walking away from a fight, nor how this might be achieved, other than to mention the discipline needed in an individual sport like boxing. Basic crime reduction figures are given for crime in the Abbotswood area of Bristol, home of Yate Boxing Club. The club has police support, but it is accepted that crime reduction levels cannot necessarily be linked to the club or to other antisocial behaviour dispersal programmes in the area.

Other evaluations discussed below are available, but they do not fall into the binary categories of 'yes, it does' or 'no, it doesn't' work. McMahon and Belur (2013) mention a couple of boxing-based programmes that have been evaluated. Laureus (2011) looks at the Boxing Academy and mentions Sampson and Vilella (2012) on Fight for Peace. Laureus's (2011: 34) figures for the Boxing Academy show that two out of eight boxers with criminal convictions reoffended. Extrapolating from this, they calculate that the academy prevented 12 crimes in 2008, with alleged savings of £81,072. It is claimed anecdotally that two young people from the academy's 2007 intake had stopped taking Class A drugs [16]

In their work on gangs in Rio and London, Sampson and Vilella found that of 33 young people in London who took part in Fight for Peace initiatives, 85% said that they were less likely to be a member of a gang, 79% that they were less likely to commit a crime and 70% that they were less likely to disrespect someone. Furthermore, in London in 2010 and 2011, 74% of those participating in intensive case work (20 out of 27 young people) desisted from offending; 42% (five out of 12 young people) ended their gang affiliations; and 75% of those who attended the Pathways programme (out of 175 young people) desisted from further offending. In Rio in 2010 and 2011, of those who attended the Pathways programmes, 15 young people were officially known offenders, and 47% (seven) subsequently desisted from offending (2012: 14). These are small numbers, subject to intensive

[16] Much the same material and pictures of sports stars meeting 'urban' kids can be found in Laureus and Ecorys (2012).

work, and differences between similar programmes in Brazil and the UK make comparisons and certainty difficult.

Big claims are made for many of these schemes but the evidence to back them up is not extensive or overwhelming. More interesting is why such schemes might work. From a Nordic perspective, but suggestive of wider application, Lander and colleagues note the following:

> Being a boy or a man, one is expected to be able to endure a certain amount of violence, both in terms of committing violence and being the victim of this, for instance on the soccer field or in the boxing gym. (2014: 7)

In other words, we might ask whether crime prevention projects that use sport work more on masculinity and not so much on criminality. No definitive answer can be given here, but we raise the same question again in the next section on joyriding.

Motor sports

The Home Office likes to claim that 'there Is no joy In "joy-riding". Joyriding is theft of a car in exactly the same way as 'shoplifting is theft from a shop' (Home Office Standing Conference on Crime Prevention, 1988: 19). Yet the theft of a car means far more than that to both the victim and the offender, both practically and symbolically (Groombridge, 1997). Our 'car culture' means that cars have become increasingly necessary for transport and personal safety reasons, particularly for women. It also offers the thief a means to 'do' a form of masculinity. The fieldwork for Groombridge (1997) was carried out at a number of motor projects associated with the probation service.

Not all of the projects had 'banger racing' as their *modus operandi*; some just offered lessons in motor mechanics and a youth club atmosphere. The classic banger project offered one night or more a week of motor mechanics and the opportunity for participating 'at-risk' or convicted car crime offenders to race the bangers they had built. Permission to race was subject to good behaviour and a record of non-offending. Anecdotally such projects 'work', although Wilkinson (1997) found:

> offenders who attend Ilderton specialize in car crime. Equally there seems little doubt that attending Ilderton is associated with lower re-arrest rates, especially for motor-vehicle offences, and offences of taking cars. This

is consistent with Ilderton providing a useful response to car crime. (1997: 579)

Perhaps the most interesting question is how such projects work rather than whether they do. Wilkinson's work is quantitative and comparative, but still gives some clues. His finding of reductions in levels of vehicle-related offending suggests they were linked to something about 'the car'. Is that 'something' just a 'hook'? Sports projects attract participants at the outset by that hooking mechanism. It also raises the issue, again, of whether there are similar crime–sport fits beyond 'car culture'. Should we recommend boxing for brawlers or, conversely, yoga, or both? Cars 'fit' many lifestyles. Cars play an enormous part in offenders' lives, legally and illegally, and will do so until public transport improves enormously and driverless cars become the norm.

Crime prevention through sport in general

Kelly notes that:

> Youth projects often benefit participants, but over-stating their ability to prevent crime and 'anti-social behaviour' can be problematic. Voluntary services with limited resources ultimately focus on receptive young people, but pressure to justify funding encourages practitioners, programme managers and policy-makers to highlight the 'riskiness' of participants and publicize the most striking successes. (2012: abstract).

McMahon and Belur survey the scene and are prepared to say:

> Sport can act as a *diversionary activity* distracting from violent and criminal activities and also as a *hook*.... But positive and negative impacts are mediated by contextual factors [the amount and stability of finances, staff and so on] .... Sports-based interventions can also have a negative impact on youth violence. (2013: 3; emphasis in original)

Even the frequently cheerleading tone in Laureus (2011) is occasionally reined in, though only in an Appendix that notes that sport alone unlikely to work (Taylor et al, 1999; Nacro, 2008) and the absence of robust data (Shields and Bredemeier, 1995).

Football

In *The Guardian*, Goldblatt reports on 'the prison where murderers play for Manchester United'.[17] He writes about Luzira Prison in Uganda which houses remand, psychiatric and death row prisoners and has a reputation as rough place. Nevertheless, it claims a 30% recidivism rate that UK prisons can't match. Organised football appears to be part of this. The prison league is organised and overseen by the prisoners; there is a constitution, a system of player registration, and rules for fair play and no 'diving'. There are spectators (over a thousand, for some matches), and there is no violence. Pick-up games in the large yard were once common, but the organised league has been operating for 20 years, with teams often named after those in the Premier League. Goldblatt notes the African nationalist tradition of activism and administration that may be part of what works at Luzira, not just the physical activity of the sport.

Space is at a greater premium in UK prisons. Here, the training and matches are more likely to be in the hands of staff, and they are often designed to have some specific effect. Prison football in Luzira seems to organic, bottom-up and autotelic, whereas that in the UK is top-down, officially controlled and often has a purpose other than rehabilitation (health, recreation, and so on).

In 2009, Sky TV showed a six-part documentary series entitled Football Behind Bars, fronted by former Arsenal and England striker, Ian Wright.[18] Episode one shows Wright running 'trials' in order to assemble a prison team and the final episode shows the team playing against a side of football 'legends', with the then justice secretary, Jack Straw, looking on.

Wright's programme took place at HMYOI Portland, as did Meek's (2014). Meek describes the four sport academies in prisons over two years accepting 79 young male prisoner (46% white, 33% black and 21% mixed race, Asian or 'other'). On average, participants were just under 20 years old and 40% had convictions for violence against the person. Though self-selected, they were 'broadly representative of the national young adult population according to sentence category' (2014: 92). Their offender group reconviction scale scores ranged

[17] David Goldblatt (28 May 2015) 'The prison where murderers play for Manchester United', *The Guardian*, www.theguardian.com/football/2015/may/28/the-prison-where-murderers-play-for-manchester-united (accessed 11 October 2015).

[18] locatetv.com (nd), www.locatetv.com/tv/football-behind-bars/6439404/episode-guide (accessed 11 October 2015).

widely from 10-85. Of the 411 prisoners released from Portland in 2010, 50% reoffended within one year against the national figure of 53%. Given all the appropriate provisos and caveats, Meek concludes: 'This suggests that academy participants are less likely to reoffend than those who haven't participated in the academy' (2014: 94). This does raise the thorny issue of what counts as working.

What works?

Meek is meticulous is listing 17 suggested indicators of success, some with sub-sections (2014: 182-3), which take us far beyond the bombast of the anecdotal claims made for (and against) sport. She also examines the 'negative aspects of prison sport' (2014: 180) such as 'narcissism', 'exploitativeness' and aggressive reactions to threat.

Farrell et al (2001) examine a project that sounds as if it might be of use to the boxing programmes discussed earlier. Three urban middle schools took part in the programme, entitled Responding in Peaceful and Positive Ways. The authors found fewer disciplinary violations and fight-related injuries on completion of the programme, as well as greater use of peer mediation. Bosworth and Espelage's (1995) work on 'impulsivity' involved a different group – university students, rather than inmates. CRIAQ and CRIME PICS 2 measures are widely used in such work. It would be interesting to know whether such measures have been used in studies with athletes.

A subsequent search[19] in the academic literature revealed over 500 hits for 'beliefs about aggression and athletes', many concerning doping and sexual violence, but only 38 for 'use of non-violent strategies and athletes', including references to using sport against violence in both Nigeria and Kenya.

A search on 'impulsivity and athletes' only returned 58 results. The top result is a reference to work by Maher et al (2015), which examines risk-taking and impulsive personality traits in proficient downhill sports enthusiasts. This speaks to the contention that sport and crime/deviance are not in a cause–effect relationship, but are fused. The authors show the extent of impulsivity among downhill skiers, including women, and even suggest ways to teach the skiers self-control. They make no mention of crime, but the parallels are intriguing. How much would the *Daily Mail* complain were joyriders sent skiing? And is there a measurable effect in countries or areas of countries where such extreme sports are the norm? Would long days on the slopes have an incapacitatory effect or the 'rush' some cathartic effect?

In offenders and potential offenders, 'impulsivity' is seen to be a bad thing. What potential downsides does Meek (2014) identify? One is narcissism, which is associated with antisocial characteristics such as low empathy (Watson and Morris, 1991), exploitativeness (Campbell et al, 2005) and aggressive reactions to threat (Bushman and Baumeister, 1998). Watson and Morris (1991) make no specific mention of any sport, but Meek suggests that the self-esteem associated with playing sport may tip over into narcissicism and low empathy. This may help explain some of the bad behaviour of sports stars, as might Campbell et al's (2005) finding that 'narcissists' harvested too much 'timber'. This was a test that sounds like an educational game. Stansfield (2015) does not mention Meek's (2014) work, but is clear on the negative effects of sport for both genders and all nationalities.

While a number of prisons now have football and rugby schemes (discussed elsewhere in the chapter), more common is the use of football in the community as crime prevention. On such programme, Kickz, began in 2006 as a partnership between the Premier League and the Metropolitan Police and now involves over 40 clubs and over 100 projects. Typically, projects involve two nights of 'football' (coaching/ competition) and one night of other activities, with the majority including a weekend night. The Premier League's website[19] claims the following of its programme 'Kicks':

- over 75% of participants live in the top 30% most deprived areas of England;
- one third live in the top 10%;
- 91% of projects include Friday and/or Saturday evening activity (local authorities struggle to register more than 5%);
- up to 60% reduction in anti-social behaviour in Kicks areas;
- up to 20% reduction in 'select crime', which are most often associated with young people;
- falling crime in key areas: 28% reduction in criminal damage and 19% in violence against the person.

Much of the initial success of a project run by Arsenal in a North London park from 2006 appears to relate to the displacement of the crime and antisocial behaviour that once beset the park (Laureus, 2011:

[19] Premier League (nd) 'Creating chances: Kicks', www.premierleague.com/en-gb/ communities/2011-12/kicks.html (accessed 28 September 2015).

22). The project organisers recognise more general falls in crime, but still claim that 579 crimes stopped in the three years 2006–09 (2011: 27).[20]

One sport better than another?

Meek (2014) examined rugby union as well as football at HMYOI Portland. The institution ran a scheme based on rugby union provided by 2nd Chance Project, which had advised on the Sky TV Football Behind Bars project. Where football academy participants completed their level 1 coaching qualification, the rugby academy participants achieved a level 2 first aid qualification and the Rugby Football Union (RFU) Rugby Ready Coaching Award. Three of the rugby academy participants also completed their RFU Young Leaders Rugby Award. Meed, wisely perhaps, attempts no comparison on the specific efficacy of rugby versus football, but noted 'the need to make greater efforts to determine which types of sport are most effective in meeting specific aims' (2014: 179-80).

Meek refers not to 'sports' but 'types of sport', so not rugby, soccer, badminton or tiddlywinks but team versus individual and contact versus non-contact sport. Given the class background of the Borstal pioneers rugby union and cross country running might have been their 'bait' but soccer or boxing are more attractive for inmates now. While rugby union and cross-country running might have once have been deemed suitable activities for young offenders, soccer and boxing are more attractive for inmates now. Meek returns to this in her conclusion that 'research also needs to concentrate on establishing which sports are more or most useful in prison' (2014: 184), although she seems to be referring to their usefulness for the authorities not for the sports participants, the prisoners.

So what other types of sport might be examined? Are there similar schemes in tennis? Schneider (2014: 9) in a review of community-based crime prevention schemes found that tennis authorities in Toronto had provided a court and free lessons for local residents. There is no information about when the scheme was implemented, and the only evaluation offered is that 120 children enrolled on the course. Basketball schemes aimed at crime prevention are more common in the US but tennis legend, Boris Becker, a Laureus Academy member, is featured in a photo in the Laureus report *Teenage Kicks* (2011) at the launch of a London midnight basketball . Mention of the league still appears on the

---

[20] With further details in Appendix 3 (2011:49).

Laureus website, but with no further details. Yet such projects existed in 1999 in London, Cardiff and Mansfield.[21] What became of them? Nichols (2007) makes no mention of basketball in his comprehensive review of sports crime prevention schemes in the UK. It may be that in the UK basketball still does not have the pulling power of football.

In the US, basketball is associated with urban black youth (Hartman, 2012). Indeed, it is suggested that basketball schemes help reinforce the perception of crime as 'black' and 'urban' even where they have helped individuals. Hartman is clear that although sport can contest assumptions around race, it also produces and maintains them. Thus:

> The idea that having young black men throw balls at metal hoops would reduce crime draws together two of the most prominent images/representations of African American men in contemporary American culture: namely, that they are either superstar athletes or, alternatively, super-predator criminals (or would-be criminals). (2012: 1012)

Hartmann also describes the three core components of 'midnight basketball' set out by the founder, G. van Standifier, in Washington DC in the late 1980s: (1) players to be men between the ages of 17 and 21; (2) no game to start before 10 pm; and (3) two uniformed police officers to be present and visible at all times. The integrity of these rules is compromised, depending on where and when the game is played. For instance, in Australia the programme appears to be popular, but matches run from 7.30 pm to midnight starting with dinner, with the proviso that players must attend a workshop in order to play – hence the slogan, 'NoWorkshop NoJumpshot®'. Farrell et al (1996) found a 30% reduction in crime in the area they examined; but not in criminality of the attendees. Despite concerns about race, Hartman and Depro, 2006) feels that such programmes should not be lightly dismissed, as they found them to be associated with reductions in property crime. Kudlac (2010) mentions anecdotal presidential support for midnight basketball and also refers to a scheme called 'badges for baseball' that uses that sport for some of the same crime prevention purposes.

Hartman and Depro recommend combining sport with other initiatives – the initial midnight basketball programmes are deemed too simple – and suggest publicity effects also to have potential to improve results:

[21] BBC (5 May 1999) 'Beating crime with basketball', http://news.bbc.co.uk/1/hi/uk/335914.stm (accessed 11 October 2015).

The public attention devoted to high-profile prevention programs like midnight basketball may have had its own independent impact on community crime rates. This could happen in one of two ways. On the deterrence side, public attention to midnight basketball programs might send a message to potential criminals of a new emphasis on crime prevention and the extent to which law enforcement and other public officials are willing to go in the fight against crime, thus creating a rational deterrent for would-be criminals. (2006: 192)

On the other hand, the creation of popular, high-profile programs like midnight basketball might send a more positive, proactive message to community members, one that puts a new emphasis on community outreach and builds trust, commitment, and solidarity. (2006: 192)

Projects desperate for money might pitch their idea at whichever scheme has money in whichever nomenclature or discourse is required. Civil servants and ministers might approve projects under pressure to be seen to be doing 'something'. Hartman and Depro (2006) quote Johnson and Bowers' (2003) work on the effectiveness of intense standalone publicity in burglary reduction schemes, even before they have been implemented. Academics may feel uneasy at their work being (mis)used or them being misquoted on the effectiveness of a scheme when data may be poor or non-existent. Others warn·

Many crime reduction tactics have a characteristic lifecycle. To begin with there may be a substantial effect, but this can fade over time. Attention to ways of sustaining effects is therefore needed. (Tilley and Laycock, 2002: v)

The earlier discussion of gangs and sport showed the centrality of basketball in US colleges, and its subsequent appearance in sport-related violence. Football, rugby and basketball and are deemed to be 'central' or close to 'central' sports. What of more marginal sports, those that are not commercially important or deemed particularly masculine, especially individual sports?

A search of the internet reveals that many US crime prevention partnerships have annual fund-raising golf matches. In one intriguing account, NBC News describes 'How golf transformed a blighted neighbourhood'.[22] The East Lake housing project in Atlanta had a crime rate 18 times the national average and the exclusive golf course that bordered it had also fallen on hard times. The razing of the project and decanting of the residents might suggest that (re)gentrification was the real agent of change and developers the beneficiaries. However, reviving the private golf course and establishing a public one, developer Tom Cousins – who had brought professional basketball and hockey to the city – built a community in which half of the 542 units are reserved for families on public assistance, and the rest for middle-income working families who pay market rates. A report by Bridgespan (nd, but probably 2011 or 2012) rightly notes:

> ... dramatic improvements are partially the result of an influx of higher-income individuals and the exclusion of those former inhabitants with the worst criminal records. However, one-time residents who lived in the East Meadows project prior to 1995, and have returned, have seen similarly impressive gains along these metrics among their children. (p 3)

So golf is clearly a totem and headline bait, but the course offers classes and employment opportunities for neighbourhood residents and the local school uses it for physical education lessons. This is because:

> 'One of the better things is (that golf) teaches integrity,' he [Cousins] said. 'In other sports, basketball, football, you break the rules and there's a penalty. But there's no moral issue there. But in golf, it's all on your personal integrity. You don't improve the ball in the rough. You don't change the position.'

He would be disappointed by the tale of golfer Scott Stallings mentioned in Chapter Three, and may have forgotten that Scott Fitzgerald's *The Great Gatsby* featured a golfer who was a cheat, but since Jordan Baker was a woman perhaps that doesn't count.

Meek (2014) suggests that the Duke of Edinburgh (DoE) award schemes that have an adventure element 'offer some promise' of

---

[22]   David C. Lewis (22 April 2008) 'How golf transformed a blighted neighborhood', CNBC TV, www.nbcnews.com/id/24185797/ns/business-cnbc_tv/t/how-golf-transformed-a-blighted-neighborhood/#.Vu_ZjOKLSUk (accessed 28 September 2015).

working, citing evaluation by Dubberley and Parry (2010). They used focus groups with 60 young people in six institutions, each groups comprising eight to 12 young people, an officer, a researcher and a DoE worker. The focus groups took place before and after the DoE activity. Expeditions form a vital part of the awards, but the inability to obtain release on temporary licenses meant that some of the map reading, camping and fire lighting was done in the grounds of the institution. But external expeditions enabled participants to see things like sheep and waterfalls for first time. Learning could be mundane but profound. As one participant said:

> 'When you do the expedition you learn to respect the nature around you. If you are in the city you eat a pack of crisps and throw it on the floor, but we carried it around with us. I know it sounds mad, but it is like a lesson in itself.' (2010: 156)

Nichols examines the work of Fairbridge, now part of the Prince's Trust, which includes challenging adventure schemes such as sailing. He found positive change in 'attitude to self', 'career' and 'personal' (2007: 104). These indicators, like Meek's (2014) measures, are a long way from the finding that funders might want – that is, 'prevents crime'. Nichols found that the programme had a 'theory of change'. That is they were clear precisely what it was about boxing or white-water rafting, for instance, that would have a predicted effect on crime and why. Many charismatically led programmes appeal to common sense notions of effectiveness evaluated by testimony and faith.

Nichols examined another, more adventurous, programme at the Haffoty Wen Outdoor Activity Centre in North Wales funded by Merseyside Probation Service from 1984. It offered activities like mountaineering, gorge scrambling and mountain biking. It had been in operation for 15 years when Nichols carried out his research. Because it was run by the probation service, attendance data was available from 1986 and could be checked against data relating to re-offending. The most extreme course involved four days of preparation for tackling all 14 peaks in North Wales over 3,000 feet in 24 hours. It was this course that Nichols (2007) examined.

Out of the total 94 offenders who had ever attended, Nichols was able to track 62 offenders who attended between 1990 and 1995. For a variety of reasons some of these had to be excluded, leaving only 28. This illustrates the difficulties of evaluation even in organisations with established systems, but one example is typical of the difficulties inherent in this type of programme: three offenders received their first conviction after attending the course. This suggests to Nichols (2007) that non-offenders had been on the course as well as offenders. This is a recurring issue and one that many such projects struggle with. The dilemma is whether you wait until someone offends to offer a programme. Depending on funding streams, separate courses for offenders and non-offenders might be the solution. Another dilemma is whether attending such a programme might lead not to desistance from, but initiation into, crime.

Of the 28 participants in Nichols' study, 46.4% were reconvicted after two years, although their predicted offender group reconviction scale (OGRS) suggested that this figure would be 68.4%. This result was statistically significant (p=0.013) and, if one was only interested in publicity, one might stop there, but Nichols (2007) performs further analysis. As a number of the offenders lived in a residential drugs hostel, they would have had less opportunity to commit crime. Removing them from the analysis raised the reconviction rate to 66.6%, the OGRS to 69.1% and the statistical significance to p=0.55. Qualitative interviews had suggested that the course was particularly appropriate for drug offenders, so running the analysis for those 11 showed 36.4% against an OGRS of 74.3%. This is an apparently stunning result with a statistical significance of p=0.09, and one that is undermined by further work that extended the period for reconviction to three years to take account of offenders' reduced opportunity to offend when in residential accommodation. This found that 63.6% had reoffended in three years from their 'index' offence against the prediction from OGRS of 74.3% reconviction within two years. With statistical significance of p=0.31, Nichols rightly concludes that statistically 'this analysis does not support the hypothesis that the course reduced re-offending' (2007: 79).

Nichols' (2007) qualitative interviews suggested that it was not the 'risk' or 'edgework' of the courses that worked for the participants – although some respondents spoke of the adrenalin rush they received from participating – but the 'situation' – that is, being brought together. The mountains were not a 'hook' or 'bait' in the same way as the boxing, football or motor projects discussed above, but simply provided a space in which the participants could work – and work on them(selves).

Holyfield and Fine (1997) investigate these issues in a ropes adventure course for adolescent offenders in Atlanta. Their talk of 'morals' and 'character' reminds of earlier, and sometimes submerged, discourses but they also mention Lyng's (1990) 'edgework' and quote, Simmel (1959) to argue, 'that to experience an adventure is to move beyond the mundane, thereby linking one to more transcendent goals' (1997:344).

The tradition of outdoor and experiential learning is voluntarism as Lasch argues 'games quickly lose their charm when forced into the service of education, character development, or social improvement' (1991: 100).

In Holyfield and Fine's (1997) ethnography, adolescents were 'sentenced' to adventure work in lieu of detention. This was not a one-off event, but a six-week course involving more than games and high-rope activities. As described earlier, it was not the actual challenges so much as the briefing, debriefing and group activity that 'works', that is, anticipating and reflecting on the action beyond remarking, for example, that is was 'scary' or 'fun'. Although we have moved from a sporting context to one of leisure or physical activity, they are similar in the sense that if they are not carried out under supervision and in an appropriate place, they may constitute criminal activity. Adventure activities provide an experience of constrained risk. Videogames allow limitless and risk-free 'risk'. Might video games make suitable alternatives to custody?

Does sport work for women?

Summing up his findings from the Fairbridge programme, Nichols concludes that 'young women were significantly more likely to benefit ... than young men' (2007: 106). Young women also participated in the programme discussed by Holyfield and Fine (1997), albeit those authors fail to address the women's experience. It is for such reasons that Hornibrook et al (1997) recommend all-female courses

Leberman (2007) examined the learning of female offenders on a 20-day, tailor-made, experiential adventure education course (Women in Action) delivered by Outward Bound New Zealand. Significantly she sees these as challenging, but different from 'boot camps' aimed at breaking down participants before building them up (and therefore more suitable for women whose offending is not seen to stem from lack of discipline (Marcus–Mendoza et al, 1998). The majority of the women on the programme were of Maori origin, aged 18-48. Their convictions carried sentences ranging from six weeks to four-and-a-half years for offences including aggravated robbery, burglary, drug- and driving-related offences and fraud. The authors interviewed the women about their experience on the course and reviewed the reports written by staff. Many of the women were still in prison at the time of interview, so reoffending was clearly never an issue. About half the women reported an increase in confidence and self-awareness, with staff reports confirming this. However, while being in prison meant that they could not offend, neither could they put into practice what they had learned.

Nicola Adams, the 2012 Olympic flyweight gold medallist, is an ambassador for Fight For Peace. She was quoted earlier in the chapter, from the foreword she wrote in the APPGB (2015) report, in which she is, not unexpectedly, fulsome in her praise for boxing. Unlike her male counterparts, however, she does not credit boxing with keeping her out of prison. But she and other boxers throughout history (Smith, 2014) have faced a double-gendered penalty. Boxing has often been illegal for men (Chapter Two), but always deviant for women. As Lindner says, 'Women's engagement in boxing is "troubling" since female boxers' embodied performance of masculinity threatens to blur already destabilised gender boundaries' (2012: 466).

Only synchronised swimming and rhythmic gymnastics are open solely to women at the Olympics. There are campaigns[23] by and for men to compete in these events, and we may be still further behind in incorporating such activities in crime prevention/desistance schemes. Indeed, given the current gender order, it might be seen as suitably shaming to sentence a young man to attend a synchronised swimming course – a type of postmodern stocks, perhaps.

Both Lindner (2012) and Caudwell (2008) mention the film Million Dollar Baby directed by Clint Eastwood (2004) and featuring a woman boxer. Caudwell, however, concentrates on the less well-known Girlfight (directed by Karin Kusama in 2000) about a young woman who gets to spar with and fight against men, including her own father. It might be instructive to both show and discuss such films in boxing intervention programmes for offenders. This might add a reflective dimension to the physicality component. This is important; in Leberman's study, for instance, seven women commented on the mental challenge of their course, and, in particular, on the reflection days immediately afterwards. The most valuable thing for this respondent was:

> The reflections actually. Cause the girls in here the other day were all looking at themselves and how they were. I took a look at myself and I thought about my reflection

[23] Associated Press (19 August 2015) 'Russia pushes to add men's rhythmic gymnastics to Olympics', *Denver Post*, www.denverpost.com/olympics/ci_28666009/russia-pushes-add-mens-rhythmic-gymnastics-olympics?source=infinite and William Kremer (21 July 2015) 'Why can't men be Olympic synchronised swimmers?', BBC, (accessed 11 October 2015).

day and what I did and the three different days we had for it. (2007: 124)

Significantly, 'the course was seen as useful in learning to apply in practice some of the skills learned on other prison courses, such as Straight Thinking and Anger Management' (2007: 126). It is suggested that transitional assistance should be given to women leave prison after courses such as these, or that release should automatically follow the course, as is the case in Canada.

Meek (2014) devotes a chapter to sport and physical activity in prison for women and girls. No yomping the moors for them; she notes that women's involvement in sport in prison is less than men's in prison and less than that of women out of prison (Plugge et al, 2006). This suggests sport is needed for more immediate reasons than any potential crime prevention or desistance effects. Meek cites Ozano's (2008) small-scale work with nine British women in prison who benefited mentally and physically from three sessions of physical activity a week. This chimes with Leberman's (2007) findings.

Meek (2014) notes such prison offerings as yoga, aerobics and weight-management programmes, with zumba dance classes much requested. Women and authorities saw physical activity as a mental and physical health and weight-management issue, not one of recreation or rehabilitation. Sport-based qualifications were seen as potentially useful in gaining employment on release. It should be noted, however, that the lack of female gym staff in prisons may have a disproportionately negative effect on Muslim and gypsy/traveller women. Quidditch is now considered a contact sport, and is played (after a fashion) by mixed teams.[24] Might any of these activities work as crime prevention or desistance measures for women? Or might they just be a way into crime? Cohen and Peachey (2015) suggest that Quidditch provided leadership skills, social gains, self-confidence and pride – a positive sporting experience to set against findings such as Stansfield's (2015) on the damaging aspects of sport.

Conclusion

Chamberlain examines similar work under the Sports Based Initiative (SBI) and concludes that:

[24] International Quidditch Association (nd) http://iqaquidditch.org/ (accessed 11 October 2015),

Sports Based Initiative advocates must seek to promote a less homogeneous idea of what an SBI is, as well as be more sensitive to the diverse needs of young people, particularly if they are to tackle the underlying structural inequalities that arguably create the social problem, that is youth crime in the first place. (2013: 1292)

None of the programmes discussed here has been aimed at preventing a particular type of crime, with the exception of the motor projects (Groombridge, 1997), which were targeted specifically at car crime. No suggestion is made by promoters and funders of such schemes that football projects be saved for football hooligans, or those who dive on the pitch. Eric Cantona's assault on an abusive fan in the stands did, by contrast, lead to a tailored punishment of a soccer-based community service coaching children (Auclair, 2009). Cantona had originally been sentenced to two weeks' imprisonment by the magistrates, but this was overturned on appeal. He was fined and suspended by his club, and fined further and suspended for a longer period by FIFA with worldwide effect. This reminds us of the double punishment that sports stars often suffer (Chapter Six), although Auclair (2009) noted that Cantona spent the earliest hours of his community service signing autographs, overseen by his probation officer.

Crabbe (2000) specifically looks at what might work for drugs. He tends to see commonalities, not contrast, between sport and crime. His research focused on Leyton Orient Community Sports Programme on a Tower Hamlets Drug Challenge Fund Project, that is, football against drugs.

He is critical of New Labour and Victorian 'muscular Christianity' alike for naively assuming that sport represents a solution to societal ills. Much of Chapter Three is in the same vein as his warning note on Maradona's life, which 'has had its fair share of sex, drugs and rock'n'roll. Only more so. For with Diego you can add poverty, corruption, conspiracy, adultery and sainthood' (2000: 381). The source of this quote and the final word are significant.

Crabbe (2000) makes the point that sport's attitude to performance-enhancing and recreational drugs is increasingly at odds with wider societal values, and that the very reasons for taking drugs are similar to the reasons for taking up sport. Thus one might take performance-enhancing drugs in one's chosen sport to avoid recreational ones. All of Crabbe's prefatory material chimes with material covered here and in Chapters One and Four. So what of the relationship between drugs and the programme he was examining?

Crabbe is clear that just saying 'no' to drugs is an inadequate response, but so would saying 'yes' to sport. He was admiring of the commitment of those attending the programme and the respect shown to one 'top geezer' on the staff. He also felt that where it worked it did so through community development in which football was only a small part. To be fair, however, it is perhaps only a scheme associated with a football club such as this that is able to provide an 11-a-side fixture on the first team's pitch before an invited audience and a buffet lunch at which 'participants were freely chatting and socialising with the invited guests' (2000: 388)

But he retains his cynicism in noting from his observations that the drug taking that was part of the participants' lives continued, but was just hidden from the project workers (as they would be from any sports coach).

Crabbe's account is more theoretical and polemic than the work of Nichols (2007) or Meek (2014), but it does remind us of the complexity of the issues and identifies his work as sports criminology. But all warn against the simple assumption that sport 'works'.

EIGHT

Conclusion: no such thing as crime, no such thing as sport

Pete Dexter once described boxing promoter Don King, a successfully rehabilitated ex-convict, as someone who 'for 15 cents will put boys in the ring and girls on the street' (cited in Johnson and Long, 2008: 122).

More of this book has been about boxing than intended. I have participated in boxing training and enjoyed it, but I am uncomfortable about the sport of boxing. This may be the result of queasiness, fear, or just knowledge of the medical evidence against it. Sex work is not unproblematic either. Supporting the right of people to do what they want with their bodies applies equally to the bodywork of boxing and to prostitution. In an unequal society, the want of '15 cents' may put you in the ring or on your back. Thinking back to the gladiators in Chapter Two, are those who take 15 cents *infami* or are they exercising their *libertas*?

Throughout the book, parallels have been noted between sport and crime. We have discussed the links with masculinity, the idea that sport is a cause of, or cure for, crime and the overlaps where crime occurs in or near sport, or have nothing to do with sport but simply feature sportspeople as victims, offenders, witnesses or even bystanders. The reasoning in *R v Brown* (1975) shows how comments about boxing (and football, rugby and ice hockey[1]) were deployed to argue about the lawfulness of the participants in gay sado-masochistic sex. Lord Jauncey of Tullichettle opined: 'None of the appellants however had any medical qualifications and there was, of course, no referee present such as there would be in a boxing or football match.' Lord Mustill, looking at the decided cases, found that boxing 'stands outside the ordinary law of violence because society chooses to tolerate it'.

It is strongly argued that sport is not a thing in itself that can cause or cure anything, but is a part of life that sociology is already, and forever, exploring and that criminology should explore. Here the

---

[1] Victoria Silverwood notes the deviant and functional in fist fights in ice hockey (2015) 'The legitimate bare-knuckle fist fight – what makes ice hockey so unique?', https://deviantleisure.wordpress.com/2015/11/09/the-legitimate-bare-knuckle-fist-fight-what-makes-ice-hockey-so-unique/ (accessed 25 November 2015).

intention has been to encourage criminologists of all stripes to add sport to their consideration, as sport and crime are the same – not just connected or parallel, but the same. 'Crime has no ontological reality', said Hulsman (1986: 64). Equally sport has no ontological reality and is also socially constructed; sports criminology, therefore, is in a sense doubly impossible.

But sport/crime can be subjected to debate, disagreement and discursive manoeuvres; indeed, even 'censure' (Sumner, 2005). Both crime and sport are socially constructed, and from much the same materials: violence, transgression, deceit, gender segregation and so on. So sport is crime. And vice versa, is crime sport? According to Briggs (1991), joyriders enjoyed 'playing' with the police. Moreover, combating financial fraud has been turned into a videogame for educational and instructional purposes.[2]

In arguing that 'sex is not a sport', Hanna (2001) examines cases in the US where men have asked the courts to treat domestic violence like sport or consensual sado-masochism – that is, something for which consent can be, and was, given. *The People v Jovanovic* appears to suggest that only consent was an issue in this case of heterosexual sado-masochism, and thus in the US *R v Brown* might have been decided differently. As Hanna says:

> Prior to this decision, courts in the United States, England, and Canada have consistently maintained that one cannot consent to any activity which could cause serious bodily injury or death, i.e. violence, with a few exceptions, voluntary participation in organized sports being the most common. (2001: 242)

Here we cannot attempt to critically analyse the state of consent to sex between jurisdictions, but we can pick up on what Hanna says about sport, as she immediately carries on to say: 'Sex is not a sport.' Yet like the judges in *R v Brown* she consistently returns to it. We do seem legally to be able to consent to more on the sports field than in the bedroom. Etter (2014) discusses the growth of adventure races and quotes Will Dean, CEO of one such well-known challenge:

> 'What Tough Mudder does well is things that shouldn't be: I'm running in fire! I'm in a dumpster full of ice! I'm

---

[2] Serious Games Market (23 June 2015) http://seriousgamesmarket.blogspot. co.uk/2015/06/serious-games-for-investigating.html (accessed 11 October 2015).

getting zapped with 10,000 volts of electricity!... People
want to leave this event with a few cuts and bruises.'

People consent to this. I have friends who have completed several such
races; they and others proudly share their experiences on Facebook.

Smart opined that the decision in *R v Brown* had 'left Britain with
a law on sexuality which states – symbolically at least – that when
women say No to rape they mean Yes, but when men say Yes to
homosexual sex they mean No' (1975: 120). Her desire to speak up
for gay men – and Hanna (2001) details both their rights and those
of lesbian women – is admirable, but she might also have raised the
difference in treatment of sport and sex.

Throughout Chapter Two and elsewhere we have seen the law's
attempts to rein in certain sports, the crowds they attract or their
behaviour. Sport has been most successful when it has have been able
to argue that its knowledge should prevail. Thus boxing's discipline or
domain is regularly challenged, but putting it in a ring and providing
referees and medical help has enabled it to continue to exist, if not
always thrive. There may be a lesson here for extreme sex participants.

Clearly more successful in fighting the disciplinary war with 'the law'
are sports like football and rugby – but particularly baseball as we saw
in Chapter Two – which have been able to confine their games to a
set of rules and their crowds to a set of increasingly high-priced seats.

Parkour presents a picture of a more 'outlaw' sport in its use of
public spaces and highly contested, privately owned semi-public spaces
(Chow, 2010). And although mass participation running events are
now sanctioned by corporate interests, they offer some resistance to
'car culture', if only for a day. Cycle use of the highway continues to
be a contested area.[3] What might be made of the cycling 'gangs' of Los
Angeles who hold legal and illegal races as well as mass rides, which
seems to keep them out of other trouble?[4]

Taking urban exploration seriously but having enormous fun, we find
'urban explorer' and ethnographer Bradley Garrett roundly declaring
the need to take back 'rights to the city from which we have been
wrongfully restricted through subversions that erode security and
threaten clean narratives about what we can and can't do' (2013: 24).

[3] I once took part in a triathlon that was stopped by the police.

[4] Rory Carroll (4 September 2015) 'Ride, hustle, kill, repeat: the underground cycle
gangs of Los Angeles', *The Guardian*, www.theguardian.com/cities/2015/sep/04/ride-
hustle-kill-repeat-the-underground-cycle-gangs-of-los-angeles (accessed 11 October
2015).

In this there will be tensions. Urban exploration (what many would call trespassing) has regularly been denounced as 'crime', but is in danger of lapsing into 'sport' – like parkour, boxing and football.

Review of chapters

Chapter One discussed sports law and sociology of sport and raised the possibility of sports criminology. It is good, therefore, to see Young argue that it is:

> ... sociologically useful, indeed sociologically necessary, to approach the full range of the subject matter as SRV [sports-related violence] rather than 'sports violence' per se. Using an approach that combines criminology, social justice and community health concerns (2015: 642)

Sports law is largely involved with disputes between players and authorities, or authorities and news media. Indeed, in the Gasquet case discussed in Chapter Three, Adam Lewis QC represented the player and Jonathan Taylor the International Tennis Federation, but they still edited a book together and presented the case jointly to a sport and law conference.[5] The Gasquet case shows how 'sport law' follows 'black letter' law traditions and sports sociology largely backs the huge anti-doping edifice heaped on sportspeople. A critical, realist, culturally informed sports criminology notes such impositions. It may come closer to Finley and Finley's (2006) *The Sport's Industry's War on Athletes*. These authors take issue with the use of the concepts of deviance and overconforming in sports sociology. They note the sacrifices made in the name of the sport's ethics and the harm that drugs, eating disorders, playing through pain, hazing, various 'isms, predatory finance and so on has on athletes. Such a mix might be of interest to zemiologists and criminologists of the harm perspective (Hillyard et al, 2004).

Much of Chapter Two and the introduction above are about boxing, because it teeters on the border between the legal and illegal over time and place. Whether legal or illegal, it always involves harm, which reminds us of ongoing debates within criminology about its core subject matter and whether to embrace zemiology. There was much hype about the Floyd Mayweather versus Manny Pacquiao fight of May 2015. This illustrates the potential harm two men might do to each,

---

[5] 30 March 2010, Montague on the Gardens.

which often overshadows the harm one of them has already done. Some would allege that the media have been easy on Mayweather (though all 'incidents' have been covered), and others would have expected the boxing authorities to have been harder on him. Comparisons may be drawn with the National Football League's eventual strong action against Ray Rice (see Chapter Six).

Chapter Two set out some of the history of sports, crime and the law, but some speculation about the future seems necessary. Concussion is a clear and anticipatable consequence of boxing, and is not infrequent in National Hunt horse racing. American football (Fields, 2014), rugby union and rugby league are now taking the risk of concussion seriously.[6] All legal actions that have so far been brought in relation to sport have been civil ones, but, as with boxing in the past, what if criminal law were applied in such cases.

Chapter Three examined a number of cases of violence and 'cheating', which set up the next three chapters on theory and justice. Such cases are often reported by the media as 'scandals' and to some we have attributed the suffix 'gate'. This media trope/meme should be of interest to media (cultural) criminologists.

The theory chapters, Four and Five, imagined what various criminological theories might say about crime and sport, but sometimes we find well-known criminologists using sport as a metaphor to explain their thinking or even talking directly about sport. It is hoped that more will come forward, particularly in the areas of harm, gender, sexuality, race and class. Methods were touched on but given the eclecticism of the field, no single method is prescribed or proscribed. Even the brief discussion of theory should indicate that mainstream, critical and right- and left-leaning versions of sports criminology are possible.

Some of the issues of sport and crime coalesce in the story of boxer Emile Griffith, who beat and killed Benny 'Kid' Paret in a welterweight world title fight in April 1962 at Madison Square Gardens. This was their third fight. Griffith was black and he was gay – not 'out' (homosexuality was still illegal) – but known to be gay. At the weigh-in, as he bent over, his Cuban opponent mimed sex with him and called him *maricón* (faggot). Although downed in the sixth round, he went on to fatally knock out Paret in the 12th. This combines issues of consent,

---

[6]   Hugh Godwin (18 April 2015) 'Is rugby starting to see sense over concussion?', *Independent*, www.independent.co.uk/sport/rugby/rugby-union/news-comment/is-rugby-starting-to-see-sense-over-concussion-10187295.html and Kieran Fox (29 April 2015) 'Lance Hohaia retires because of 'recurrent concussion symptoms', BBC, www.bbc.co.uk/sport/0/rugby-league/32525472 (accessed 11 October 2015).

gender, sexuality, ethnicity and the referee's powerlessness. There was spectacle too – the loving slow-mo replays of the fatal blows, until broadcasters eventually realised they were showing the death of a man.[7]

Chapter Six looked at the justice systems of sport through the lens of Kraska and Brent's (2011) metaphors and then at corruption, performance-enhancing drugs and issues of sports 'extraterritoriality'.

As one respondent, 'Ken', told Sefiha (2012), taking drugs is not cheating:

> 'Bike racing is hard enough as it is. For many of these guys, they are just trying to hang on [in the races]. Trying to keep their jobs. It's not like drugs are going to make them start winning a bunch of races.' (2012: 228)

The miscarriages and rough justice of most sport procedures suggest that, just as some criminologists (Stevens, 2011) would support decriminalisation of drugs in society, if only because of the damage done in the 'war on drugs', so peace should be declared in sport. The use of drugs in sport should be a medical issue. My contention is that cheats are those like runner Julius Njogu or modern pentathlete Boris Onishenko. In 2015, Njogu tried to claim second prize in the Nairobi Marathon after joining it with only a kilometre to go.[8] Onishenko was found to have used a rigged épée at the 1976 Olympics to score at will. The sword had a button that allowed him to replicate the hit, and was detected by the technology of the time (Tibballs, 2003).

In writing this book, I was tempted to obtain Modafinil to assist my concentration.[9] Would that have been cheating? Why didn't I do so? – lack of opportunity and distrust of proffered sources on the internet. A proposal to legalise drug use in sport is not new, but among Savulescu's

[7]   Donald McRae (10 September 2015) 'The night boxer Emile Griffith answered gay taunts with a deadly cortege of punches', *The Guardian*, www.theguardian. com/sport/2015/sep/10/boxer-emile-griffith-gay-taunts-book-extract (accessed 11 October 2015).

[8]   Associated Press (26 October 2015) 'Man sneaks in for last kilometre of Nairobi marathon to win second place', *The Guardian*, www.theguardian.com/world/2015/ oct/26/kenya-man-cheats-nairobi-marathon-second-place (accessed 25 November 2015).

[9]   Helen Thomson (20 August 2015) 'Narcolepsy medication modafinil is world's first safe "smart drug"', *The Guardian*, www.theguardian.com/science/2015/aug/20/ narcolepsy-medication-modafinil-worlds-first-safe-smart-drug (accessed 11 October 2015).

arguments for legalisation is the arbitrariness of genetic advantage that saw Finnish cross-country skier Eero Mäntyranta win seven medals at three Olympics.[10] He had a genetic mutation causing him to have over 50% more red blood cells than his competitors. Savulsecu concluded that sport is built around a set of fairly arbitrary rules that harm people and cause injustice, and so should be changed.

Some see the use of performance-enhancing drugs as a form of corruption – of the noble pursuit of sport – yet it might best be seen as a part of sport. Corruption such as match fixing, spot fixing, exploitation of players and fixing over locations for tournament staging all are major and growing forms of corruption, with national and transnational policing and criminal justice implications that should interest criminology and not just be side-lined as sport-related or sports criminology.

Foster argues that law is increasingly invasive, but that sport 'uniquely offers a field in which the constitutive power of regulation and law is easily studied, and where the arguments over legal intervention are not yet closed' (2006: 155). Much the same argument might be made for criminology. Indeed, sport might be seen to be a different country where they do things differently, thereby enabling the national-based criminologist to practice some transnational criminology. Sport's criminal justice systems, as we have seen, have tended to operate separately and now impinge on real-life criminal justice.

Criminology needs to push back. But perhaps criminology and criminal justice systems might also learn. Might the vanishing spray (the return of the 'deadline'?) now used to police free kicks have a wider societal use? The 'law of the code' (Lessig, 1999) in videogames, or the semi-automaticity of tenpin bowling 'justice', shows the increased use of technology for control and judgement, and not necessarily a comfortable one. Does this make 'Hawkeye' or goal-line technology a human rights issue?

Some sporting metaphors have been used in this book. In wider society, their use is sometimes seen as exclusionary for those not versed in field or pitch vernacular. The flow of 'British' sport to the rest of the world has been considerable, but that to Britain from the US has not. One malign import, though, is the baseball metaphor taken up by Michael Howard when he was Home Secretary. He was enamoured of the game, 'stepped up to the plate' and proposed 'three strikes and

---

[10] Julian Savulescu (1 September 2015) 'Opinion: Why it's time to legalise doping in athletics', The Conversation, http://m.medicalxpress.com/news/2015-09-opinion-legalise-doping-athletics.html (accessed 11 October 2015).

you're out' (Jones and Newburn, 2006). To use a golf metaphor, it was a 'one-club' policy. We should also avoid becoming the 'referees of deviance'!

Chapter Seven looked at 'cures' for, or ameliorations of, crime through sport, yet Jones' (2000) survey of violent crime has little to say about sport other than its association with violence and its potential to prevent crime. Some of the work discussed shows promise, but evaluation of preventive or rehabilitative programmes is very difficult. There are practical issues that make the comparisons and evaluations discussed in the chapter especially difficult. You don't have to be a left realist to follow Jock Young's (1992: 40) insistence on 'the principle of specificity'. He was speaking of the specifics of crime, different crimes, different places, different cultures. Kudlac (2010: xiii) is more prosaic:

> It is nearly impossible to talk about athletes in general because of the many differences that can encompass them, from a wrestler to a football player ... there are vast differences between a high school football player who rarely makes it into a game and a starting quarterback in the NFL.

In his analysis, Kudlac tends to undermine his argument by concentrating on the male, revenue-generating sports of football, baseball and basketball. Individual sports, meanwhile, have their supporters. Jenkins and Ellis's research into Taekwondo martial arts training leads them to conclude the following:

> It has shown that combat sport participation can act as a protective factor which distances participants from socio-cultural and individual risk factors in the behavioural, economic and social spheres. It has shown that combat sport represents an appropriate activity to be utilised within crime reduction strategies that aim to address these risks. Furthermore, it has indicated that combat sport has the potential to help treat violent offenders, gang/group offenders and emotionally charged impulsive offenders. (2011: 129)

They note Trulson's (1986) finding that combat sport work better if allied to the tradition and philosophy of that sport, but don't present their results in a way that shows the difference between the different groups of traditional and non-traditional martial arts clubs. Their study also covered a good proportion of women and the results held up for them too.

Ways forward for sports criminology

This chapter has drawn together some of the arguments of previous chapters and suggests connections with traditional and emerging criminologies (social harm, green, cultural and queer). It also sets out some potential areas for other researchers to take forward. The short trajectories of both green and queer criminologies offer some notes of caution. Green criminology has largely become a criminology of 'making the polluter pay', and queer criminology a victimology of the rainbow nation. Thus, despite the arguments presented in this book, sports criminology will likely come to be about football hooliganism (see Hopkins and Treadwell, 2014, for a broader picture) and condemnation of the off-field behaviour of sports stars. The intention is wider. The intention is not to carve out a specialist area within criminology for sports fans, but to say something to and about criminology more generally. Just as policing scholars have come to look beyond the 'boys in blue', so sports criminologists might examine the policing done by referees, and match officials and so on.

Giulianotti and Klauser (2010: 49) argue that an interdisciplinary research approach is required to understand security governance at sports mega-events that:

> ... brings together three particular strands: first, a sociological approach that explores the 'security field,' drawing in part on Bourdieu; second, critical urban geographical theory, which contextualizes security strategies in relationship to new architectures of social control and consumption in urban settings; and third, different strands of risk theory, notably in regard to reflexive modernization, governmentality, and cultural sociological questions.

Their work is highly relevant, particularly in respect of the need for interdisciplinary work, though much of what they propose could be seen as 'surveillance studies'. Sports criminology might overlap with cultural criminology, crime and media perspectives and corporate crime, but other approaches are possible too.

Atkinson and Young (2008) talk of theoretical intersections; for others, sports criminology is the sociology of masculinities with which the best sport sociology engages. Those interested in environmental perspectives – in criminology and elsewhere – would do well to examine issue such as the growth of sports mega-events in the Global South and plans to fell forests for unnecessary golf courses.[11] This chapter mentions other perspectives, and it is hoped that other commentators will find more.

CCTV has been used for many years in sports stadia as an aid for crowd control and identifying criminal activity; critical criminologists and sports sociologists rightly see this as evidence of social control. Others focus more on the effectiveness of the wider street use of CCTV (Groombridge, 2008b). Yet despite the presence at sports venues of cameras, spectators in their tens of thousands and dedicated official 'capable guardians', various types of cheating appear to be endemic. Here sport is an example of an 'experiment' that might not be sanctioned in real life.

Throughout this book I have been trying to practise a reflexive critical sports criminology, a criminology that questions the basis of its own production, constantly asking what sport is and what criminology is. Thus Chapters Four and Five explored the extent to which crime might be 'caused' by sport and Chapter Seven discussed how crime might be prevented by, or resisted through, sport. However, questions about the nature of sport and crime rather miss the point, and not just because logically they appear to cancel each other out.

The difficulty with these questions is that you cannot separate sport out from other influences for or against crime. It is impossible, for example, to work out what effects (good or bad) the media has on society in a media-saturated culture (Gauntlett, 1998) and sport is fully integrated into that media/society nexus. As Chapter Two showed, even before the growth of mass media sport was part of local and national cultures. A critical sports criminology cannot answer whether sport does or doesn't encourage crime or desistance; rather, it reminds sport and its participants that sport is not above the law, and reminds criminology that breaches of the law, deviance and harm can be found everywhere. They can be found in the one thing we might have turned to when not 'being' criminologists – our recreation.

Kudlac (2010, 144) piously concludes his book as follows: 'Thus, to truly change the image of sports in the United States, an effort to *avoid* [emphasis added] criminal behaviour must be made by every participant in the sports world – athletes, coaches, and fans alike.'

---

[11] John Watts (23 April 2010) 'All the tees in China: Golf boom threatens rainforest' *Guardian* website available at http://www.guardian.co.uk/environment/2010/apr/23/ endangered-habitats-china (accessed 11 October 2015)

Jamieson and Orr (2009) offer similar heartfelt thoughts and examples. Such handwringing marks these studies out as mainstream sports criminologies rather than critical sports criminologies.

If it has not been obvious, in many respects this book has doubts about its own title. There has been much discussion of sport and of criminology. Whether the book has successfully argued for a sports criminology is moot. The intention has always been to avoid crimes merely associated with sport, but I have had to allude to them often. Most of those crimes are already, or should be, the subject of criminology. Drug use, fraud, bribery and international law and policing are the stuff of modern sport, and so need criminological examination.

When Hanna (2001) says that sex is not a sport she is urging us to take sex seriously by contrasting it to sport. This book has taken sport, crime (and sex) seriously. All require strenuous social construction. Crime and sport often involves implicit consent, but sport often requires more explicit consent. The consensual requirements of everyday life are often played down until you face hospital admission for surgery.[12] More should be made of the issue of consent. Who can consent and in what circumstances?

The difficult methodological, epistemological and ontological issues of sport and crime cannot clear nor condemn sportsmen of violence outside sport, particularly sexual violence, often towards women. Making more explicit the issue of consent in stepping onto the field or into the ring might help in establishing a discourse and practice where sportspeople are sensible of consent when stepping from the bar to the bedroom.

---

[12] Or an ethics committee.

Cases and legislation

Arbitral Award Court of Arbitration for Sport CAS 2009/A/1926 ITF v Richard Gasquet

CAS 2009/A/1930 WADA v ITF and Richard Gasquet, http://jurisprudence.tas-cas.org/sites/CaseLaw/Shared%20 Documents/1926,%201930.pdf (accessed 22 July 2015)

Commonwealth v Collberg 119 Mass 350353 (1876)

Enderby Town FC v The Football Association [1971] Ch 591 at 605

London Olympic and Paralympic Games Act 2006, www.england-legislation.hmso.gov.uk/acts/acts2006/ukpga_20060012_en_1 (accessed 22 July 2015)

International Tennis Federation Independent Anti-Doping Tribunal Decision in the Case of M. Richard Gasquet, July 2009

R v Brown [1993] 2 All ER 75

References

AA (Automobile Association) (1992) *'Safe' and 'Unsafe' – A Comparative Study of Younger Male Drivers*, Basingstoke: AA Foundation for Road Safety Research.

Abel, Richard L. (1982) *The Politics of Informal Justice: Volume 2 Comparative Studies*, New York, NY: Academic Press.

ACC (Australian Crime Commission) (2013) 'Threats to the integrity of professional sport in Australia. Crime profile series, Organised crime in professional sport', www.crimecommission.gov.au/sites/default/files/Threat%20s%20to%20the%20integrity% 20of%20professional%20sport%20in%20Australia%20JULY%202013.pdf (accessed 7 June 2014).

Adler, Freda Schaffer and Adler, Herbert Marcus (1975) *Sisters in Crime: The Rise of the New Female Criminal*, New York, NY: McGraw-Hill.

Advisory Council on the Misuse of Drugs (2009) *Annual Report 2008/9*, London: Home Office.

Agnew, Robert (1992) 'Foundation for a general strain theory of crime and delinquency', *Criminology*, 30(1): 47-87.

Agnew, Robert (2012) 'The ordinary acts that contribute to ecocide: a criminological analysis', in Nigel South and Avi Brisman (eds) (2012) *Routledge International Handbook of Green Criminology* London: Routledge.

Akers, R. L. (1998) *Social Learning and Social Structure: A General Theory of Crime and Delinquency*, Boston, MA: Northeastern University Press.

Alcoff, Linda and Gray, Laura (1993) 'Survivor discourse: transgression or recuperation?', *Signs* 8(2): 260-90.

Alpert, Geoff, Rojek, Jeff, Hansen, Andy, Shannon, Randy L. and Scott Decker H. (2011) 'Examining the prevalence and impact of gangs in college athletic programs using multiple sources: final report', www.biol.sc.edu/crju/pdfs/gangs_and_student_athletes_final.pdf (accessed 30 September 2015).

Anderson, Elijah (2001) *Code of the Street: Decency, Violence and the Moral Life of the Inner City* New York, NY: Norton.

Anderson, Jack (2007) *The Legality of Boxing: A Punch Drunk Love?*, Abingdon: Birkbeck Law Press.

Anderson, Jack (2013) 'Doping, sport and the law: time for repeal of prohibition?', *International Journal of Law in Context*, 9: 135-59.

Atencio, Matthew and Wright, Jan (2008) '"We be killin' them": hierarchies of black masculinity in urban basketball spaces, *Sociology of Sport Journal*, 25: 263-80.

Atkinson, Michael (2009) 'Parkour, anarcho-environmentalism, and poiesis', *Journal of Sport and Social Issues*, 33(2): 169-94.

Atkinson, Michael (2011) 'Physical cultural studies [Redux]', *Sociology of Sport Journal*, 28(1): 135-44.

Atkinson, Michael and Young, Kevin (2008) *Deviance and Social Control in Sport*, Leeds: Human Kinetics.

Auclair, Philippe (2009) *Cantona: The Rebel Who Would Be King*, London: Pan Macmillan.

Baron, L., Straus, M.A., and Jaffe, D. (1988) 'Legitimate violence, violent attitudes, and rape: a test of the cultural spillover theory', in R.A. Prentky and V.L. Quinsey (eds) *Human Sexual Aggression: Current Perspectives*, New York, NY: New York Academy of Sciences.

Beashel, Paul, Taylor, John and Alderson, John (1996) *Advanced Studies in Physical Education and Sport*, Cheltenham: Thornes Nelson.

Becker, Howard S. (1963) *Outsiders: Studies in the Sociology of Deviance*, New York, NY: The Free Press of Glencoe.

Bellos, Alec (2003) 'The president wins the midfield battle', *New Statesman*, 3 November.

Benedict, Jeff (1997) *Public Heroes, Private Felons: Athletes and Crimes against Women*, Boston, MA: Northeastern University Press.

Benedict, Jeff (2004) *Out of Bounds: Inside the NBA's Culture of Rape, Violence and Crime*, New York, NY: Harper Collins.

Benedict, Jeff and Yaeger, Don (1999) *Pros and Cons: Criminals Who Play in the NFL*, New York, NY: Time Warner Books.

Berlin, Isaiah (1978) *Karl Marx: His Life and Environment*, New York, NY: Oxford University Press.

Birley, Derek (2013) *A Social History of English Cricket*, London. Aurum Press Ltd.

Birrell, Susan (1981) 'Sport as ritual: interpretations from Durkheim to Goffman', *Social Forces* 60(2): 354-76.

Bissinger, H. G. (2005) *Friday Night Lights: A Town, a Team, and a Dream*, London: Yellow Jersey Press.

Blackshaw, T. and Crabbe, T. (2004) *New Perspectives on Sport and Deviance: Consumption, Performativity and Social Control*, London: Routledge

Bloom, Gordon A. and Smith, Michael D. (1996) 'Hockey violence: a test of cultural spillover theory', *Sociology of Sport Journal*, 13(1): 65-77.

Blumstein, A. and Benedict, J. (1999) 'Criminal violence of NFL players compared with the general population', *Chance* 12(3): 12-15.

Bonger, Willem Adriaan (1969) *Race and Crime*, Montclair, NJ: Patterson Smith.

Bonger, Willem Adriaan (2015) *Introduction to Criminology*, London: Routledge.

Bosworth, K. and Espelage, D. (1995) *Teen Conflict Survey*, Bloomington, IN: Centre for Adolescent Studies Indiana University.

Bosworth, Mary and Hoyle, Carolyn (eds) (2011) *What is Criminology?*, Oxford: Oxford University Press.

Bowling, Ben and Sheptycki, James (2012) *Global Policing*, London: Sage Publications.

Box, Stephen (1971) *Deviance, Reality and Society*, London: Holt, Rinehart and Winston.

Boyle, P. and Haggerty, K. (2009) 'Spectacular security: mega-events and the security complex', *International Political Sociology*, 3(3): 257-74.

Braithwaite, John and Drahos, Peter (2000) *Global Business Regulation*, Cambridge: Cambridge University Press.

Bricknell, Samantha (2015) *Corruption in Australian Sport*, Trends and Issues in Crime and Criminal Justice, No 490, Canberra: Australia Institute of Criminology.

Bridgespan (nd) 'Case study: East Lake, Atlanta: needle-moving community collaboratives', www.bridgespan.org/getmedia/9db0fc5e-231e-4904-bd28-9df134b70ef1/Community-Collaboratives-CaseStudy-Atlanta.pdf.aspx (accessed 29 August 2015).

Briggs, J. (1991) 'A profile of the juvenile joyrider and a consideration of the efficacy of motor vehicle projects as a diversionary strategy', MA Dissertation Thesis, University of Durham: Department of Sociology and Social Policy.

Brissonneau, Christophe (2015) 'The 1998 Tour de France: Festina, from scandal to an affair in cycling', in Verner Møller, Ivan Waddington and John M. Hoberman (eds) *Routledge Handbook of Drugs and Sport*, Abingdon: Routledge.

Brohm, Jean-Marie. (1987) *Sport: A Prison of Measured Time*, London: Pluto Press.

Brookes, C. (1974) 'Cricket as a vocation: a study of the development and contemporary structure of the occupation and career patterns of the cricketer', PhD Thesis, University of Leicester.

Brooks, Graham, Aleem, Azeem and Button, Mark (2013) *Fraud, Corruption and Sport*, London: Palgrave Macmillan

Brown David (2013) 'Losing my religion': reflections critical criminology in Australia', in Russell Hogg and Kerry Carrington (eds) *Critical Criminology*, Abingdon: Routledge.

Bunsell, Tanya (2014) *Strong and Hard Women: An Ethnography of Female Bodybuilding, Abingdon:* Routledge.

Burgess, Ernest (1925) 'The growth of the city', in Robert E. Park, Ernest W. Burgess and Roderick D. McKenzie (eds) *The City*, Chicago, IL: University of Chicago Press.

Bushman, Brad J. and Baumeister, Roy F. (1998) 'Threatened egotism, narcissism, self-esteem, and direct and displaced aggression: does self-love or self-hate lead to violence?', *Journal of Personality and Social Psychology*, 75(1): 219-29.

Butler, Brin-Jonathan and Emhoff, Kurt (nd) 'Gold in the mud: the twisted saga of jailhouse boxer James Scott's battle for redemption', www.sbnation.com/longform/2014/3/12/5496096/james-scott-jailhouse-boxer-profile (accessed 21 August 2015).

Campbell, Bea (1993) *Goliath: Britain's Dangerous Places*, London: Methuen.

Campbell, W. Keith, Bush, Carrie Pierce, Brunell, Amy B. and Shelton, Jeremy (2005) 'Understanding the social costs of narcissism: the case of the tragedy of the commons', *Personality and Social Psychology Bulletin*, 31(10): 1358-68.

Card, D. and Dahl, G. (2011) 'Family violence and football: the effect of unexpected emotional cues on violent behaviour', *The Quarterly Journal of Economics*, 126(1): 103-43.

Carrabine, Eamonn, Cox, Pamela, Fussey, Pete, Hobbs, Dick, South, Nigel, Thiel, Darren, Turton, Jackie (2013) *Criminology: A Sociological Introduction* (3rd edn), Abingdon: Routledge.

Carrington, Ben and McDonald, Ian (eds) (2009) *Marxism, Cultural Studies and Sport*, Abingdon: Routledge.

Carter, Rubin (2011) *Eye of the Hurricane: My Path form Darkness to Freedom*, Chicago, IL: Lawrence Hill Books.

Caudwell, Jayne (2008) 'Girlfight: boxing women', *Sport in Society: Cultures, Commerce, Media, Politics*, 11(2-3): 227-39.

Chamberlain, J. M. (2013) 'Sports-based intervention and the problem of youth offending: a diverse enough tool for a diverse society?', *Sport in Society: Cultures, Commerce, Media, Politics*, 16(10): 1279-92.

Chow, Broderick D. V. (2010) 'Parkour and the critique of ideology: turn-vaulting the fortresses of the city', *Journal of Dance and Somatic Practices*, 2(2): 143-54.

Christie, Nils (2000) *Crime-Control as Industry: Towards GULAGS Western Style*, Abingdon: Oxford University Press.

Cloward, Richard A. and Ohlin, L. E. (2013) *Delinquency and Opportunity: A Study of Delinquent Gangs*, London: Routledge.

Coakley, Jay and Pike, Elizabeth (2009) *Sports in Society: Issues and Controversies*, New York, NY: McGraw Hill.

Cohen, Adam and Peachey, Jon Welty (2015) 'Quidditch: impacting and benefiting participants in a non-fictional manner', *Journal of Sport and Social Issues*, 39(6): 521-44.

Cohen, Kircidel Albert (1955) *Delinquent Boys: The Culture of the Gang*, New York, NY: Free Press.

Cohen, Stanley (2011) *Folk Devils and Moral Panics* (3rd edn), Abingdon: Routledge.

Committee on Climate Change (2015) 'Reducing emissions and preparing for climate change: 2015 progress report to parliament', www.theccc.org.uk/publication/reducing-emissions-and-preparing-for-climate-change-2015-progress-report-to-parliament (accessed 5 July 2015).

Connell, R.W. (1995) *Masculinities*, Cambridge: Polity Press.

Connolly, Chris (2011) 'A warning to disciplinary panels of regulatory bodies: the impact of "Bloodgate" goes beyond sport', LawinSport, www.lawinsport.com/articles/regulation-a-governance/item/a-warning-to-disciplinary-panels-of-regulatory-bodies-the-impact-of-bloodgate-goes-beyond-sport (accessed 25 March 2016).

Corteen, K. and Corteen, A. (2012) 'Dying to entertain? The victimization of professional wrestlers in the USA', *International Perspectives in Victimology*, 7(1): 47-53.

Crabbe, Tim (2000) 'A sporting chance? Using sport to tackle drug use and crime', *Drugs Education, Prevention and Policy*, 7(4): 381-91.

Craig, Kellina M. (2000) 'Defeated athletes, abusive mates? Examining perceptions of professional athletes who batter', *Journal of Interpersonal Violence*, 15(11): 224-1232.

Croall, Hazell (1992) *White Collar Crime: Criminal Justice and Criminology*, Buckingham: Open University Press.

Crosset, Todd W., Benedict, Jeffrey R. and McDonald, Mark A. (1995) 'Male student-athletes reported for sexual assault: a survey of campus police departments and judicial affairs offices', *Journal of Sport and Social Issues*, 19(2): 126-40.

Crowley, Annie, Brooks, Oona and Lombard, Nancy (2014) *Football and Domestic Abuse: A Literature Review Report No. 6/2014*, Glasgow: Scottish Centre for Crime and Justice Research.

Cuyler, P.L. (1980) *Sumo: From Rite to Sport*, New York, NY: Weatherhill.

Cycling Independent Reform Commission (2015) *Cycling Independent Reform Commission Report to the President of the Union Cycliste Internationale*, Lausanne: UCI.

Dart, Jon (2014) 'Sports review: a content analysis of the International Review for the Sociology of Sport, the Journal of Sport and Social Issues and the Sociology of Sport Journal across 25 years', *International Review for the Sociology of Sport*, 49(6): 645-68.

Day, Frederick J. (2005) *Sports and Courts: an introduction to principles of law and legal theory using cases from professional sports*, Lincoln, NE: iUniverse Inc.

Delaney, Tim and Madigan, Tim (2009) *The Sociology of Sports: An Introduction*, Jefferson, NC: McFarland and Co.

Dimeo, Paul (2007) *A History of Drug Use in Sport: 1876-1976: Beyond Good and Evil*, Abingdon: Routledge.

Donnermeyer, Joseph F. and DeKeseredy, Walter (2013) *Rural Criminology*, Abingdon: Routledge.

Donziger, Stephen R. (1996) *The Real War on Crime: Report of the National Criminal Justice Commission*, New York, NY: Harper Perennial.

Douglas, M. (1966) *Purity and Danger: An Analysis of the Concepts of Pollution and Taboo*, London: Routledge.

Downes, David and Rock, Paul (1998) *Understanding Deviance*, Abingdon: Oxford University Press.

Dubberley, S. and Parry, O. (2010) '"Something we don't normally do": a qualitative study of the Duke of Edinburgh's Award in the secure estate', *Research, Policy and Planning: The Journal of the Social Service Group*, 27(3): 151-62.

DuBois, W. E. Burghardt (1944) 'My evolving program for Negro freedom', in Rayford W. Logan (ed) *What the Negro Wants*, Chapel Hill, NC: The University of North Carolina Press.

Duggan, Mark and Levitt, Steven D (2002) 'Winning isn't everything: corruption in sumo wrestling', *American Economic Review*, 92(5): 1594-605.

Dunning, Eric (1999) *Sport Matters: Sociological Studies of Sport, Violence, and Civilization*, London: Routledge.

Dunning, Eric and Malcolm, Robert (2003) *Sport: Critical Concepts in Sociology*, London: Routledge.

Eitzen, D. Stanley (2012) *Fair and Foul: Beyond the Myths and Paradoxes of Sport* (5th edn), Lanham, MD: Rowman and Littlefield Publishers.

Elias, N. and Dunning, E. (1986) *Quest for Excitement: Sport and Leisure in the CivilizingProcess*, London: Blackwell.

Ericson, Richard V. (2007) *Crime in an Insecure World*, Cambridge: Polity.

Etter, Lauren (2014) 'The few, the proud, the extreme: extreme recreational sports are more popular than ever, bringing with them growing numbers of injuries and deaths', *ABA Journal*, June, www.abajournal.com/magazine/article/extreme_sports_are_more_popular_than_ever_prompting_questions (accessed 30 September 2015).

Eysenck, Hans Jürgen (1997) *Repel With a Cause: The Autobiography of Hans Eysenck*, New Brunswick, NJ: Transaction Publishers.

Eysenck, Hans Jürgen (2013) *Crime and Personality*, Abingdon: Routledge.

Farrell, Albert D., Meyer, Aleta L. and White, Kamila S. (2001) 'Evaluation of Responding in Peaceful and Positive Ways (RIPP): a school-based prevention program for reducing violence among urban adolescents', *Journal of Clinical Child Psychology*, 30(4): 451-63.

Farrell, Graham (2010) 'Situational crime prevention and its discontents: rational choice and harm reduction versus "cultural criminology"', *Social Policy and Administration*, 44(1): 40-66.

Farrell, Walter C. Jr., Johnson, James H. Jr., Sapp, Marty, Pumphrey, Roger M. and Freeman, Shirley (1996) 'Redirecting the lives of urban black males: an assessment of Milwaukee's Midnight Basketball League', *Journal of Community Practice*, 2(4): 91-107.

Feeley, Malcolm and Simon, Jonathan (1992) 'The new penology: notes on the emerging strategy of corrections and its implications', *Criminology*, 30(4): 449-74.

Felson, Marcus (1998) *Crime and Everyday Life*, Thousand Oaks, CA: Sage Publications.

Fields, Sarah K. (2014) 'Legislating sport: does law aid, abet or hinder national pastimes?', *International Journal of the History of Sport*, 31(1-2): 203-223.

Finley, Peter S. and Finley, Laura L. (2006) *The Sports Industry's War on Athletes*, Westport, CT: Greenwood.

Fletcher, Ralph (1846) *A Few Notes of Cruelty to Animals: On the Inadequacy of Penal Law, On General Hospitals for Animals*, London: Longmans and Co.

Forbes, G. B., Adams-Curtis, L. E., Pakalka, A. H. and White, K. (2006) 'Dating aggression, sexual coercion, and aggression: supporting attitudes among college men as a function of participation in aggressive high school sports', *Violence Against Women*, 12(5): 441-55.

Forman, James Jr. (2009) 'Exporting harshness: how the war on crime helped make the war on terror possible', *N.Y.U. Review of Law and Social Change*, 33(3): 331-74.

Foster, Ken (2006) 'Juridification of sport', in Guy Osborn and Steve Greenfield (eds) *Readings in Law and Popular Culture*, Abingdon: Routledge.

Fotheringham, William (2009) *Fallen Angel: The Passion of Fausto Coppi*, London: Yellow Jersey Press.

Fraser, David (2005) *Cricket and the Law: The Man in White is Always Right*, Abingdon: Routledge.

Fussey, Pete, Coaffee, Jon, Armstrong, Gary and Hobbs, Dick (2012) 'The regeneration games: purity and security in the Olympic city', *British Journal of Sociology*, 63(2): 260-84.

Gage, Elizabeth Ann (2008) 'Gender attitudes and sexual behaviors: comparing center and marginal athletes and nonathletes in a collegiate setting', *Violence Against Women*, 14(9): 1014-32.

Gantz, Walter, Wang, Zheng and Bradley, Samuel D. (2009) 'Televised NFL games, the family, and domestic violence', in Arthur A. Raney and Jennings Bryant (eds) *Handbook of Sports and Media*, Abingdon: Routledge.

Gardiner, Simon, O'Leary, John, Welch, Roger, Boyes, Simon and Naidoo, Urvasi (2006) *Sports Law*, Abingdon: Routledge.

Garland, David (2002) *The Culture of Control: Crime and Social Order*, Chicago, IL: University of Chicago Press.

Garrett, Bradley L. (2013) *Explore Everything: Place-Hacking the City*, London: Verso.

Gaskew, Tony (2012) 'Mann Act', in Wilbur R. Miller (ed) *The Social History of Crime and Punishment in America: An Encyclopedia*, Thousand Oaks, CA: Sage Publications.

Gauntlett, David (1998) 'Ten things wrong with the "effects model"', in Roger Dickinson, Ramaswani Harindranath and Olga Linné (eds) *Approaches to Audiences – A Reader*, London: Arnold.

Gibson, Timothy A. (2014) 'Property outlaws in cyberspace and meatspace? Examining the relationship between online peer production and support for private property violations', *Communication, Capitalism and Critique: Journal for a Global Sustainable Information Society*, 12(2): 876-90.

Gibson, William (1984) *Neuromancer*, New York, NY: Ace.

Girdwood, John (2009) 'Discovering inconspicuous exploitation: applying the theories of W. E. B. DuBois to American sports sociology', www.academia.edu/203156/Discovering_Inconspicuous_Exploitation_Applying_the_Theories_of_W._E._B._DuBois_to_American_Sports_Sociology (accessed 23 July 2015).

Giulianotti, Richard (2005) *Sport: A Critical Sociology*, Cambridge: Polity.

Giulianotti, Richard and Klauser, Francisco (2010) 'Security governance and sport mega-events: toward an interdisciplinary research agenda', *Journal of Sport and Social Issues*, 34(1): 49–61.

Global Alliance Against Traffic in Women (2011) 'What's the cost of a rumour? A guide to sorting out the myths and the facts about sporting events and trafficking', www.gaatw.org/publications/WhatstheCostofaRumour.11.15.2011.pdf (accessed 23 July 2015).

Glueck, Sheldon and Glueck, Eleanor (1950) *Unraveling Juvenile Delinquency*, Boston, MA: Harvard University Press.

Goode, Erich (2011) *Sports Doping as Deviance: Anti-doping as Moral Panic*, Copenhagen: International Network of Humanistic Doping Research/Books on Demand.

Goring, Charles (1913) *The English Convict*, London: HMSO.

Gorn, Elliott J. and Goldstein, Warren Jay (2004) *A Brief History of American Sports*, Chicago, IL: University of Illinois Press.

Graham, M., Ryan, Paul, Baker, Julien, Davies, Bruce, Thomas, Non-Eleri, Cooper, Stephen-Mark, Evans, Peter, Easmon, Sue, Walker, Christopher, Cowan, David and Kicman, Andrew (2009) 'Counterfeiting in performance- and image-enhancing drugs', *Drug Test and Analysis*, 1(3): 135–42.

Groombridge, Nic (1997) 'The car and crime: critical perspectives', Unpublished PhD Thesis, Middlesex University, http://eprints.mdx.ac.uk/6692/ (accessed 23 July 2015).

Groombridge, Nic (2007) 'Criminologists say: an analysis of UK national press coverage of criminology and criminologists and a contribution to the debate on "Public Criminology"', *Howard Journal of Criminal Justice*, 46(5): 459–75.

Groombridge, Nic (2008a) 'Playing around with crime and criminology in videogames: exploring common themes in games studies and criminology', *Papers from the British Criminology Conference*, 8: 18–32, www.britsoccrim.org/volume8/2Groombridge08.pdf (accessed 30 September 2015).

Groombridge, Nic (2008b) 'Stars of CCTV? How the Home Office wasted millions – a radical Treasury/Audit Commission view', *Surveillance and Society*, 5(1) 73–80.

Groombridge, Nic (2015) 'A modest contribution: tattoos and "tatistics"', *CRIMSOC: The Journal of Social Criminology, Report 4: Gender, Victimology and Restorative Justice*, ed. Walter De Keseredy and Liam Leonard, www.researchgate.net/profile/Walter_Dekeseredy/publication/277871183_CRIMSOC_The_Journal_of_Social_Criminology_CRIMSOC_REPORT_4_Gender_Victimology__Restorative_Justice_edited_by_Walter_DeKeseredy_and_Liam_Leonard/links/5575928808ae7521586ac5a3.pdf (accessed 23 July 2015).

Grow, N. (2012) 'In defense of baseball's antitrust exemption', *American Business Law Journal*, 49(2): 211-73.

Haberfeld, M. J. and Abbott, John (2014) 'Introduction: match fixing as a modality of sports related crimes', in M. R. Haberfeld and Dale Sheehan (eds) *Match-Fixing in International Sports: Existing Processes, Law Enforcement, and Prevention Strategies*, Cham: Springer.

Hall, Steve and Winlow, Simon C. (2012) *New Directions in Criminological Theory*, Abingdon: Routledge.

Hallsworth, Simon (2006) 'Review of "Cultural Criminology Unleashed"', in *Criminology and Criminal Justice*, 6(1): 147.

Hanna, Cheryl (2001) 'Sex is not a sport: consent and violence in criminal law', *Boston College Law Review*, 42(2): 239-90.

Harding, Simon (2014) *Unleashed: The Phenomena of Status Dogs and Weapon Dogs*, Bristol: Policy Press.

Hartley, Hazel (2009) *Sport, Physical Recreation and the Law*, Abingdon: Routledge.

Hartley, Hazel (2013) 'Modahl v British Athletic Federation', in Jack Anderson (ed) *Leading Cases in Sports Law*, Cham: Springer.

Hartmann, Douglas (2003) *Race, Culture, and the Revolt of the Black Athlete: The 1968 Olympic Protests and their Aftermath*, Chicago, IL: University of Chicago Press.

Hartmann, Douglas (2012) 'Beyond the sporting boundary: the racial significance of sport through midnight basketball', *Ethnic and Racial Studies*, 35(6): 1007-22.

Hartmann, Douglas and Depro, Brooks (2006) 'Rethinking Sports-Based Community Crime Prevention: A Preliminary Analysis of the Relationship Between Midnight Basketball and Urban Crime Rates', *Journal of Sport and Social Issues*, 30(2): 180-196.

Hawkins, Ed (2015) *Lost Boys: Inside Football's Slave Trade*, London: Bloomsbury.

Hayward, Keith (2004) 'Space – the final frontier: criminology, the city and the spatial dynamics of exclusion', in Jeff Ferrell, Keith Hayward, Wayne Morrison and Mike Presdee (eds) *Cultural Criminology Unleashed*, Abingdon: Routledge.

Hayward, Keith (2007) 'Situational crime prevention and its discontents: rational choice theory versus the "culture of now"', *Social Policy and Administration*, 41(3): 232-50.

Healey, Deborah (2009) *Sport and the Law*, Sydney: University of New South Wales Press.

Heidensohn, Frances and Gelsthorpe, Lorraine (2007) 'Gender and crime', in Mike Maguire, Rod Morgan and Robert Reiner (eds) *The Oxford Handbook of Criminology* (4th edn), Abingdon: Oxford University Press.

Henne, Kathryn, Koh, Benjamin and McDermott, Vanessa (2013) 'Coherence of drug policy in sports: illicit inclusions and illegal inconsistencies', *Performance Enhancement and Health*, 3(2): 48-55.

Henning, A. D. (2014) '(Self-)surveillance, anti-doping, and health in non-elite road running', *Surveillance and Society*, 11(4): 494-507.

Herrnstein, R. and Murray, C. (1994) *The Bell Curve: Intelligence and Class Structure in American Life*, New York, NY: The Free Press.

Hill, Declan (2010) *The Fix: Soccer and Organized Crime*, Toronto: McClellan and Stewart.

Hillyard, Paddy, Pantazis, Christina, Tombs, Steve and Gordon, Dave (eds) (2004) *Beyond Criminology: Taking Harm Seriously*, London: Pluto Press.

Hirschi, Travis (1969) *Causes of Delinquency*, Berkeley, CA: University of California Press.

Hirst, Paul Q. (1975) 'Marx and Engels on law, crime and morality', in Ian Taylor, Paul Walton and Jock Young (eds) (1975) *Critical Criminology*, London: Routledge Kegan Paul.

Holt, Richard (1990) *Sport and the British: A Modern History*, Oxford: Clarendon Press.

Holyfield, Lori and Fine, Gary Alan (1997) 'Adventure as character work: the collective taming of fear', *Symbolic Interaction*, 20(4) 343-63.

Home Office Standing Conference on Crime Prevention (1988) *Report of the Working Group on Car Crime*, London: Home Office.

Hopkins, Matt and Treadwell, James (eds) (2014) *Football Hooliganism, Fan Behaviour and Crime: Contemporary Issues*, Basingstoke: Palgrave Macmillan.

Hopkins-Burke, Roger (2013) 'Theorizing the criminal justice system: four models of criminal justice development', *Criminal Justice Review*, 38(3) 277-90.

Hornibrook, T., Brinkert, E., Parry, D., Seimens, R., Mitten, D. and Priest, S. (1997) 'The benefits and motivations of all women outdoor programs', *Journal of Experiential Education*, 20(3): 152-8.

Hornung, Ernest William (1905) 'The criminologists' club', in *A Thief in the Night*, London: Chatto and Windus.

Huggins, M. (2004) *The Victorians and Sport*, New York, NY: Palgrave Macmillan.

Hughes, Robert and Coakley, Jay (1991) 'Positive deviance among athletes: the implications of overconformity to the sport ethic', *Sociology of Sport Journal*, 8(4): 307-25.

Hughes, Stephanie and Shank, Matt (2005) 'Defining scandal in sports: media and corporate sponsor perspectives', *Sports Marketing Quarterly*, 14: 207-16.

Hulsman, Luk (1986), 'Critical criminology and the concept of crime', *Contemporary Crises*, 10(1): 63-83.

Hylton, Kevin (2009) *'Race' and Sport: Critical Race Theory*, London: Routledge.

IeSF (International e-Sports Federation) (2015) 'IeSF, Partnership with Athletics for a Better World, powered by IAAF, one of the world's leading international sports federations', http://ie-sf.com/bbs/board.php?bo_table=iesf_news&wr_id=43 (accessed 22 July 2015).

Ifekwunige, Jayne O. (2009) 'Venus and Serena are "doing it" for themselves: theorising sporting celebrity, class and Black feminism for the Hip-Hop generation', in Ben Carrington and Ian McDonald (eds) *Marxism, Cultural Studies and Sport*, Abingdon: Routledge

Ireland, Richard W. (2013) 'Criminology, class and cricket: Raffles and real life', *Legal Studies*, 33(1): 66-84.

Jackson, Arrick, Gilliland, Katherine and Veneziano, Louis (2006) 'Routine activity theory and sexual deviance among male college students', *Journal of Family Violence*, 21: 449-60.

Jackson-Jacobs, Curtis (2004) 'Taking a beating: the narrative gratifications of fighting as underdog', in Jeff Ferrell, Keith Hayward, Wayne Morrison and Mike Presdee (eds) *Cultural Criminology Unleashed*, Abingdon: Routledge.

James, C.L.R. (1963) *Beyond a Boundary*, London: Hutchinson.

James, Mark (2010) *Sports Law*, Basingstoke: Palgrave Macmillan.

Jamieson, Lynn and Orr, Thomas (2009) *Sport and Violence: A Critical Examination of Sport*, Abingdon: Routledge.

Jarvie, Grant (2007) 'Sport, social change and the public intellectual', *International Review for the Sociology of Sport*, 42(4): 411-24.

Jefferson, Tony (1998) 'Muscle, "hard men" and "iron" Mike Tyson: reflections on desire, anxiety and the embodiment of masculinity', *Body Society*, 4(1): 77–98.

Jeffery, C.R. (1965) 'Criminal behavior and learning theory', *Journal of Criminal Law and Criminology*, 56(3): 294–300.

Jenkins, Craig and Ellis, Tom (2011) 'The highway to hooliganism? An evaluation of the impact of combat sport participation on individual criminality', *International Journal of Police Science & Management*, 13(2): 117–31.

Jhally, S. (1989) 'Cultural studies and the sports/media complex', in L. Wenner (ed) *Media, Sports and Society*, London: Sage Publications.

Johnson, John and Long, Bill (2008) *Tyson-Douglas: The Inside Story of the Upset of the Century*, Dulles, VA: Potomac Books.

Johnson, Shane D. and Bowers, Kate J. (2003) 'Opportunity is in the eye of the beholder: the role of publicity in crime prevention', *Criminology and Public Policy*, 2(3): 497–524.

Jones, Stephen (2000) *Understanding Violent Crime*, Abingdon: Open University Press.

Jones, Trevor and Newburn, Tim (2006) 'Three strikes and you're out: exploring symbol and substance in American and British crime control politics', *British Journal of Criminology*, 46(5): 781–802.

Jump, Deborah (2015) 'Fighting for change: narrative accounts on the appeal and desistance potential of boxing', *Howard League Early Career Network Bulletin 26*, www.academia.edu/11955240/Howard_League_of_Penal_Reform (accessed 22 August 2015).

Jupp, Victor (2001) 'Hidden crime', in Eugene McLaughlin and John Muncie (eds) *The Sage Dictionary of Criminology*, London: Sage Publications.

Kappeler, V.E. (2004) 'Inventing criminal justice: myth and social construction' in P.B. Kraska and J. J. Brent (eds) *Theorizing Criminal Justice: Eight Essential Orientations*, Grove, IL: Waveland Press.

Kane, Pat (2005) *The Play Ethic*, London: Pan MacMillan.

Katz, Jack (1988) *Seductions of Crime: Moral and Sensual Attractions in Doing Evil*, New York, NY: Basic Books.

Kelly, Laura (2008) 'Sport-based crime prevention', in Barry Goldson (ed) *Dictionary of Youth Justice*, Cullompton: Willan.

Kelly, Laura (2012) 'Representing and preventing youth crime and disorder: intended and unintended consequences of targeted youth programmes in England', *Youth Justice*, 12(2): 101–17.

Kent, Steven (2010) *The Ultimate History of Video Games: From Pong to Pokemon and Beyond … The Story Behind the Craze that Touched our Lives and Changed the World*, New York: Three Rivers Press.

Kerr, Clark (2001) *The Gold and the Blue: A Personal Memoir of the University of California, 1949-1967, Volume 1*, Berkeley, CA: University of California Press.

Kidder, Jeffrey L. (2013) 'Parkour: adventure, risk, and safety in the urban environment', *Qualitative Sociology*, 36: 231-50.

Kietlinski, Robin (2011) *Japanese Women and Sport: Beyond Baseball and Sumo*, London: Bloomsbury.

King, C. Richard (2008) 'Toward a radical sport journalism: an interview with Dave Zirin', *Journal of Sport and Social Issues*, 32(4): 333-44.

Kirby, Stuart, Francis, Brian and O'Flaherty, Rosalie (2014) 'Can the FIFA world cup football (soccer) tournament be associated with an increase in domestic abuse?', *Journal of Research in Crime and Delinquency*, 51(3): 259-76.

Kohlberg, L. (1963) 'The development of children's orientations toward a moral order', *Human Development*, 6: 11-33.

Kraska, Peter B. and Brent, John J. (2011) *Theorizing Criminal Justice* (2nd edn), Grove, IL: Waveland Press.

Kretschmer, Ernst (1921) *Körperbau und Charakter*, Berlin: Springer Verlag.

Krien, Anna (2013) *Night Games: Sex, Power and a Journey into the Dark Heart of Sport*, London: Yellow Jersey Press.

Kudlac, C. S. (2010) *Fair or Foul: Sports and Criminal Behavior in the United States*, Santa Barbara, CA: Praeger/ABC-CLIO.

Kuhn, Gabriel (2011) *Soccer vs the State: Tackling Football and Radical Politics*, Oakland, CA: PM Press.

Lamb, Sharon (1991) 'Acts without agents: an analysis of linguistic avoidance in journal articles on men who batter women', *American Journal of Orthopsychiatry*, 61(2): 250-7.

Lander, I., Ravn, S. and Jon, N. (2014) *Masculinities in the Criminological Field: Control, Vulnerability and Risk-Taking*, Farnham: Ashgate Publishing Limited.

Larkin, Ralph W. (2007) *Comprehending Columbine*, Philadelphia, PA: Temple University Press.

Lasch, Christopher (1991) *The Culture of Narcissism: American Life in an Age of Diminishing Expectations*, New York, NY: W. W. Norton and Company.

Laureus (2011) 'Teenage kicks: the value of sport in tackling crime', www.thinknpc.org/publications/teenage-kicks (accessed 24 August 2015).

Laureus and Ecorys (2012) 'Sport scores: the costs and benefits of sport for crime reduction', Laureus Sport for Good Foundation and Ecorys, www.laureus.com/sites/default/files/publications/laureusecoryssportscores211112.pdf (accessed 24 August 2015).

Leberman, Sarah (2007) 'Voices behind the walls: female offenders and "experiential learning"', *Journal of Adventure Education and Outdoor Learning*, 7(2): 113-30.

Lee, Sherman A., Gibbons, Jeffrey A. and Short, Stephen D. (2010) 'Sympathetic reactions to the bait dog in a film of dog fighting: the influence of personality and gender', *Society and Animals*, 18(2): 107-25.

Lefever, Katrien (2012) *New Media and Sport: International Legal Aspects*, The Hague: T.M.C. Asser Press.

Lessig, L. (1999) *Code and other Laws of Cyberspace*, New York, NY: Basic Books.

Lewis, Adam and Taylor, Jonathan (2008) *Sport – Law and Practice*, Haywards Heath: Bloomsbury Professional.

Lewis, Michael (2014) *Flash Boys*, New York, NY: Norton.

Lewis, Robert M. (1987) 'Cricket and the beginnings of organized baseball in New York city', *International Journal of the History of Sport*, 4(): 315-32.

Lindner, Katharina (2012) 'Women's boxing at the 2012 Olympics: gender trouble?', *Feminist Media Studies*, 12(3): 464-7.

Loader, Ian (2008) 'The anti-politics of crime', *Theoretical Criminology*, 12(3): 399-410.

London Councils/GLE (2011) 'The 2012 Games and human trafficking: identifying possible risks and relevant good practice from other cities', http://lastradainternational.org/lsidocs/The2012GamesandHumanTrafficking.pdf (accessed 23 July 2015).

Lyng, Stephen (1990) 'Edgework: a social psychological analysis of voluntary risk taking', *American Journal of Sociology*, 95(4): 851-86.

Lyng, Stephen (2005) 'Sociology at the edge: social theory and voluntary risk taking', in Stephen Lyng (ed) *Edgework: The Sociology of Risk-Taking,* Abingdon: Routledge.

Macdonald, H. (2014) *H is for Hawk*, London: Jonathan Cape.

Maennig, Wolfgang (2005) 'Corruption in international sports and sport management: forms, tendencies, extent and countermeasures', *European Sport Management Quarterly*, 5(2): 187-225.

Maennig, Wolfgang (2008) 'Corruption in international sports and how it may be combated', IASE NAASE Working Paper Series, Paper No. 08-13, http://college.holycross.edu/RePEc/spe/Maennig_Corruption.pdf (accessed 16 August 2015).

Maher, Amelia M., Thomson Cynthia J. and Carlson Scott R. (2015) 'Risk-taking and impulsive personality traits in proficient downhill sports enthusiasts', *Personality and Individual Differences,* 79: 20-24.

Majumdar, Boria and Brown, Sean (2007) 'Why baseball, why cricket? differing nationalisms, differing challenges', *The International Journal of the History of Sport,* 24(2): 139-156.

Maguire, J. (1991) 'The media-sport production complex: the case of American football in Western European Societies', European Journal of Communication, 6(3): 315–335.

Malcolm, Dominic (1999) 'Cricket spectator disorder: myths and historical evidence', *The Sports Historian,* 19(1): 16-37.

Malcolm, Dominic (2014) 'The social construction of the sociology of sport: a professional project', *International Review for the Sociology of Sport,* 49(1): 3-21.

Manzenreiter, Wolfram (2014) 'Cracks in the moral economy of sumo: beasts of burden, sport heroes, national icons and living gods in disgrace', *International Journal of the History of Sport,* 31(4): 459-73.

Marcus-Mendoza, S. T., Klein-Saffran, J. and Lutze, F. (1998) 'A feminist examination of boot camp prison programs for women', *Women and Therapy,* 21(1): 173-85.

Martinson, R. (1974) 'What works? Questions and answers about prison reform', *The Public Interest,* 35: 22-54.

Matza, David (1964) *Delinquency and Drift,* New Brunswick, NJ: Transaction Publishers.

McFee, G. (2004) *Sport, Rules and Values: Philosophical Investigations into the Nature of Sport,* Abingdon: Routledge.

Meek, Rosie (2012) 'The role of sport in promoting desistance from crime: an evaluation of 2nd Chance project rugby and football academies at Portland Young Offender Institution', Second Chance. Report available at http://eprints.soton.ac.uk/210815/1/Meek_2nd_Chance_Portland_Evaluation_Final_Report.pdf (accessed 19 February 2016).

Meek, Rosie (2014) *Sport in Prison: Exploring the Role of Physical Activity in Penal Practices: Exploring the Role of Physical Activity in Correctional Settings,* Abingdon: Routledge.

Merton, Robert K. (1938) 'Social Structure and Anomie', American Sociological Review, 672-682.

Messerschmidt, J. W. (1993) *Masculinities and Crime: Critique and Reconceptualisation of Theory,* Lanham, MA: Rowman and Littlefield.

Messner, Michael A. (1990) 'When bodies are weapons: masculinity and violence in sport', *International Review for the Sociology of Sport,* 25(3): 203-20.

Messner, Michael (2002) *Taking the Field: Women, Men, and Sports*, Minneapolis, MN: University of Minnesota Press.

Miller, Toby (2009) 'Michel Foucault and the critique of sport', in Ben Carrington and Ian McDonald (eds) *Marxism, Cultural Studies and Sport*, Abingdon: Routledge.

Millie, Andrew, Jacobson, Jessica, McDonald, Eraina and Hough, Mike (2005) 'Anti-social behaviour strategies: finding a balance', Institute for Criminal Policy Research. Report available at https://www.jrf.org.uk/report/anti-social-behaviour-strategies-finding-balance (accessed 19 February 2016).

Milling, Lynn (nd) 'The Connecticut institutional furlough program: a research report of the Connecticut Department of Correction', www.ncjrs.gov/pdffiles1/Digitization/61706NCJRS.pdf (accessed 21 August 2015).

Miracle, Andrew W. and Rees, C. Roger (2003) *Lessons of the Locker Room: The Myth of School Sports*, Amherst, NY: Prometheus Books.

Moller, Verner, Waddington, Ivan and Hoberman, John M. (2015) *Routledge Handbook of Drugs and Sport*, Abingdon: Routledge.

Mooney, Lauren (2007) 'The man', *Bicycling*, 8(5), June, Burbank, CA: Rodale Press.

Morgan, Rod and Newburn, Tim (2007) 'Youth justice', in Mike Maguire, Rod Morgan and Robert Reiner (eds) *The Oxford Handbook of Criminology*, Abingdon: Oxford University Press.

Morris, Leesa, Sallybanks, Jo and Willis, Katie (2003) *Sport, Physical Activity and Antisocial Behaviour*, Australian Institute of Criminology Research and Public Policy Series No. 49. Available at http://www.aic.gov.au/media_library/publications/rpp/49/rpp49.pdf (accessed 19 February 2016).

Morris, Paul H. and Lewis, David (2009) 'Tackling diving: the perception of deceptive intentions in association football (soccer)', *Journal of Nonverbal Behavior*, 34(1): 1-13.

Nacro (2008) *Youth Crime Briefing: Sport, Recreational and Physical Activity Programmes and Youth Justice*, London: Nacro.

Nadir, Urvasi (2013) 'Cheating in sport: is increased regulation the answer?', *Sport and Law Journal*, 21(2): 29-36.

Nathan, Daniel A. (2003) *Saying It's So: A Cultural History of the Black Sox Scandal*, Chicago, IL: University of Illinois Press.

Nelson, Mariah Burton (1995) *The Stronger Women Get, The More Men Love Football: Sexism and the American Culture of Sports*, San Diego, CA: Harcourt Brace.

Newburn, Tim and Stanko, Betsy (1994) 'When men are victims', in Tim Newburn and Betsy Stanko (eds) *Just Boys Doing Business? Men, Masculinities and Crime*, Abingdon: Routledge.

Newburn, Tim (2013) *Criminology*, Abingdon: Routledge.

Nichols, Geoff (2007) *Sport and Crime Reduction: The Role of Sports in Tackling Youth Crime*, Abingdon: Routledge.

Ozano, Kimberley A. (2008) 'The role of physical education, sport and exercise in a female prison', MA Dissertation, University of Chester, http://chesterrep.openrepository.com/cdr/handle/10034/84838 (accessed 31 August 2015).

Packer, Herbert L. (1964) 'Two models of the criminal process', *University of Pennsylvania Law Review*, 113(1): 1-68.

Palmer, Catherine (2011) 'Violence against women and sport: a literature review', www.endviolenceagainstwomen.org.uk/resources/22/violence-against-women-and-sport-a-literature-review-by-dr-catherine-palmer (accessed 23 July 2015).

Paoli, L. and Donati, A. (2014) *The Sports Doping Market: Understanding Supply and Demand, and the Challenges of their Control*, New York, NY: Springer.

Pappa, Evdokia and Kennedy, Eileen (2012) '"It was my thought … he made it a reality": normalization and responsibility in athletes' accounts of performance-enhancing drug use', *International Review for the Sociology of Sport*, 48(3): 277-94.

Park, Robert E. (1925) 'The city: suggestions for the investigation of human behaviour in the urban environment', in Robert E. Park, Ernest W. Burgess and Roderick D. McKenzie (eds) *The City*, Chicago, IL: University of Chicago Press.

Pearce, Fred (1993) 'How green is your golf?', *New Science*, 139: 30-36.

Pearson, Geoffrey (1983) *Hooligan: A History of Respectable Fears*, Basingstoke: Palgrave.

Penfold-Mounce, Ruth (2010) *Celebrity Culture and Crime: The Joy of Transgression*, Basingstoke: Macmillan Palgrave.

Perelman, Marc (2012) *Barbaric Sport: A Global Plague*, London: Verso.

Perrin, Benjamin (2007) *Faster, Higher, Stronger: Preventing Human Trafficking at the 2010 Olympics*, Vancouver: The Future Group.

Perryman, Mark (ed) (2001) *Hooligan Wars: Causes and Effects of Football Violence*, Edinburgh: Mainstream Sport.

Pfleegor, Adam G. and Roesenberg, Danny (2014) 'Deception in sport: a new taxonomy of intra-lusory guiles', *Journal of the Philosophy of Sport*, 41(2): 209-31.

Picart, Caroline Joan (Kay) and Greek Cecil (eds) (2004) *Monsters In and Among Us: Towards a Gothic Criminology*, Cranbury, NJ: Associated University Presses.

Plugge, Emma, Douglas Nicola and Fitzpatrick, Ray (2006) *The Health of Women in Prison Study Findings*, Oxford: Department of Public Health, University of Oxford.

Pollak, Otto (1950) *The Criminality of Women*, Philadelphia, PA: University of Pennsylvania Press.

Pollard, Richard (2008) 'Home advantage in football: a current review of an unsolved puzzle', *The Open Sports Sciences Journal*, 1: 12-14.

Poulton, Emma (2001) 'Tears, tantrums and tattoos, framing the hooligan', in Mark Perryman (ed) (2001) *Hooligan Wars: Causes and Effects of Football Violence*, Edinburgh: Mainstream Sport.

Pronger, Brian (1998) 'Post-sport: transgressing boundaries in physical culture', in G. Rail (ed) *Sport and Postmodern Times*, Albany, NY: State University of New York Press.

Qureshi, H. and Verma, A. (2013) 'It is just not cricket', in M. R. Haberfeld and Dale Sheehan (eds) *Match-Fixing in International Sports: Existing Processes, Law Enforcement, and Prevention Strategies*, Cham: Springer.

Rafter, Nicole Hahn (1990) 'The social construction of crime and crime control', *Journal of Research in Crime and Delinquency*, 27(4): 376-89.

Rafter, Nicole Hahn (ed) (2009) *The Origins of Criminology: A Reader*, Abingdon: Routledge.

Rasmussen, Kristian (2005) 'The quest for the imaginary evil: a critique of anti-doping', *Sport in History*, 25(3): 515-35.

Reichel, Philip and Albanese, Jay (eds) (2013) *Handbook of Transnational Crime and Justice*, London: Sage Publications.

Redhead, Steve (2015) *Football and Accelerated Culture: This Modern Sporting Life*, Abingdon: Routledge.

Rojek, Chris (2000) *Leisure and Culture*, Basingstoke: Macmillan.

Rojek, Chris (2004) *Celebrity*, London: Reaktion Books.

Roth, Amanda and Basow, Susan A. (2004) 'Femininity, sports, and feminism: developing a theory of physical liberation', *Journal of Sport and Social Issues*, 28(3): 245-56.

Rowe, D. (1997) 'Apollo undone: the sport scandal', in J. Lull and S. Hinerman (eds) *Media Scandals: Morality and Desire in the Popular Culture Marketplace*, Cambridge: Polity.

Rowe, D. (2013) *Sport, Scandal, Gender and the Nation*, Institute for Culture and Society Occasional Paper Series, Volume 4, Number 3, Sydney: Institute for Culture and Society, University of Western Sydney.

Runciman, W.G. (1966) *Relative Deprivation and Social Justice: A Study of Attitudes to Social Inequality in Twentieth-Century England*, Berkeley, CA: University of California Press.

Russell, Gordon W. and Mustonen, Anu (1998) 'Peacemakers: those who would intervene to quell a sports riot', *Personality and Individual Differences*, 24(3): 335-39.

Sabo, Donald F. and Ross Runfola (eds) (1980) *Jock: Sports and Male Identity*, Englewood Cliffs, NJ: Prentice-Hall.

Sarre, Rick (1999) 'Beyond "What works?" A 25 year Jubilee retrospective of Robert Martinson', Paper presented at the History of Crime, Policing and Punishment Conference, Australian Institute of Criminology in conjunction with Charles Sturt University, Canberra, 9-10 December.

Sampson, Alice and Vilella, Maria Rita (2012) *Fight for Peace in Rio and London – Assessing their Progress and Impact*, London: Centre for Institutional Studies, University of East London.

Saville, Stephen John (2008) 'Playing with fear: parkour and the mobility of emotion', *Social and Cultural Geography*, 9(8): 891-914.

Schneider, Stephen (2014) *Crime Prevention: Theory and Practice*, Boca Raton, FL: CRC Press.

Scraton, Phil (1999) *Hillsborough: The Truth*, Edinburgh: Mainstream.

Sefiha, Ophir (2012) 'Bike racing, neutralization, and the social construction of performance-enhancing drug use', *Contemporary Drug Problems*, 39(2): 213-45.

Shaw Clifford R. and McKay Henry D. (1942) *Juvenile Delinquency in Urban Areas*, Chicago: University of Chicago Press.

Sheldon, William Herbert. (1949) *Varieties of Delinquent Youth: An Introduction to Constitutional Psychiatry*, New York: Harper and Brothers.

Shields, D.L.L. and Bredemeier, B.J.L. (1995) *Character Development and Physical Activity*, Leeds: Human Kinetics Publishers.

Silk, M.L. and Andrews, D.L. (2011) 'Toward a physical cultural studies', *Sociology of Sport Journal*, 28(1): 4-35.

Sillitoe, Alan (1959) *The Loneliness of the Long Distance Runner*, London: W. H. Allen.

Simmel, Georg (1959) *Essays on Sociology, Philosophy, and Aesthetics* (edited by Kurt Wolff), New York, NY: Harper and Row.

Simon, Jonathan (2007) *Governing Through Crime: How the War on Crime Transformed American Democracy and Created a Culture of Fear*, Oxford: Oxford University Press.

Simon, Rita James (1975) *Women and Crime*, Lexington, MA: Lexington Books.

Sikka, Annuradha (2014) 'Trafficking In Persons And The Canadian Response: Looking For A "Victim"' PhD Thesis University of Ottawa.

Smart, Carol (1990) 'Feminist approaches to criminology or postmodern woman meets atavistic man', in Loraine Gelsthorpe and Allison Morris (eds) *Feminist Perspectives in Criminology*, Milton Keynes: Open University Press.

Smart, Carol (1995) 'Law, feminism and sexuality: from essence to ethics?', *Law, Crime and Sexuality: Essays in Feminism*, London: Sage Publications.

Smith, Andrew (2011) 'All bets are off: match fixing in sport – some recent developments', *Entertainment and Sports Law Journal*, 9: 1 www2.warwick.ac.uk/fac/soc/law/elj/eslj/issues/volume9/smith/smith.pdf (accessed 6 October 2015).

Smith, Andy and Waddington, Ivan (2004) 'Using "sport in the community schemes" to tackle crime and drug use among young people: some policy issues and problems', *European Physical Education Review*, 10(3): 279-98.

Smith, D. and Stewart, S. (2003) 'Sexual aggression and sports participation', *Journal of Sport Behaviour*, 26(4): 384-95.

Smith, M. (1983) *Violence and Sport*, Toronto: Butterworths.

Smith, Malissa (2014) *A History of Women's Boxing*, Lanham, MD: Rowman and Littlefield.

Snyder, Eldon E. (1994) 'Interpretations and explanations of deviance among college athletes: a case', *Study Sociology of Sport Journal*, 11(3): 231-48.

South, Nigel and Brisman, Avi (eds) (2013) *Routledge International Handbook of Green Criminology*, Abingdon: Routledge.

Squires, Peter (2015) 'From Dunblane to Duggan: the rise and fall of British gun crime?', *Criminal Justice Matters*, 100: 32.

Standen, Jeffrey (2009) *Taking Sports Seriously: Law and Sports in Contemporary American Culture*, Durham, NC: Carolina Academic Press.

Stansfield, Richard (2015) 'Teen involvement in sports and risky behaviour: a cross-national and gendered analysis', *British Journal of Criminology*, advanced publication online at http://bjc.oxfordjournals.org/content/early/2015/10/19/bjc.azv108.full (accessed 15 November 2015).

Stevens, Alex (2011) *Drugs, Crime and Public Health: The Political Economy of Drug Policy*, Abingdon: Routledge.

Stewart, Bob and Smith, Aaron C.T. (2008) 'Drug use in sport: implications for public policy', *Journal of Sport and Social Issues*, 32(3): 278-98.

Straus, Murray Arnold (1994) *Beating the Devil Out of Them*, New Brunswick, NJ: Transaction Publishers.

Sumner, Colin (1994) *The Sociology of Deviance: An Obituary*, Milton Keynes: Open University Press

Sumner, Colin (2005) *Violence, Culture and Censure*, Abingdon: Taylor and Francis.

Sutherland, Edwin H. (1949) *White Collar Crime*, New York, NY: Dryden.

Sutherland, E. H., Cressey D.R. and Luckenbill D. (1995) 'The theory of differential association', in N. J. Herman (ed) *Deviance: A Symbolic Interactionist Approach*, Lanham, MD: General Hall.

Sykes, Gresham M. and Matza, David (1957) 'Techniques of neutralization: a theory of delinquency', *American Sociological Review*, 22(6): 664-70.

Taylor, Ian and Walton, Paul (1975) 'Radical deviancy theory: a reply to Paul Q. Hirst', in Ian Taylor, Paul Walton and Jock Young (eds) *Critical Criminology*, London: Routledge Kegan Paul.

Taylor, Ian, Walton, Paul and Young, Jock (1973) *The New Criminology: For a Social Theory of Deviance*, London: Routledge Kegan Paul.

Taylor, Ian, Walton, Paul and Young, Jock (eds) (1975) *Critical Criminology*, London: Routledge Kegan Paul.

Taylor, P., Crowe, I., Irvine, D. and Nichols, G. (1999) *Demanding Physical Activity Programmes for Young Offenders under Probation Supervision*, London: Home Office.

Theberge, Nancy (1981) 'A critique of critiques: radical and feminist writings on sport', *Social Forces*, 60(2): 341-53.

Thelin, John R. (1994) *Games Colleges Play: Scandal and Reform in Intercollegiate Athletics*, Baltimore, MA: John Hopkins University Press.

Thrasher, Frederic Milton (1927) *The Gang: A Study of 1,313 Gangs in Chicago*, Chicago, IL: University of Chicago Press.

Tibballs, Geoff (2003) *Great Sporting Scandals*, London: Robson.

Tilley, Nick and Laycock, Gloria (2002) *Working Out What to Do: Evidence-Based Crime Reduction*, Crime Reduction Research Series Paper 11, London: Home Office.

Timming, Andrew R. (2014) 'Visible tattoos in the service sector: a new challenge to recruitment and selection', *Work, Employment and Society*, 29(1): 60-78.

Tomlinson, Richard (2015) *Amazing Grace: The Man who was WG*, London: Little, Brown.

Tomsen, Stephen (1997) 'A top night: masculinity and the culture of drinking violence', *British Journal of Criminology*, 37(1): 90–102.

Triviño, José Luis Pérez (2012) 'Strategic intentional fouls, spoiling the fame and famesmanship', *Sport, Ethics and Philosophy*, 6(1): 67–77.

Trulson, Michael E. (1986) 'Martial arts training: a novel "cure" for juvenile delinquency', *Human Relations*, 39(12): 1131–40.

Tsui, V. (2014) 'Male victims of intimate partner abuse: use and helpfulness of services', *Social Work*, 59(2): 121–30.

United Nations (nd) 'Peacebuilding through sports: engaging the youth of Somalia', http://so.one.un.org/content/unct/somalia/en/home/presscenter/International%20Youth%20Day%202015/peacebuilding-through-sports--engaging-the-youth-of-somalia.html (accessed 19 August 2015).

Valiér, Claire (1998) 'Psychoanalysis and crime in Britain during the inter-war years', *Papers from the British Criminology Conference*, Loughborough University, 18-21 July, http://britsoccrim.org/volume1/012.pdf (accessed 23 July 2015)

von Essen, Erica and Allen, Michael P. (2015) 'Reconsidering illegal hunting as a crime of dissent: implication for justice and deliberative uptake', *Criminal Law and Philosophy*, 1–16.

Wacquant, Loïc J.D. (1995) 'Pugs at work: bodily capital and bodily labour among professional boxers', *Body Society*, 1(1): 65-93.

Walsh, David (2013) *Seven Deadly Sins: My Pursuit of Lance Armstrong*, New York, NY: Simon and Schuster.

Waddinton, Ivan and Smith, Andy (2009) An Introduction to Drugs in Sport: Addicted to Winning?, Abingdon: Routledge.

Waterhouse-Watson, Deb (2013) *Athletes, Sexual Assault, and 'Trials by Media': Narrative Immunity*, Abingdon: Routledge.

Watson, P.J. and Morris, Ronald J. (1991) 'Narcissism, empathy and social desirability', *Personality and Individual Differences*, 12(6): 575–79.

Weber, Max (2012) *The Protestant Ethic and the Spirit of Capitalism*, New York, NY: Dover.

Webb, Tom and Thelwell, Richard (2015) "He's taken a Dive": Cultural Comparisons of Elite Referee Responses to Reduced Player Behaviour in Association Football', *Sport Business and Management: An International Journal*, 5(3): 242-258.

Welch, Michael (1997) 'Violence against women by professional football players: a gender analysis of hypermasculinity, positional status, narcissism, and entitlement', *Journal of Sport and Social Issues*, 21(4): 392-411.

West, Mark D. (2005) *Law in Everyday Japan: Sex, Sumo, Suicide, and Statutes*, Chicago, IL: University of Chicago Press.

Wheen, Francis (2012) *Karl Marx*, London: Harper Collins.

Wiener, Martin J. (2006) *Men of Blood: Violence, Manliness, and Criminal Justice in Victorian England*, Cambridge: Cambridge University Press.

Wilkinson, John (1997) 'The impact of Ilderton motor project on motor vehicle crime and offending', *British Journal of Criminology*, 37(4): 568-81.

Williams, Damien J., Neville, Fergus G., House, Kirsty, Donnelly, Peter D. (2013) 'Association between Old Firm football matches and reported domestic (violence) incidents in Strathclyde, Scotland', *SAGE Open*, September 3(3).

Williams, Jack (2012) *Cricket and England: A Cultural and Social History of Cricket in England*, Abingdon: Routledge.

Wilson, David and Groombridge, Nic (2009) '"I'm making a TV programme here!": reality TV's banged up and public criminology', *Howard Journal of Criminal Justice*, 49(1): 1-17.

Yar, Majid (2014) *Crime, Deviance and Doping: Fallen Sports Stars, Autobiography and the Management of Stigma*, Basingstoke: Palgrave Pivot.

Yochelson, S. and Samenow, S. E. (1976) *The Criminal Personality, Volume I: A Profile for Change*, Northvale, NJ: Jason Aronson.

Young, Jock (1969) 'The zookeepers of deviance', in Colin Ward (ed) *A Decade of Anarchy: Selections from "Anarchy" 1961-70*, London: Freedom Press.

Young, Jock (1988) 'Radical criminology in Britain', *British Journal of Criminology*, 28(2): 159-83.

Young, Jock (1992) 'Ten points of realism', in J. Young and R. Matthews (eds) *Rethinking Criminology: The Realist Debate*, London: Sage Publications.

Young, Jock (2004) 'Voodoo criminology and the numbers game', in Jeff Ferrell, Keith Hayward, Wayne Morrison and Mike Presdee (eds) *Cultural Criminology Unleashed*, Abingdon: Routledge.

Young, Kevin (2013) *Sport, Violence and Society*, Abingdon: Routledge.

Young, Kevin (2015) 'Assessing the sociology of sport: on sports violence and ways of seeing', *International Review for the Sociology of Sport*, 50(4-5): 640-44.

Young, T.R. (1986) 'The sociology of sport: structural Marxist and cultural Marxist approaches', *Sociological Perspectives*, 29(1): 3-28.

Zaksaite, Salomeja (2013) 'Match-fixing: the shifting interplay between tactics, disciplinary offence and crime', *International Sports Law Journal*, 13: 287-93.

Zalman, Marvin (2007) 'The search for criminal justice theory: reflections on Kraska's theorizing criminal justice', *Journal Of Criminal Justice Education*, 18(1): 163-81.

Zamanian, Faezeh, Zameni Leila, Forouzandeh Elham and Haghighi, Mina (2012) 'Effects of sports participation on social delinquency reduction among adolescents', *Annals of Biological Research*, 3(1): 660-67.

Zatz, Marjorie S. (1987) 'Chicano youth gangs and crime: the creation of a moral panic', *Contemporary Crises*, 11(2): 129-58.

Index